Reading the DIFFICULTIES

Reading the Difficulties

Dialogues with Contemporary American Innovative Poetry

Edited by Thomas Fink and Judith Halden-Sullivan

THE UNIVERSITY OF ALABAMA PRESS
Tuscaloosa

The University of Alabama Press
Tuscaloosa, Alabama 35487-0380

Manufactured in the United States of America

Typeface: Minion and Gill Sans

Cover art: Thomas Fink, *Reading the Difficulties,* 11" x 14". Acrylic on canvas, 2012
Cover design: Todd Lape / Lape Designs

∞

The paper on which this book is printed meets the minimum requirements of American National Standard for Information Sciences—Permanence of Paper for Printed Library Materials, ANSI Z39.48-1984.

Library of Congress Cataloging-in-Publication Data

Reading the difficulties : dialogues with contemporary American innovative poetry / edited by Thomas Fink and Judith Halden-Sullivan.
pages cm. — (Modern and Contemporary Poetics)
Includes bibliographical references.
ISBN 978-0-8173-5752-8 (quality paper : alk. paper) — ISBN 978-0-8173-8720-4 (e book)
1. American poetry—History and criticism. 2. Poetics. 3. Poetry—Explication. 4. Discourse analysis, Literary. I. Fink, Thomas, 1954– editor of compilation. II. Halden-Sullivan, Judith, 1955– editor of compilation.
PS305.R43 2014
811.009—dc23

2013020494

Contents

Acknowledgments

An earlier version of Eileen R. Tabios's essay in this volume, entitled "Eileen Tabios Engages *2nd NOTICE OF MODIFICATIONS TO TEXT OF PROPOSED REGULATIONS* by John Bloomberg-Rissman," was published in *Galatea Resurrects* 15 (Dec. 2010) Web. http://galatearesurrection15.blogspot.com/2010/12/2nd-notice-of-modifications-to-text-of_05.html

"Thank You for Saying Thank You" was published in *Girly Man*, University of Chicago Press, © by Charles Bernstein. Permission to reprint given by the author.

The editors wish to thank their best beloved ones: Edward Sullivan, Glenn and Joanne Halden, and Molly, Ariana, and Maya Mason.

Reading the DIFFICULTIES

Reading the Difficulties

Thomas Fink and Judith Halden-Sullivan

In the soothing (and parodic) voice of the self-help guru, Charles Bernstein reassures readers in his "The Difficult Poem" that "*Difficult poems are normal.* They are not incoherent, meaningless, or hostile" (*Attack of the Difficult Poems* 4). He also helps readers identify whether they have encountered a difficult poem by providing a handy checklist of five questions. This checklist asks the reader whether he or she is struggling with hard-to-understand vocabulary and syntax or feeling "inadequate or stupid" as a reader. But the checklist concludes with a question of transformation: "Is your imagination being affected by the poem?" (*Attack* 4). While funny and frequently self-deprecating as a creator, teacher, and critic of difficult poetry, Bernstein tips his hand with this final question. There is much more to the experience of "difficult" verse than deciphering non-traditional surface features.

What is a "difficult" poem? Certainly difficult poems have always been with us. Listen to students of literature; they find poetry daunting, regardless of time period and prosody. The work of Emily Dickinson can be "difficult" with its spare metaphoric compression. The tapestries of cultural referents in both Eliot's and Pound's verse also can be "difficult." But what difficulty characterizes contemporary innovative American poetry? According to Marjorie Perloff, this poetry is so challenging that much critical discourse either "dismisses the new work out of hand as simply too opaque, obscure, and disorganized to reward any kind of sustained attention" or emphasizes the work's relation to "a particular theory or an alternate discourse" and thus sidesteps the poem itself (*Differentials* xix). The contributors to *Reading the Difficulties*—both academics and non-academics, many of them poets—eschew such critical misdirection. Through readings and responses that are both typical and atypical of interpretive essays, they ponder what sort of stances open up readers to verse that deliberately removes comfortable cues that lead to comprehension. They seek to characterize the aesthetics of reception for innovative poetry, and they frequently encourage encounters with innovative verse in ways *commensurate with* their poetics. As Bruce Andrews claims, "A writing that is itself a 'wild reading' *solicits* wild reading" (*Paradise & Method* 54-55). The contributors to this volume probe what such readings might be and how *reading* innovative verse might in manifold ways be "re-staged," to borrow Andrews's verb ("Poetry as Explanation" 670).

The "difficult" verse of the following poets inspires the writing of our contributors: Ron Silliman, Hank Lazer, Charles Bernstein, Tan Lin, Sheila E. Murphy, John Bloomberg-Rissman, Harryette Mullen, Stephen Ratcliffe, Myung Mi Kim, Lisa Robertson, Tom Beckett, Mei-mei Berssenbrugge, bpNichol, and Lisa Jarnot. Some of these poets are considered Language poets, others can be classified as Conceptual poets, and the rest might be broadly characterized by the catch-all descriptor "post-Language." Even in such a diverse group, their common difficulty may stem from their resistance to expectations for a relatively unified vision of dominant cultural values. They avoid expressivist cohesion; rarely in their poetry does a single unified self lend coherence. Instead many selves may compete for attention, and, if a distinctive self appears, it quickly morphs into something other. Innovative difficult verse also is frequently non-narrative and not personally disclosive in a confessional sense; however, private references drawn from lived experiences of worlds may abound. As Bernstein asserts, "difficult" poetry "may actually provide a good deal more immediacy and affect than much of the more 'I am my subject matter and don't you forget it' variety" ("Poetry Scene Investigation" *Attack* 245). In addition, difficulties in contextualization mark innovative poems—not that they are devoid of context; instead the collaging of multiple contexts invites unexpected context-building. Innovative verse problematizes referentiality to deliver worlds in abundance; it's not the "death" of the referent, *per se*, but "rather a recharged use of the multivalent referential vectors that any word has" (Bernstein, "Semblance," *Content's Dream* 34). Innovative verse's difficulty is hardly formlessness; instead, especially in the cases of Conceptual, concrete, and Oulipo poetries, it is often driven by experimentation and play with acknowledged prosodies and formulae. As Oulipian-influenced poet Christian Bök explains, the innovative poem "makes a Sisyphean spectacle of its labor, willfully crippling its language in order to show that, even under such improbable conditions of duress, language can still express an uncanny, if not sublime, thought" (qtd. in *The /n/oulipian Analects* 76). Here "sublime" is a surprising Romantic retrofit that evokes transformative experiences with language.

What is perhaps most difficult about difficult innovative poetry is its relation to language—its commitment to experiences with language that valorize the unexpected, not the accessible. Language poet Bruce Andrews explains that what motivates difficult innovative poetry is a demand "for a social, political dimension in writing—embracing concern for a public, for community goods, for overall comprehension & transformation" that, in turn, "intersects an overall concern for language as a medium: for the conditions of its makings of meaning, significance or value, & sense" ("Poetry as Explanation, Poetry as Praxis" 669). Transparency, Andrews qualifies, "will not be found in words. That classical ideal is an illusion—one which recommends that we repress the process of production or cast our glance away"; instead Andrews pursues "a poetry that is a reading which acknowledges, or faces up to, its material base as a rewriting of the language" (669-670). Like the difficult post-Language poets with whom he shares kinship, Andrews seeks to enact "formal celebration, a playful infidelity, a certain illegibility *within* the legible" (670). In other words, Andrews posits the "re-staging" of language in verse to lay bare its methods of signification. Such verse does not provide an "extension of the dominant values in American culture," but instead offers multiple alternatives, alternatives that are "often messy, inchoate, disturbing, unhappy—indeed sometimes *worse*—alternatives to boot" (Bernstein, "Poetry Scene Investigation" *Attack* 243).

To warn readers of the "tendency to idealize the accessible poem," Bernstein demonstrates the danger by *writing* one ("The Difficult Poem" *Attack* 5). Initially published in *Girly Man* (2006) and reprinted to set the tone for this anthology, Charles Bernstein's wickedly hilarious poem, "Thank You for Saying Thank You," marshals an opening defense of "the difficulties" by satirizing the pseudo-populist position that poetry must provide simple, direct, reassuring, and emotionally predicable communication—which is allegedly regarded as respect and appreciation for the audience—to become effective and prove its value. Purveying a double-voiced discourse that damns intellectual difficulty, abstraction, supercilious elitism, and perverse deviations from a "common speech" or "plain style" norm, Bernstein invites readers to consider how such prescriptive and proscriptive attitudes result in dangerous foreclosures. For example, as much of Bernstein's other poetry—as well as work considered by the contributors herein—demonstrates, such condemnation of "theory" and "abstraction" is based on questionable, problematically *abstract*, untested theories that see writing as the transparent representation of speech with a direct connection to feelings. This theory would hold that those feelings are accessible, as though the unconscious has no force. Further, this belief would ignore whatever brings into question both the emotional coherence of a "self" and its full "communication" with other "selves."

Bernstein demonstrates that to "banish" difficulty while promoting the illusion of transparent referentiality is to settle for self-congratulation, reciprocal flattery, and sometimes, shared social prejudice. Does pandering constitute respect? Can't reader and "difficult" writer establish a sense of mutual trust and respect based on the values of expansive imagination and cognitive/affective/social exploration?

These questions motivate the catalogue of declarations and manifestos that were written between the "first utopian, radical, optimistic phase" of "the Modernist era"—during which, as Marjorie Perloff asserts, "the great literary inventions of our time—collage, simultaneity, free verse and verse-prose combinations, genre-mixing, indeterminacy of image and syntax—were born" ("Modernism Now")—and the present. To cite a very partial list, such efforts to define the decidedly "difficult" relationships among poets, readers, and language—in other words, American innovative poetics—include: Olson's dictums in "Projective Verse" about the breath, spacing, and the movement of perception; New York School icon John Ashbery's commentary about the poem as a reproduction of "the polyphony that goes on inside [the poet]," reflecting the fact that "one is constantly changing one's mind and thereby becoming something slightly different" (390); Language poet Ron Silliman's delineation of *The New Sentence*; Lyn Heijinian's commitment to "escape within the sentence . . . a medium of arrivals and departures" (*Language* 195-196); poetic formulae by Conceptual and Oulipo practitioners as described in *The /n/oulipian Analects*; and Mark Wallace's assertion that "[t]he primary value of postlanguage poetry is its ability to extend a fundamental theoretical insight of the language poets—that language constitutes and is constituted by cultural production—to a growing array of possibilities for poetry." *Writing* the difficulties and *reading* the difficulties both enact the difficult poetic text, whatever its form—electronic, hard-copy, or multimedia (text accompanied by art and music)—*as event*: a dynamic, spontaneous experience of language, without monolithic meaning, bountiful in terms of interpretative possibilities, often political but not hegemonic, decentered, sometimes multivocal—a moment in thought in which "re-staged" language permits the experience of what is not obvious.

Tenets of "new," difficult poetry abound, but what of "new" reading? One persistent attribute of difficult poetry is the interpretive leeway it permits its readers as co-creators. Reader response theorists of the 1970s and 1980s asserted this notion about readers—now a commonplace in contemporary aesthetics. According to Wolfgang Iser, since the text offers "various perspectives," the reader can "relate the patterns and the 'schematized views' to one another" and thus set "the work in motion" (275). Works of literature "lead" the reader "to shade in the many outlines suggested by the given situations, so that these take on a reality of their own," though it is "the reader's imagination" that animates "these 'outlines'" (276). For example, a retrospective comprehension of temporal structure, "the product of the reader's mind working on" the work's "raw material," can yield the text's "potential multiplicity of connections" (278). "Each individual reader," Iser holds, "will fill in the gaps in his own way, thereby excluding the various other possibilities" (280).

About the same time that Iser, Jane Tompkins, David Bleich, and Stanley Fish, building on the earlier work of Louise Rosenblatt, were developing reader-response perspectives, Language poets utilized reader-centered rhetoric to champion contemporary experimental work. In a 1981 essay originally given as a talk, Charles Bernstein valorizes the kind of "text" that "calls upon the reader to be actively involved in the process of constituting its meaning" because it "formally involves the process of response/interpretation and in so doing makes the reader aware of himself or herself as producer as well as consumer of meaning" ("Writing and Method" 595). The insistence that perception must be accompanied by "interpretation" is brought "into view rather than" exploited "passively" through deletion of "its tracks." In the oft-cited 1985 essay "The Rejection of Closure," Lyn Hejinian criticizes the coerciveness of the "closed text . . . in which all the elements of the work are directed toward a single reading of the work" (270) and valorizes "the open text," which "invites participation, rejects the authority of the writer over the reader and thus, by analogy, the authority implicit in other (social, economic, and cultural) hierarchies" (272). She also supports the development of "a reader/writer collaboration" from the evolution of "ideas and meanings" (272).

Hejinian and Bernstein's ideas seem to indicate that the reader's authority over her reading has much to do with what the writer does in the first place to facilitate the exercise of that power. In the aforementioned essay "The Difficult Poem"—which is modeled on typical treatises about "difficult" children, parents, bosses, co-workers et al.—Bernstein acknowledges that the reader may take the poet's offer of "liberation" as quite the opposite. However, as a pseudo-therapist and an actual professor of poetry, Bernstein believes that the reader who sets aside his or her preconceptions and prejudices can benefit from the encounter with "difficulty." Bernstein writes: "The difficulty you are having with the poem may suggest that there is a problem not with you the reader nor with the poem but with the relation between you and the poem," and in fact, "learning to cope with a difficult reading of a poem will often be more fulfilling than sweeping difficulties under the carpet" (*Attack* 5). Even if the glibness of his persona elicits mistrust, Bernstein implies that a reader willing to work on this "relationship" can gain a sense of empowerment that enables critical receptivity—one that is not necessarily "conversion" or bowing to a superior authority. Difficult poems instead invite readers to *play*; they encourage "a willingness to jump into the middle of the flow of experience" just as one encounters "that other world we sometimes call everyday life" (Bernstein, "Poetry Scene Investigation" *Attack* 252).

So how do we read the difficult poem? Bernstein advises that readers start by getting "the hang" of the poem rather than try to figure it out; "obscure references" can be pondered later ("Poetry Scene Investigation" *Attack* 250). This need not be an atomized, private experience. In her study *Everybody's Autonomy* (2001), Juliana Spahr focuses on difficult work that encourages connections to "large, public worlds that are in turn shared with readers" (4); she is involved in "deciphering . . . what sorts of communities [these] works encourage" (5). Spahr characterizes contemporary innovative poetry as distinct from modernist verse in its pursuit of "work that is public and yet at the same time nonappropriative . . . a move to share authority with readers and an accompanying abandoning of authorial privilege" (*Autonomy* 53). While she makes a case for reader-centered verse as the most democratic and empowering, Spahr's commentary is hardly utopian, as she makes clear in calling "freedom . . . impossible to even imagine as a concept related to reading (and even the most utopian rhetoric in language writing merely envisions form guiding toward a sort of localized emancipation for the individual reader . . .)"; instead she identifies "connection" as "the crucial value," along with "generative thinking" (59). Spahr articulates carefully those "connections" in her book, but she is not particularly direct about possibilities innovative texts create for readers' "generative thinking."

Like Spahr, Erica Hunt in "Notes for an Oppositional Poetics" looks at the interrelationship between difficult writing and the community. Hunt sees in the interpretations of discrete, often oppositional communities a "contiguity" (qtd. in Hinton 2); she locates the interconnections among these various audiences for innovative verse, and then defines common ground in their responses. Laura Hinton and Cynthia Hogue, editors of the 2002 collection *We Who Love to Be Astonished: Experimental Women's Writings and Performance Poetics*, use Hunt's approach for their anthology because it "suggests new reading and writing practices" that acknowledge commonality and yet maintain and respect various groups' oppositions. This fosters "a broadening sense of community"(2). Hinton and Hogue see their text as creating a "capillary network" that weaves together diverse discourses to "reframe the way in which we speak about the avant-garde in general" (12).

Like Hinton and Hogue, Charles Altieri in his 1998 *Postmodernisms Now* shares concerns for dialogues about differences. However, like Spahr, Altieri is skeptical about the idea that readers can enjoy untrammeled freedom, as he believes that "models of reading" should impel us to "try out identifications with how others construct meanings for situations" (173). Altieri speculates about a kind of "connectivity" between reader and contemporary "difficult" text and an understanding of "generative thinking" that cannot rely on simple notions of authorial intention and does not discard but complicates notions of agency. As we seek to "reflect on what our languages make of us as we fold and unfold their ways of mediating blindness and insight," he suggests that "we . . . treat agency as if it had something close to independent force, then imagine agents as provisional human constructs that we try to get into harmonious relations with the forces of agency that do not require any vocabulary shaped by positive ideals of reflexivity and will. Lyric agents are those who are learning how to let themselves explore agential forces that they neither control nor even quite contain within their individual psyches" (192).

In divergent ways, the contributors to *Reading the Difficulties* respond to the challenges that Altieri cogently articulates. Sharing Altieri's concerns, Sheila E. Murphy addresses general resolutions to difficulties in difficult verse in a poem she composed for this anthology—a bookend to Bernstein's "Thank You for Saying Thank You." In "Extrapolatia"—the title an exemplary Murphyian word-coinage—Murphy explores just what audiences should pull or not pull out of a text. Perhaps the poem is marked as a field, a neighborhood, galleria, or mall for readers' extrapolation of sound, visual pattern, and meaning, or perhaps it is an ensemble of words containing the poet's own extrapolations from diverse experiential and/or textual sources. Nine chiseled tercets feature brief, fragmentary narratives that do not form a discernible temporal sequence; each foregrounds a problem in the interpretation of social experience. The poem opens with the smashing of representations of otherness as enforcement of "the culture's" arbitrary demand for "homogamy." Murphy goes on to contrast "the shallows" of such monocultural trends with "our ancestry," undoubtedly more heterogeneous than the enforcers admit and so distinct from present configurations as to appear to comprise "another species." This is a difficulty of recognition, as when "homogamous" notions of patriarchal standardization and division police gender arrangements, for some, threatening to "oust" feminine impulses. Speaking of "literal fracking," Murphy offers a quintessential trope of a solution to problems of apparently diminished resources that can exacerbate difficulties in a different, potentially deadly way. Here, the analogy to reading is that extrapolation of determinate meaning based on principles of "homogamy," while providing energy or cultural capital for some, also engenders the perils of determinacy, the "smudged veracity" emblemized by the bygone Remington typewriter. In her eighth tercet, the poet responds to hegemonic forces with the hopeful assertion that skill—whether aesthetic, conceptual, or more broadly social—can "remove prevailing code." Such skill persists even in the face of reader resistance: "*I can't hear you.*"

The other contributors to *Reading the Difficulties* further Murphy's impetus, revealing their variegated listening skills in each chapter. In "Reading and Reading," Elizabeth Robinson analyzes re-reading and its role as disruptive and transformative of poetry, particularly innovative, difficult verse in which readers' interactions can modify the text itself to invite further re-readings. If readers are co-creators of texts, then it seems plausible that continued re-readings of any given text renew the material indefinitely. Robinson investigates how the reader achieves both intimacy and estrangement from a text (or assimilation of material and resistance to it) through repeated readings, as well as how re-readings can be undertaken through deliberate misreadings and what the impact of such procedures may be. She considers how re-reading may be enacted through writing to, through, or against a given text and what results from placing an individual reading in conversation with communal or group readings of texts. The theory of schemata developed by Murray Gell-Mann informs her analysis. This theory of schemata investigates the tendency of systems to function in a state of (dis)equilibrium that oscillates between stability and disruption. A system thus may maintain vitality by governing both operations and alterations that may take it over a tipping point so that it must reconstitute itself; this process is akin to Joan Retallack's discussion on the "swerve" in *The Poethical Wager* (2003). Investigating the practices apparent in Flarf and Oulipo writings as examples, Robinson explores ways that repeated readings of a text operate variously within a schema that may entrench its meaning or radically destabilize it.

Like Robinson, Hank Lazer in "Of Course Poetry Is Difficult/Poetry Is Not Difficult" invites the reader to linger longer in observation and questioning, as he provides question heuristics to respond to the declaration often heard from readers of innovative poetry: "I don't get it." Lazer's modes of inquiry offer viable reading strategies that open possibilities for understanding difficult verse and persistently resist closure. Referring to his books, *INTER(IR)RUPTIONS* (1992) and *Days* (2002), and aspects of his ongoing poetic project, "The Notebooks," begun in 2006, Lazer addresses the problems of how to proceed in reading these texts, especially when they have disruptive visual elements. He explains the performative and improvisational necessity of such writing, as the reader takes on the reading or sounding out of the page. Lazer treats the page as a unit of composition, and thus the form of the writing often varies radically from page to page, with each page being a new performance of the possible shapes suggested by the particular dimensions at hand. The shape of the poem on the page, often involving overwriting, immediately puts into question the sequence of reading as well as the assumption of a single reading voice. While Lazer's chapter focuses on examples of visually innovative uses of the page and the kinds of questions these poems raise for the activity of reading, it begins with a consideration of how to read innovative poetry more generally, with particular attention to the kinds of assumptions that can block the enjoyment of innovative writing.

Stephen Paul Miller in "Articulating a Radical and a Secular Jewish Poetics: Walter Benjamin, Charles Bernstein, and the Weak Messiah as Girly Man" re-envisions Charles Bernstein's purposive "difficulty" as he defines a lexicon of poetic practices that support the Language poet's kinship with philosopher-historian-critic-poet Walter Benjamin. Miller grounds his piece by arguing the intellectual border-crossing that distinguishes both the poetic/historical/literary criticism of Benjamin and this philosopher's critical poetizing. Miller locates in Benjamin's insights a call for a new messiah, who, from the catastrophe of World War II, needs to take up the accomplishments of Moses and achieve them all again in the post-war days to follow in secular Jewish culture, in radical secular Jewish poetics. Bernstein, who pays tribute to Benjamin overtly in his *Shadowtime* and implicitly in many other texts, answers the call, claims Miller, by echoing Benjamin's stylistic practices in his own use of nonsensuous similarity, cleaving, dynamic biblical parallelism, and structures of intensification, among other techniques.

Burt Kimmelman in "Reading the Posthuman Subject in *The Alphabet*" argues that one can meet the challenge of Ron Silliman's long poem *The Alphabet* by setting aside earlier strategies for reading (modernist) long poems. Even if it includes numerous personal references, Kimmelman declares that it is futile to read this encyclopedic and, arguably, epic work—which he considers comparable in scope, ambition, and focus (on the relation of knowledge and language) to the early medieval Isidore of Seville's *Etymologiae* and other temporally distant achievements—either as autobiography or as the record of worldly phenomena's presence. Citing Katherine N. Hayles's cybernetic, "posthuman" criticism, Kimmelman argues that *The Alphabet*, saturated with the discourse of information theory, needs to be read according to the paradigm of pattern-randomness. Silliman's proceduralism, aligned with the innovative play that characterizes what he terms "the new sentence," is not only the deployment of pattern that elicits randomness but also one that discloses material aspects of language frequently concealed in the search for expected conventional forms of meaning and for the full expression of the unified subject. For Kimmelman, attention to how the contemporary world of game theory, data streaming, and information theory informs the epistemology of Silliman's grand project allows the difficulties of this "postmodern" "encyclopedia" to become legible.

Kimmelman's insistence on the importance of transforming reading habits to do justice to innovative poetry is crucial to various chapters in this book, including Kristen Gallagher's "How to Read Tan Lin's *Seven Controlled Vocabularies*." Tan Lin often talks about wanting to make reading easier and more relaxing by creating a smoother textual surface than what his readership had become accustomed to with Language poetry, and Gallagher asserts that this text is the smoothest yet; this smoothness helps induce readings toward more direct modes like theory, autobiography, or restaurant review. According to Gallagher, Lin's text, which alternately teases at being a book of aesthetic theory or straightforward stylized autobiography, involves multiple frameworks. Descriptors locating the book within American library databases provide clues for how to read it; they activate its poetics. Lin then foregrounds these headings by moving them from their usual place, tucked into the unreaderly front matter, to the cover. The descriptors include poetry, engagements with mass media, family relationships, cookbooks, book design, and the product standards of the publishing industry—among other topics. As Gallagher argues, keeping these frameworks in mind twists, turns, and changes one's approach to reading.

A poet who, like Tan Lin has practiced varieties of appropriative composition, Eileen R. Tabios acknowledges the conceptual challenge of regarding wholesale appropriation of a single text—a seemingly simple process—as something worthy of being treated as poetry. To illustrate the challenge and her contention that it can be successfully met, Tabios, who also refers to Kenneth Goldsmith and Vanessa Place's conceptual work, analyzes *2nd NOTICE OF MODIFICATIONS TO TEXT OF PROPOSED REGULATIONS, REGULATION AND POLICY MANAGEMENT BRANCH, CALIFORNIA DEPARTMENT OF CORRECTIONS AND REHABILITATION* (2010) by John Bloomberg-Rissman, a poem resulting from the poet's decision to utilize a PDF file that he received unexpectedly. Indeed, she makes much of the fact that Bloomberg-Rissman received the text because he already had a "profile" of political involvement related to the document's subject matter. Tabios offers dramatic examples of how the text's "migration" from the "signature" of an institution to that of a poet can foster a double (literal/ironic) reading with conflicting ideological perspectives. Further, as Tabios manifests, Bloomberg-Rissman's indications in the book that his source includes editing changes (deletions, additions, and word substitutions) permit readers to recognize rhetorical effects used to justify political decisions—about execution procedures. The poem's audience can also perceive how, in their editing, the writers avoid connotations that make regulations seem morally suspect. Even the document's decentered form, Tabios notes, reflects the decentralizing of responsibility for executions.

The use of constraints has often been associated with poetry that disrupts lyric and narrative continuities and, thus, poses obstacles for readers of mainstream verse. As the title of her chapter "Bursting at the Seams: Exploding the Confines of Reification with Creative Constraints in *Sleeping with the Dictionary*" announces, Carrie Conners discusses how Harryette Mullen's humor-charged, constraint-based (but felicitously rule-bending) 2002 volume enables readers to examine and contest reifying uses of language—most notably, American English. Invoking Georg Lukacs's theorizing of reification, Conners applies the term to Mullen's poetic critique of contemporary U.S. commodity capitalism, power relations involving gender and race, and religious institutions, as well as intersections among these areas. Mullen's poems expose the impact of humor that reinforces domination *and* utilize satirical humor that highlights the absurdity and immorality of reified forms of thinking. Further, the tracing of a Mullen poem to a specific configuration based on an Oulipian procedure, anagram, or parodistic structure offers joys of recognition without resulting in discovery of univocal meaning. Indeed, according to Conners, the "explosion" stemming from (and out of) arbitrary constraints results in an uncontainable plurality of meaning, a refusal of containment analogous to the experience of new social freedom for members of oppressed groups, such as African Americans and women. What some would lament as "difficulty" can be experienced as pleasure, release, and reclamation.

Judith Halden-Sullivan explores the "event" of difficulty in "The Game of Self-Forgetting: Reading Innovative Poetry Reading Gadamer," in which she conceptualizes the temporal nature of innovative verse with the aid of Hans-Georg Gadamer's later aesthetic theories. She focuses on Gadamer's sense of the "event" of both poetic creation and interpretation, and the questions this simple yet dynamic characterization can provoke about reading innovative poetry, along with applying other Gadamerian terms such as "play," "game," *energeia*, "self-forgetting," and "nearness." Halden-Sullivan enacts the event of open reading with the work of two innovative poets, the first being the most elaborate of event-planners and the second the most deliberately minimalist: the mixed media poetry-happenings currently sponsored by Stephen Ratcliffe and the spare, implosive texts of Myung Mi Kim. Gadamer's aesthetics, she argues, provides those who read innovative poetry with terms of engagement befitting a mode of experience that invites both innovative verse and open readers to *be* and continue *becoming*.

In "The Utopian Textures and Civic Commons of Lisa Robertson's Soft Architecture," Christopher Schmidt argues that Canadian poet Lisa Robertson's style is a "hybrid," combining earlier European aesthetic topoi with the difficulty of such innovative writing as "Language" poetry and the "New Narrative," while resisting assimilation into any school. In his chapter, Schmidt's emphasis on Robertson's own theory (and blueprint for praxis) situates the difficulties of her poetry in cultural/historical frames that substantially facilitate readers' entry into the work. He links reversal of the subordination of style to content, of ornament (or surface) to structure in Robertson's lyrically charged analytic prose in *Occasional Work and Seven Walks from the Office for Soft Architecture* (2003) to the poetics informing *XEclogue* (1993) and other poetry collections. Rem Koolhaas's architecture, where ornamentation often determines structure, the well-traveled berry-plant *Rubus armeniacus*, and the concept of "scaffolding" provide Robertson with cogent illustrations of her contention that "soft" surface features are more significant in architecture, urban existence, and poetry than "hard" structure. In "soft architectural" poetry and criticism, Robertson as "dandy" and *flaneuse* resists commodity culture's promotion of "the new" by making excess and waste re-function as "secondhand" material, even if briefly. Robertson's critique discloses how cities like her own Vancouver are saturated with heterogeneous fragments of international influence; local and global are not separable. Not seduced by the re-construction of pastoral spaces and motifs, she indicates how waning imperial powers (with enduring economic strength) exploit notions of the pastoral to produce fantasies that counter their collective anxieties in postcolonial times. Pastoral "palimpsests" obscure struggle over power relations and historical change.

As Stephen Paul Miller reads Bernstein with Benjamin and Judy Halden-Sullivan uses Gadamer as a lens to explore innovative poetry's complexity, Thomas Fink employs the work of another continental philosopher/cultural theorist to situate ways of accounting for poetic difficulty. Fink's "Problems of Context and the Will to Parsimony: Reading 'Difficult' Recent U.S. Poetry" places Jacques Derrida's deconstructive insistence in "Signature Event Context" (1971) that the boundlessness of context poses severe obstacles for interpretation beside Ron Silliman's claim in "Migratory Meaning" (1982) that concise, coherent reading depends on the often reductive functioning of Charles Fillmore and Paul Kay's "Parsimony Principle." Reading three highly self-reflexive poetic texts, Fink suggests how Derrida's and Silliman's findings impinge on theorizing about authorial intention or the reader's freedom. While Tom Beckett's "This Poem" posits a text articulating itself without help from writer or reader, Fink traces how a complex consideration of how the three principals interact in the production of reading thwarts the attempted exclusion. A section of the long poem *Toccatas in the Key of D* serves to illustrate how Sheila E. Murphy rings complex, unanticipated changes on the opposition of inside/outside while striving to define what constitutes a "home." In Mei-mei Berssenbrugge's "Concordance," a labyrinthine flux of meditation and imagery reveals myriad problems involved in a writer's opening determination to achieve full, intimate communication with her audience. Fink sketches out possibilities for forms of close reading that neither privilege nor ignore pressures to go in the direction of parsimony and of proliferation. The poems' intricacies are best served by approaches that attempt to mark developments of contextualization, decontextualization, and recontextualization in their temporal unfolding.

Like Gallagher and Schmidt, among others in this volume, Paolo Javier in "Some Notes on bpNichol, (Captain) Poetry, and Comics" considers the implications of how seemingly disparate discursive realms collide in poetry. Javier, who writes poetry comics himself, challenges the notion that poetry is a "high art," comics dwell in "lowbrow" culture, and the two should not meet. Therefore, "difficulty" resides for many readers in fathoming how these "high" and "low" forms can defy the proscription. Before discussing the history of poets drawing on comics in their work, Javier indicates how Seth, Richard Hahn, Grant Morrison, and other prominent writers of comics establish points of common ground between the two practices. These include similarities between the "rhythm" of dialogue, sentence distribution, and shape placement in the comic panels and a poem's patterns of sound pattern, meter, free verse, other constraints, and visual orientation on pages. Further, Morrison makes material from modern poetry part of his narratives. As Javier notes, bpNichol, on the other hand, asserts the influence of the content of comics on his long poem *The Martyrology*, and he speaks of Dadaist and Surrealist resources in texts of particular comics writers. Javier points to fragmentation and instability—disjunctions between visual/verbal—in the reading of comics as enabling conditions for Nichol's predominantly non-narrative poetic comics. Nichol identifies (and Javier describes) his treatment of poetry comics' first superhero in *Captain Poetry Poems Complete* (1971, 2011) as both a parody of macho attitude in Canadian poetry and appreciation for the character's endearing idiosyncrasies. Also, for Javier, the book's visual and verbal components clear a space in which various figures can engage in dialogue to explore multifarious facets of their "otherness."

Finally, in the phenomenology of music, Jessica Lewis Luck locates a paradigm for the process of reading difficult innovative verse. In "Crossing the Corpus Callosum: The Musical Phenomenology of Lisa Jarnot," Luck tests Lisa Jarnot's experimental poems' ability to engage a deep musical phenomenology within the reader who encounters her difficulties. She uses theories of literary emotion from Patrick Colm Hogan, the work of cognitive linguist Reuven Tsur on how the brain processes language sounds, and studies of musical emotion from cognitive scientist Oliver Sacks to argue that Jarnot's use of musical language promotes a kind of cognitive border-crossing in the reader, from the more logical left cortex to the more emotional and musical right cortex. According to Luck, the rollicking rhythms, traditional forms, and musical intonations of Jarnot's poems engage older, more emotional mechanisms of the brain, enabling a kind of readerly ecstasy of dance, much like the avant-garde sound poems of bpNichol or Steve McCaffery. She also considers how Jarnot's poems question that ecstasy even as they invoke it, recrossing the corpus callosum from right to left, in order to harness that readerly feeling of *jouissance* to résistance, similar to the songs of one of Jarnot's influences, Bob Dylan. The strangeness of experimental poetry such as Jarnot's disrupts the linguistic and perceptual habit-body of the reader, working not as a mirror or a lamp, but as a virus, subtly reshaping the brain from the inside out via a gestural micro-politics of disruption.

Contemporary American innovative poetic texts frequently change the reader and reading, shift boundaries in thinking, transform experiences of language, and elicit revealing resistances in themselves and their audience. The contributors to *Reading the Difficulties*—a title that pays tribute both to Charles Olson's poetic line from "Maximus, to himself" and to Tom Beckett's Language-inflected magazine of the 1980s—capture these metamorphoses in critical language. New questions and reading strategies unfold for the audiences of innovative verse, and new paradigms for aesthetic reception are engaged. This book does not homogenize innovative, difficult verse with ready how-to reading tips, but locates language that accounts for readers' thinking about these texts—language that befits their creation. *Reading the Difficulties* aspires to generate and apply a lexicon of poetic engagement commensurate with contemporary American innovative poetics and the dynamic verse it makes possible.

Thank You for Saying Thank You

Charles Bernstein

This is a totally
accessible poem.
There is nothing
in this poem
that is in any
way difficult
to understand.
All the words
are simple &
to the point.
There are no new
concepts, no
theories, no
ideas to confuse
you. This poem
has no intellectual
pretensions. It is
purely emotional.
It fully expresses
the feelings of the
author: *my feelings,*
the person speaking
to you now.
It is all about
communication.
Heart to heart.
This poem appreciates

& values you as
a reader. It
celebrates the
triumph of the
human imagination
amidst pitfalls &
calamities. This poem
has 90 lines,
269 words, and
more syllables than
I have time to
count. Each line,
word, & syllable
has been chosen
to convey only the
intended meaning
& nothing more.
This poem abjures
obscurity & enigma.
There is nothing
hidden. A hundred
readers would each
read the poem
in an identical
manner & derive
the same message
from it. This
poem, like all
good poems, tells
a story in a direct
style that never
leaves the reader
guessing. While
at times expressing
bitterness, anger,
resentment, xenophobia,
& hints of racism, its
ultimate mood is
affirmative. It finds
joy even in

those spiteful moments
of life that
it shares with
you. This poem
represents the hope
for a poetry
that doesn't turn
its back on
the audience, that
doesn't think it's
better than the reader,
that is committed
to poetry as a
popular form, like kite
flying and fly
fishing. This poem
belongs to no
school, has no
dogma. It follows
no fashion. It
says just what
it says. It's
real.

Reading and Reading

Elizabeth Robinson

It's a truism that any text worth reading is worth reading again. This is particularly the case with difficult texts such as formally experimental poetry. Yet it's worthwhile in any case to give close consideration to what happens to the text and reader after multiple readings. One might expect, from a more conventionally oriented standpoint, that subsequent readings help the reader "to establish a text which, in the now universally accepted formulation, most nearly represents the author's original (or final) intentions" (McGann 81). (McGann acknowledges, however, that readings that focus primarily on establishing authorial intention presume that the author is the locus of textual authority, and "the work is critically simplified through this process. . . . The result is that the dynamic social relations which always exist in literary production . . . tend to become obscured." [81])

The strategy for interpreting the text based on authorial intention seems to understand the material in something like literalist or originalist terms. Its textual history is traced, respected, and therefore further instantiated, with each reading. As McGann notes, "all acts of information transmission produce various sorts of corruption from the original material" (81), and ostensibly the best reading is one which offers the "purest" version of that original. One can grant that the "originalist" approach has value, especially as it abets the reader in accessing useful historical and other contextual information. Yet an alternative approach, one that understands texts as points of departure and poses the challenges of innovative poetry, for example, also merits attention.

There are ancient traditions that not only attend to texts differently and more dynamically but with markedly less preoccupation and loyalty to the "trueness" of the original. Consider the practice of Lectio Divina, which is thought to have started with Origen and the other desert fathers in the third century. By way of repeated readings of sacred texts, Origen and his followers hoped to enter into meanings frankly beyond those offered by the literal text. (The practice was, by the fifth century, institutionalized in the Rule of St. Benedict.) Granted, the religious read toward and for divine meaning, but that they labeled this "anagnosis" (reading) makes clear they welcomed ambiguity, surprise, and even a troubling of the text.

One contemporary monastic website discusses the way that Lectio Divina radicalizes the practice of reading (and rereading): "One does not engage in Lectio Divina to acquire disinterested, intellectual knowledge. The intent of Lectio Divina is to make the reading of Scripture . . . a two way street for God and us. Cyprian of Carthage put it perfectly: 'Be assiduous in prayer and in reading. In the one you speak to God, in the other God speaks to you'" ("Lectio Divina"). What is germane here is that this ancient practice of reading and rereading insists on a sense of reciprocity between reader and text: each is involved in an interchange whose outcome, meaning, and value cannot be ascertained beforehand and which is subject to change with each reading—as when one element of the constellation (text, reader, or instance of reading) differs from that of a previous occasion. As Hank Lazer notes in his essay in this collection, if one defers a consideration of what a text means and what its theme is and instead continues to make observations and pose questions about it, its "'difficulty'" can be a source of interest and pleasure, not just an "obstacle." The reading and rereading of a text then become interactive and variable.

A contemporary version of such a reading practice can be extrapolated from Murray Gell-Mann's theory of the "complex adaptive system." Such systems are not static but undergo continual evolution; they change and they learn. Returning to a text, rereading it, demonstrates to the reader how perception and apprehension (indeed, content itself) are themselves variable. Such an approach justifies Harold Bloom's assertion that criticism (and here I would substitute "reading" for "criticism") "may not be an act of judging, but it is always an act of deciding, and what it tries to decide is meaning" (3). As a reader reconsiders a poem multiple times, but each time with varying insights and valuations, her investment in the process of reading is likely to increase. This does not ensure, however, that meaning becomes more stable: what emerges is that there is no final reading for, or of, any given text. The act of reading has become relational, malleable: reading *again* is thus an excellent demonstration of the workings of a complex adaptive system. Reading again clarifies that the text "is not usually a constant [but that it changes] with time and [is] often coevolving, so that a landscape would keep shifting" (Gell-Mann 14). In what follows, I will give examples of how re-reading enriches the reader's experience of a poem (or other text). Reading as a complex adaptive system redistributes the authority of meaning-making back and forth between reader and text so as to create a dynamic and productive disequilibrium.

It's necessary to insist on *re*reading as a means of circumventing our tendency to encounter even intricately patterned texts (such as poems) in a linear and assimilative manner. At a first reading, the reader tries to grasp the work before him. That is likely to entail forming a general understanding of the content of the poem as well as its basic formal elements (for example, its sound, puns, and use of the page as a visual field). This kind of interaction with a poem shouldn't be viewed pejoratively. Indeed, Gell-Mann discusses "compression" as one central (and probably initial) aspect of interacting with a complex adaptive system. Compression occurs as a sort of generalization. In the case of the poem, "[w]hen the compression took place, regularities were abstracted from experience and compressed. The rest of experience, ascribable to chance or to regularities too subtle to recognize, cannot be compressed and does not typically form part of the schema. When the unfolding takes place, new material is adjoined, much of it again largely random, as 'present data' or input data from the real world" (10). Thus, compression assists the reader in distilling regularities or patterns from the material into a schema or "theory." This inevitable process makes the poem more comprehensible but at a loss to the larger richness of the poem and its operations. Readers may mistakenly omit consideration of seemingly extraneous elements or overemphasize features that most readily fit with their own preexisting schemata.

Yet it's possible to apply pressure to the reader's dilemma in a productive rereading of a poem. One example that's been useful for me as a teacher has been to give students excerpts from long poems, sans any contextual information. This deliberately frustrates their efforts to read poetry in the way they are accustomed to reading it. (My favorite texts for this purpose come from famously "difficult" writers such as Charles Bernstein, Susan Howe, Ron Silliman, and Rosemarie Waldrop.) Students are first asked to read the poetry and then comment on it. Responses are most often sputtered and indignant, though there are always readers who are game to find patterns and pleasures in work that is foreign to their readerly habits. I then ask students to reread the poem and underline one or two lines or phrases that speak most acutely to them, no matter the reason. This is an extreme form of compression and, once again, students are likely to respond with indignation. Apparently, they perceive enough shape in even these crudely excerpted non-narrative works to feel uncomfortable with reducing them to a single line or phrase.

This is not the end of the reading process, however. We then circle the room, each student reading aloud the line they have selected. I usually ask students to underline a line each time it is spoken so they have a graphic representation of how parts of the text are weighted in the communal rereading. It is fascinating to see the poem reemerge under these conditions. Without fail, some lines will garner multiple repetitions, while other lines, often odd and anomalous selections, get thrown into the mix. If the page is a score, the underlined phrases indicate loci of "meaning" for students, but the compression refuses ultimate tidiness. Very few readers will come to agree on the central meaning of the poem even though compression reveals bigger and communally recognized emphases. I then ask the readers to read their lines again except this time in reverse order (that is, we start with the person who read last and go backward around the circle). By now, we have read the poem, or versions of it, four times. This reverse-order reading will disrupt patterns and elisions that occurred in the first oral reading but it will also instate new ones. In this manner the poem proves elastic and alive with a variety of possibilities. At the same time, my previously baffled readers have engaged the text in a way that gives them fresh pleasure and authority.

In this particular act of compression, reading becomes a collective act that severs the possibility of settling upon the original author's intentions. This act of compression swells authorship because it would be patently unsatisfactory to substitute a *single* line or phrase for the whole. It's only amid the *collaborative* rereading that an alternative poetic pattern or schema can emerge. Nonetheless, I've rarely heard a student complain that this kind of communal-reading-cum-communal-authorship straightened their reading of a difficult work. On the contrary, the result is more often a sense of authorial camaraderie among students who are excited by new access to a work that had previously seemed impermeable. Here, the communal rereadings evince what Hank Lazer tells us of his work with students, namely that a poem—unlike texts that are consumed primarily for facts—is incomplete, resists the finality of any reading, and thus calls for the reader to come back.

Forms of communal rereading can upend our conceptions of text and content in other ways. The practice of lifting lines from a text produced by a single author creates a reasonably coherent, albeit alternative, etude. Flarf works, on the other hand, invert this process. Flarf writings are, arguably, rereadings of popularly available texts where the practices of rereading and (re)writing occur simultaneously. That is, while Flarf texts could be argued to compress the works of multiple authors, they jumble these sources together into a sort of word collage that shows writing and reading as not only coincident with each other but also proliferative. Consider (one of!) Gary Sullivan's definitions of Flarf: "Flarf (2): The work of a community of poets dedicated to exploration of 'flarfiness.' Heavy usage of Google search results in the creation of poems, plays, etc., though not exclusively Google-based. Community in the sense that one example leads to another's reply is, in some part, contingent upon community interaction of this sort. Poems created, revised, changed by others, incorporated, plagiarized, etc., in semi-public" (Sullivan).

An author might Google an eccentric conjunction of terms—Rod Smith's "Dick Cheney, dead kitties" comes to mind as one felicitous example—and then sift through the results to collage together a poem from his findings. As Sullivan notes, this process invites plagiarism and therefore rejects the idea of authorial integrity or intention. Who is reading and who is writing? The distinction between reader and writer is blurred.

Loopy and intractable to boundaries, Flarf poetry functions as a complex adaptive system. Flarf demonstrates the tendency of rereading to evolve during a process of selection and mutation. The serendipity of what a Flarfist finds and reads opens popular or nonliterary texts to startling rereadings. The resultant free-for-all of rereading and rewriting conforms to Gell-Mann's sense of chaos as "infinitely sensitive to changes in initial conditions" (9). Obviously, no two "authors" would construct identical (or even necessarily similar) texts even if they were to put the same terms into a search engine.

Gell-Mann asserts that in schematic "selection pressures in linguistic evolution . . . favor what is adaptive for communication" (10). Of course, the communicative effectiveness of an aesthetic project is subject to controversy. However, Gell-Mann emphasizes that complex adaptive systems show "how one kind of evolution or learning spawns another as an alternative way of 'solving problems'" (9). Rather than beg the question of what "communication" is, one might instead judge such problem-solving based on the system's overall efficacy as communicative and its ongoing relevance. Gell-Mann cites three strands as intrinsic to the given system's unfolding, evolutionary process. First, the system will include basic rules. These rules might be as simple as a shared grammar or shared assumptions about grammar held by the author and readers, even though the text goes on to deviate radically from these conventions. Second, the system will have incorporated some "frozen historical accidents." The example that comes to mind is the way writing from before (approximately) the 1970s always referred to any generic individual with masculine pronouns (e.g., "When one is in Rome, he must always do as Romans do"). Third, the system will evolve to encompass the emergence of what is adaptive. Anyone who has ever read a challenging poem will recognize that this is exactly what makes rereading a satisfying process. If literary activity constellates around a cycle of pattern-making, pattern-recognition, and pattern-disassembly (all of which operate cyclically), then it effectively enacts the workings of a complex adaptive system and, in so doing, generates novel ways of solving problems. Gell-Mann's sensitivity to the role of interpolation and extrapolation are especially relevant to rereading. The allusiveness, intertextuality, and frequently collaborative authorship of innovative poetries largely presuppose that the very act of *making* a poem is the result of multiple readings. Thus, the rereading and resituation of textual material that goes into the construction of the poem burgeons onward into the reader's encounters with the work.

A poem reread many times based on "basic rules" or a schema and subject to the aforementioned compression will likely, for a traditional reader, submit itself to summary and offer a general meaning. We've established, though, that even as straightforward a process as compression and summary can be defamiliarized through deliberate mis/re/readings. Recall the *reciprocity* that is considered inherent in Lectio Divina: not only do author and reader speak back and forth to each other but subsequent readings also interact in reciprocal and responsive ways. In Gell-Mann's terms, the complex adaptive system reacts to each instance. One might therefore revise "communication" as a process that radiates outward rather than as linear movement. Provocatively, he notes that given "the presence of new information from the environment, the compressed schema *unfolds* to give prediction or behavior or both" (10).

While I find Harold Bloom's one-note theory of literary influence largely unproductive and even tiresome, he does propose an intriguing and relevant analogy that suggests (re)reading as akin to Lurianic Kabbalism. Citing Gershom Scholem's work with the Kabbalistic tradition, Bloom observes that "Scholem's own descriptions of Kabbalah emphasize its work of *interpretation*, of revisionary replacements of Scriptural meaning by techniques of *opening*," all of which direct the reader/interpreter toward the "perverse necessities of misprision" (4). Lurianic Kabbalism envisions creation not as emanative but as the result of the Creator's withdrawal, "so as to make possible a creation that is not himself." As a result, there is a "breaking-apart-of-the-vessels, a vision of creation-as-catastrophe." In the third movement of this Kabbalistic process, there is a restitution or restoration (5). Understood in terms of reading and criticism, this process produces movement through stages of limitation. The reader rereads in a willfully bounded manner in order to re-see the text, and from this rereading emerges a new estimation of the material—in effect, a substitution of one reading for another. The ultimate "restitution" of meaning doesn't guide the (re)reader to a site of ultimacy (despite the fact that Bloom's theory would have all readings redound to a question of a precursor's influence) but rather helps the reader understand that each substitutive reading models rereading, and by extension, remeaning, as an evolutionary process.

A literal example of such substitution is Oulipian writing. Oulipian writing presents a fertile model for rereading in that it embraces exactly the kind of limitation that Bloom suggests through Lurianic Kabbalism. In Oulipian writings, "it is clearly in the resort to complex systems of constraints, to strategies of progressive demonstration, and to ceremonials of revelation and dissimulation that the distinction is created between the 'five finger exercises' of elementary pieces written according to constraints and creation that is truly literary; and it is only at this level that the Oulipo has earned the right to be considered a genuine literary movement" (Matthews and Brotchie 24).

The assertion here is that the disruption and deformation of constraints is exactly what raises the Oulipian text above the level of parlor game and makes possible a bona fide work of art. The constraints that an Oulipian text practices on a preexisting text are strategies of reading and deliberate misreading that compel the reader to reconsider their assumptions about how a text is made and, by extension, how it is read. Oulipo writings presuppose multiple readings because to read is not merely to absorb material critically but to ask what the terms of construction are. Consider Raymond Queneau's experiment with sonnets by Stéphane Mallarmé: Queneau lifted only the line-endings from these sonnets to create new and quite pleasing alternative poems (Matthews and Brotchie 216-217). Another Oulipian experiment, called the "homosemantic translation," retains the sense of the host text while its vocabulary is changed. Thus, Hamlet's famous question "to be or not to be?" becomes "should I live or no?" (196). I am particularly fond of the "chimera" that establishes intimacy with a text by transgressing brutally against it: "The chimera of Homeric legend—lion's head, goat's body, treacherous serpent's tail—has a less forbidding Oulipian counterpart. It is engendered as follows. Having chosen a text for treatment, remove its nouns, verbs, and adjectives. Replace the nouns with those taken in order from a different work, the verbs with those from a second work, the adjectives with those from a third" (Matthews and Brotchie 124).

To carry out such a project entails precise attention to the structure of the original. Even as the chimera profoundly alters and defamiliarizes the host text, it forces the reader to remain unusually alert to that original. I have used a related process successfully for pedagogical purposes. Often students write poems that are weighed down by an excess of, especially, adjectives or prepositional phrases. They may be only half conscious of the decisions they have made and how they impact the prosody and meaning of the poem. Under these circumstances, I ask the author to go back to the poem and add an adjective to modify *every* noun, or to interpolate a prepositional phrase in *every* line or syntactic structure. The way these constructions overdetermine the rhythm of the piece and (often) make its expression gloppy suddenly becomes absurdly evident. The author may even choose to retain the poem in its altered state. The point is that these efforts and exchanges within rereading do disrupt the stability of the poem as an organism; they constitute a form of "writing-as-catastrophe" (or perhaps, more accurately, "reading-as-catastrophe") that erupts into the restoration, if not restitution, of the text as a dynamic and interactive agent. The reworkings of a text as it comes repeatedly before the reader when it is reread in an enlivening manner and perhaps even manipulated show exactly the kind of opening or unfolding that Gell-Mann and Bloom consider necessary to a system in which meaning is being decided.

By contrast, all readers are aware of the ways that repeated readings can make a text stale and can deaden it. A childhood of enforced memorization taught me how, in essence, to make a text invisible through acts of repetition. The monotony of repetition can enact a form of erasure. Even now, I can rattle off an Emily Dickinson poem or the books of the Bible, which I had to memorize for Sunday school, but I do so with a sense of distaste for the sing-song rhythm imported ineradicably into those materials as a result of their rote memorization. All avid readers must, at some point, have had the experience of rereading a text until it closes down and ossifies. Because of this, one can see the absolute necessity of developing strategies for reading that keep the text capable of generating its own self-restoring energy. True, the basic schema of any given text suggests some baseline of stable meaning, but that meaning, as the aforementioned examples have proven, is subject to change. Gell-Mann notes that these changes typically stem from "random processes and . . . competition with other schemata. *The outcome of the unfolding leads to events in the real world that affect the survival of the schema or of related schemata*" (11).

This is an interesting turn in theorizing a practice of rereading. One might argue that such practices as Flarf and Oulipo inflict "random processes" on texts that certainly do force changes upon the text and their meanings. But how might a reader consider a text competing with itself or with other texts, and how would this impact the schema of the text? Juliana Spahr offers an illuminating reading of Teresa Cha's multi-genre book, *Dictee,* that is pertinent to this investigation. Acknowledging that "all languages are narrative and construction" (131), Spahr looks into the ways that *Dictee* fractures narrative and mixes in image, foreign language, multiple histories, multiple cultures, and multiple historical eras. The multi-textured nature of the text forces readers to find more than one dimension in the "history" the book represents, which forces readers to consider "what kinds of readers [the book can] enable or construct" (143). The conflicting voicings, histories, images and cultures that co-exist in *Dictee* do, in a sense, compete with each other for the reader's attention and precedence. Factors such as its "alliances with nonstandard speakers of languages" will unearth many assumptions about reading as mastery even as "it points to the importance of forms of reading that are not mastery-dependent" (144). In short, our reading and rereading of a text such as *Dictee* makes evident that, always, "we are reading someone else's reading" (144). Reading then manifests itself as disruptive. But this disruption doesn't thwart the practice so much as create a more complex unfolding in which elements vie with each other, differently at different readings, for priority within schematic patterning. Difficulty is then allied with pleasure (or so one hopes) as the reader rereads for varying arrays of meaning or pattern. Gell-Mann remarks this kind of static and overlap as valuable as the thinker/reader erects a working schema for a system/text: "in the case of creative thinking, the trick is then to have just enough 'noise' around to jar the system out of relative optima with only modest payoffs so as to attain relative optima with much better payoffs or even absolute optima" (14).

Not surprisingly, Spahr encourages the reader to continue reading, reading *again*, through both our own and "someone else's reading" as they occur in a text. Spahr believes this "unsettled reclamation" subtly shocks the reader toward a reading practice that jolts "the reader out of particularism without reestablishing the absorptive reading practices of universalism" (189-190). Certainly, Spahr is guiding us toward a reading that recognizes and augments the political potency of the text; at the same time, this mode of rereading helps the reader to place potentially competitive practices or meanings into a schema that keeps that system activated and vital.

Murray Gell-Mann sums up complex adaptive systems by insisting that they are schema that cannot be successfully analyzed by generalizing a structure from any atomized set of properties that might individually apply. The reader (of a system or text) can't just extrapolate from elements in order to form a comprehensive picture. Rather, it is necessary to look at the whole system, even if that means taking a crude look, and then allowing possible simplifications or complications to *emerge* from the work. In this I perceive something parallel to Joan Retallack's poethical wager, in which the trajectory of any given system is liable to sudden and unanticipated shifts that redefine the system in revelatory ways. Gell-Mann, in fact, makes a statement that could easily have appeared in Retallack's work: "Likewise, getting a valuable creative idea may involve escaping from some well-established way of thinking that has entrenched itself without being completely correct. Such a pattern tends to dig itself in and attract the thinking process to itself. Getting a better idea involves breaking out of that 'basin of attraction' into others that may be more suitable" (14).

In rereadings, we can encourage people to break down artificial barriers to understanding by making connections that don't follow logically from convention or the rules of previously established systems—those which often privilege a narrower set of patterns for deciding meaning and value.

The whole that a reader construes and creates at any given reading can hardly avoid altering the schema or model that develops through, for example, compression—and this may threaten to universalize the meaning of the text. It is preferable to consider rereading as a way to develop *many* speculative or experimental wholes that can be considered alongside each other in productive competition. The ostensible barriers that define a text can be studied in rereadings, but they can also be breached in a manner that, as Lazer suggests, places value on areas in which we lack mastery. In that way, rereadings help us to understand that all barriers are in some sense artificial and that the unfolding of a system permits new connectivity that might initially seem absurd or even offensive. Juliana Spahr gets to the heart of this when she acknowledges the complex social role that reading has. She notes, "It is one of the most important ways human beings take in knowledge, learn, and go about the business of what Stein could call, with her fondness for gerunds, being human. Without a reading that pursues ideals, all this is at risk. Without pursuing reading's renewal, we hazard no longer thinking of ourselves as doers or undoers, as shifters of patterns of thought" (149).

Practices of rereading are with us from ancient times and arise in sacred and secular contexts in response to texts that are both easily assimilable and strenuously resistant to schematization. For those whose primary reading occurs within poetry or other challenging texts, it's tempting to agree with Gell-Mann that complex adaptive systems like us humans, or like our preferred texts, "keep searching for patterns in such a way that finding them is to some extent their own reward "(14). Nonetheless, the practice of rereading demonstrates itself as both innovative and necessary when the reader's interaction with the text modifies the text itself and, in so doing, paves the way for further rereadings and adaptations.

Of Course Poetry Is Difficult / Poetry Is Not Difficult

Hank Lazer

For some reason, students and teachers of poetry—often unwilling readers of poetry who are reading the poem because it is "required" or because it has been "assigned"—feel compelled to announce, "I don't get it." Let's think about that claim. What would it mean to "get" a poem? If we interrogate the language of "I get it" and "I don't get it," we'll find ourselves in the realm of a binary understanding of language and meaning. Oddly, we know from our experience of a wide-range of other art genres that we don't approach other arts with this binary in mind. Who says after a concert (where the band may have played twenty songs) "I didn't get it"? Especially from our experience of music, we know that aesthetic experience is infinitely variable. If we listen to a favorite song ten times, we have ten different experiences of the song; our focus and attention changes and we hear (and ignore or miss) different elements in each sustained encounter. So it is with poetry. When I attend a reading, I move in and out of attention. When I read a poem, I move in and out of attention. When I give a reading from my own poetry, I move in and out of attention (and have different experiences of the poems even though I have a deep and sustained familiarity with them).

The "I don't get it" remark does have a place that makes great sense in the language of understanding: as a response to a joke. If I say, "what do you call a nun who walks in her sleep?" and then I tell you the answer is "a Roman Catholic" (playing on the pun of "roamin'" and "Roman"), it makes perfect sense for you to "get it." Similarly, if I ask, "what did one fish say to another when they smacked into a wall?" and then I tell you that the answer is "dam" (punning on "damn"), you will likely "get it."

But the nature of meaning in most poetry is a different order of complexity, and to become obsessed with "getting it" is to misunderstand both the nature of that meaning and the process of engagement with poetry. Aesthetic experience is infinitely malleable. There are many plausible meanings for a poem. This does not mean that you can say a poem means anything you want it to mean; there are interpretations of poems—professions of what a poem means—that are better than others.

Initially, let us grant that poetry is difficult, but let us consider why that is so and what it means for poetry to be accused of difficulty, as if somehow the description "difficult" also carried with it an accusation that the poet has failed in her task of "writing clearly," as in a newspaper story or an advertisement or dialog for a TV show. The two finest writers I have encountered on this alleged problem of difficulty are the contemporary French poet-critic Jacques Roubaud and the American poet Gertrude Stein. In a brief essay written as dialogue, Roubaud writes, "'Poets are not read, are hardly ever read, because they are difficult. How do you respond?' 'First response: "When a man wants to drown his dog, he says it has rabies." You find poetry difficult because you don't understand why there should be poetry in the first place'" (272). Or, as Roubaud continues: "You say poetry is difficult. Especially if you know nothing about the poetry that is being written. Stay in bed for three solid months and you'll think that walking is difficult too" (276).

By the time a student enters a university and we begin to have these conversations about the nature of poetry, the nature of meaning, the peculiarities and necessity of poetry's difficulty, the student (usually) already bears the scars of a horrific pedagogy that has been inflicted by teachers who do not read, write, buy, or have an interest in contemporary poetry. What do we expect in such circumstances? Of course, many middle school and secondary school teachers resorted to some sort of answer book, tried to steer students toward the "correct" interpretation, and babbled on about the theme of the poem, what the poet was really trying to say, the deep hidden meaning of the poem, and pointed out (thanks to the guide book) a series of terms and labels for devices that occur in the poem. In such an environment, to paraphrase Marianne Moore, I too hate poetry. For years, students have been taught wrong-headed, ill-informed, and damaging ways of approaching an engagement with poetry, as if the poem were a mysterious object in need of some sort of decoder ring that when waved near the poem will yield that ever elusive "true meaning" of the poem (which often turns out to be a rather vapid theme-statement, such as, "death at an early age is a bummer" or "love is full of unexpected difficulties") and allow the reader to "get it." Roubaud explains, "The chief difficulty of poetry today is that it is poetry. What is difficult to accept, to hear, and to understand (and always has been more or less, though it is extremely so under current conditions), is that there is still this particular way of treating language which constitutes poetry. That is the first difficulty. Any other are secondary. Of course that is due to the very special nature of the notion of meaning in poetry" (279-280).

Thus historically, particularly in the U.S., we find ourselves in an age where students are taught poetry by teachers who are either hostile or indifferent to the genre. We have, as a culture, lost any sense that poetry might in fact be an exploratory domain—the R&D (research and development) sector—for our dwelling, as languaged beings, in language. Poetry is not primarily a super-enhanced version of *USA Today* prose. It is an occasion for an *other* relationship to/in/with language.

I am often asked (as part of an introductory undergraduate course on contemporary arts) to talk about how to read, enjoy, and listen to contemporary poetry.[1] One of my poems that I hand out is "INTER(IR)RUPTIONS 5."

INTER(IR)RUPTIONS 5

BEING bahbahbahbahBAH peninsula probe tender caress exploratory HOLD
HALF OF touch tactus eruditus KB saw the import of dr. williams' deft re ONTO
A COUPLE moval of a thorn from the paw of the limping dog "the political YOUR
IS NICE power of poetry is not measured in numbers it instructs us to count HAT!
IN A WHOLE differently" import / impact / imprint friends see fricasee YOUR
LOT OF WAYS. frenzy silly bull stamps the borders "if a person is hit hard SIZ-
YOUR BOY- enough even if she stands she falls" if you have a bad tongue ZLING
FRIEND'S made to say these words put words in your/my mouth with SUMMER IS A-
FRIENDS BE- flame throwers and rifles troops reclaimed the square but BOUT TO GET
COME YOUR for whom and in whose name the comforter belonged to my gra JUST THAT
FRIENDS; HIS ndmother the rocker was my father's his family settled h MUCH HOTTER.
GROUP BECOMES ere three generations ago we are proud of our family's pioneer IT'S
YOUR GROUP. tradition yes reflected in the bold way we decorate our YOUR TURN
YET den certain of seepage and slippage crossing the fosters ferry TO BURN IN
WHILE THE bridge with his nine month old son in the back black angus gra BLAZING-
FEAR OF "GROUP- zing old eutaw highway strange hand-painted signs BRIGHT CLOTHES
LESSNESS" IS baby dozing driver bemused by odd printing and power of THAT COMBINE
UNDERSTANDABLE, proper names wherever i am when i sit and listen THE BEST OF
IT'S A LOUSY to a steady rain: feel half asleep party to Le parti pris THE ZEST:
REASON TO STAY des choses party dress fleadip is a chemical form SPANISH, SOUTH-
WITH THE WRONG PER- of spellcheck she had been having OF-THE-BORDER, EVEN INDIAN
SON. I WON'T TELL those spells "she" goes more often INFLUENCES, RICH WITH AU-
YOU THAT ENDING THINGS than "he" with "spells" (like THENTIC PEASANT TOUCHES.
WITH TED WAS EASY FOR chains of plastic pop-beads) "spells" STRIKE A MATCH WITH A
CINDY. SHE WAS LONELY goes with "dizzy" "attacks" MIDRIFF-BARING RIBBED SWEATER
FOR A WHILE. SLOWLY, goes with "anxiety" or "panic" imbal IN POTENT PINK (NOTICE
HOWEVER, SHE REDIS- ance vs. more radical dread how dare you i THE MEXICAN-STYLE
COVERED ALL THE cut no deals he weighs his options after the chin TRIM AT THE
PRE-TED ese army slaughtered thousands of students & civilians drove NECKLINE) AND
FRIENDS SHE a tank over a six year old girl machine-gunned boys CROPPED CALYPSO
HAD NEGLECTED on bicycles deng xiaoping (in the analysis of PANTS IN A PRIMITIVE
DURING HER RO- henry kissinger) must weigh two oppo PRINT. RAISE SOME TEMPERATURES
MANCE AND MADE sing forces first he spawned these demo --AND A FEW EYEBROWS--WITH
A FEW NEW FRIENDS cratic partisans (for which he himself under mao MAKEUP IN SOFT,
AS WELL. NOW spent ten years in prison subject to rehabili DUSTY SHADES AND ETHNIC
SHE'S LESS tation for his capitalist leanings) but two CLOTHES IN RICH, RADIANT
LIKELY TO during the cultural revolution he had already seen a mill COLORS. EXTRA
FORGET HER- ion people in the square & then the crowd had thrown his son IMPACT: A
SELF AND out a third story window leaving him a paraplegic for life deng SASH IN
HER LIFE IN fears chaos more than he loves reform so in bed with pro RED-HOT RED
HER NEXT state cancer he ordered the troops to attack in the name of AROUND
RELA- a quality for all in the past a crackdown (to assure conservative elem THE
TION- ents of government control & stability) has preceded reform hiding be WAI-
SHIP. hind overturned buses and tanks [THESE] are not subjective creations ST.

And though the students have had a very short time to read the five-to-ten-page poetry handout, we often begin our classroom conversation (at the request of the students) with this particular poem. I also have begun telling the students that whatever questions they have will be highly illuminating and will be fully sufficient to lead us into a different relationship to poetry.

Why begin with this poem? First, it defamiliarizes the act of reading. That is, we do not know, with complete confidence, how we are "supposed" to read the poem. Truly, the poem forces us to ask how to read it. So, I begin by asking the class for suggestions on how to read the poem, and eventually we might decide to have a couple of students join me in a three-voice simultaneous reading aloud of the poem. I would suggest that this reading aloud enactment is a perfect way to short-circuit limited or finite notions of understanding and meaning. After the reading, I ask the other students in the class to describe what they heard. Obviously, when I ask them what they heard, there are no wrong answers. (Yes, we are deferring a discussion of meaning; yes, we are beginning with a kind of radical empiricism, which rhymes with both the scientific method and with the Zen Buddhist concept of "beginner's mind.")[2]

What we find in the ensuing discussion is that each person hears and becomes attached to something somewhat different in the poem. It becomes evident rather quickly (and quite literally) that what one hears depends on where (and how) one is listening. No one hears it all. In every sense of the word, what one hears (or what one "gets") from a poem is inevitably *partial.* If we can set aside judgment—those pronouncements about whether the work of art in question is "good" or "bad"—in favor of sustained observation, we can better experience the poem and learn how our questions instruct us. Indeed, this radical attentiveness is, as discussed in Judy Halden-Sullivan's chapter in this book, very much akin to Gadamer's sense of openness that remakes the ground of understanding. Similarly, as Halden-Sullivan points out by means of Gadamer's *Truth and Method*, the art of asking questions is a primary means for preserving an orientation toward openness.

What's at stake in a poem like "INTER(IR)RUPTIONS 5," and in many innovative or truly contemporary poems (and works of art), is a new version of *realism*. When students complain about poems being "difficult," what needs fleshing out is what they are assuming poems should be like, or what they consider to be "realism." Interestingly, my experience in conversations with introductory contemporary arts classes and with non-arts majors leads to results quite similar to the assumptions held by many (supposedly better-prepared) creative writing students. The implicit assumption is that a plain-spoken, single-voice, brief poem that ends with an emotional epiphany shall be deemed "realistic." One might parody this prevailing mode of "realism":

I woke up this morning
and I looked out the window
and saw the bare oak tree
with one last leaf
fluttering in the December breeze,
and I thought of the last time
that I saw my grandfather.

It is fun to get hyperbolic in criticizing the assumption that such a poetry—which, alas, is still the core formula for the main product being taught and produced today in the creative writing industry—constitutes a fit "realism." One other implicit assumption of this outmoded notion of "realism" is that poetry's primary purpose is self-expression. Much so-called difficult poetry would align itself with Robin Blaser's observation: "No serious poetry can be described as self-expression" (23).

For the students we teach today, even though I wrote "INTER(IR)RUPTIONS 5" in 1989, their language-reality is much closer to the simultaneous multi-voice experience of "INTER(IR)RUPTIONS 5." You may find a typical student sitting in the student union building with an iPod plugged in one ear, listening to some music, holding a cell phone and reading a text message, while talking to the person across the table. At the same time this student is also glancing down to absorb some information from the student newspaper on the table and hearing in the background other music or news playing as well as what is of paramount interest (the couple at the table behind her arguing and breaking up). All the while this student is having her own ongoing thoughts and consciousness with its own inner voice. Quite obviously, we live in what a good Marxist critic would tell us is an overdetermined world—one in which our verbal/linguistic comprehension occurs in a storm of language that cannot in any certain or conclusive manner yield to a unified understanding, much less a statement of the moment's "theme."

Even so, after a detailed conversation about what students hear and notice in INTER(IR)RUPTIONS 5, we move toward discussions of meaning, form, technique, etc. The poem is, in fact, a collage poem, and the outer two capitalized columns are, as students often guess, from a girl's teen magazine (*Seventeen*; if it had been from *Cosmopolitan* there would have been more discussion of sex). And ultimately the central section of the poem resolves to be a description and analysis of the events that took place in Tiananmen Square. Thus, the poem's square shape. For the "difficulty" of this poem to become something other than an obstacle, it is crucial to stay much longer on the level of observation and questioning, *before* moving to the more habitual discussions of "meaning" and "theme." Otherwise it's easy to lose sight of how much of the poem lies beyond or beside those meaning-centered reductions. Indeed, I often think of the meaning-centered or theme-based analysis of the poem as analogous to strip-mining. There is this gorgeous, complex verbal terrain, and we're going to strip it down to extract its theme. The Tiananmen Square observations exist within the wash and backwash of many other simultaneous thoughts, perspectives, advertisements, and claims upon our interest. It is this conflicted verbal environment that may constitute one aspect of a contemporary version of "realism."

For your science students, this extended dwelling in observation without judgment should be understandable as an instance of scientific method. No good biology student in a lab, when observing a paramecium, is encouraged to decide whether or not that paramecium is "good" or "bad," nor is the student asked to come up with a pithy statement of what the paramecium "really means," nor does it make sense within the scientific method to label the paramecium as "difficult." I have found, though, that it is truly difficult for students at all levels to escape their habit of rendering judgment of the art object and thinking that the mark of a successful engagement with the art object is their ability to arrive at and defend that judgment. I often tell students (and myself), "I don't care whether you like the poem (or film or jazz piece or dance piece) or not. In fact, I'm not interested at all in whether or not you like it."

Truly, reading, even reading poetry, even reading innovative contemporary poetry, is not difficult. If there is a difficulty, it lies with the reader's assumptions (often unconscious or unarticulated) about what the nature of the reading experience *should* be. "Difficulty" (frequently accompanied by the assertion of "I don't like it") masks a discomfort with reading a kind of writing that may be unfamiliar. The rejection of the new and the unfamiliar constitutes a form of xenophobia—fear of otherness. At its heart, the problem I'm describing is one of contemporaneity. As David Antin is fond of pointing out, there is nothing so difficult to locate as the (artistic) present. Most of what gets read (poetry and fiction) is formally/aesthetically nostalgic and retrospective. As Gertrude Stein points out in her 1926 lecture "Composition as Explanation," "the characteristic quality of a classic is that it is beautiful" (496). But our sense of the beautiful typically depends on familiarity: in poetry, one already knows how to read the poem because it sounds like other poems one has already read and perhaps admired (or poems that one has repeatedly been told are good or *great* poems). Stein laments that the new composition—the work of an "outlaw"—in the arts is initially refused, and then, startlingly quickly, it is accepted. Stein suggests "it is so very much more exciting and satisfactory for everybody if one can have contemporaries, if all one's contemporaries could be one's contemporaries" (496). And that is why this issue of alleged "difficulty"—particularly with the new poem—is important: readers who refuse to engage the new, who reject it is "bad" or "difficult" or "incomprehensible," are in fact disengaging from their own present moment in time. According to Stein, the reason for this lack of engagement with the (artistic) present is simple: "If every one were not so indolent they would realize that beauty is beauty even when it is irritating and stimulating, not only when it is accepted and classic" (497). The new work of art is a portal to our sense of the present—an indication and an engagement with what it is like to be alive now, of what contemporary consciousness is. It is not so much a summary of contemporary experience as an act of discovery and a tentative manifestation of it. The new poem is a location—a dwelling place in language—for us to reflect upon what human being is now.

If, in fact, what I am urging as a way to read begins with a different goal—a radically engaged empiricism rather than a rapid movement toward a restatement or summary of the poem—then how might we begin such a process and thus evade some of the initial frustrations of experiencing the poem as something off-putting and difficult? Perhaps the best advice is to begin by taking a sounding of the poem. This means simply to sound it out like our first and second grade teachers taught us when, for radically different reasons, we found reading certain words to be difficult. Let's take the following poem, from my book *Days*, as an example:

84

4/15/95 slow to slogan

voracious to

veracity amen

to mendacity

flesh to pleasure

legs to legendary

costly to apostle

mesh to measure

& i wake up

next to you (unpaginated)

In this particular poem, it is through reading the poem aloud (and through looking carefully at the words on the page) that the kinship of paired words becomes apparent. One might begin to talk about the kinds of kinship, closeness, similarity and difference, the overlaps and divergences of the spelling, and the sounds of spoken words. One might, by analogy, begin to think about the variety of human pairings that one sees in the world. One might even speculate on when or how one might "wake up/ next to you." One might ask how such a series of paired words might lead to waking up. Waking up to what? But all such discussion would stem from an education *by means first of sound or the music of the words themselves*. It is only later in the process of engaging the poem that we might begin to make use of what we've learned from dwelling with the sounds.

Perhaps the fear of poetry—particularly of the new poem—may stem from a common pedagogical error. The way that poetry has traditionally been taught conflates reading and interpreting. Reading, as I have been arguing, should be conceived (initially, especially) as a kind of phenomenological activity: a radically attentive empiricism that is all about noticing without the presumption to judge.

As students begin college, their introductory language lessons focus on lucidity, clear communication, making your point, and effective (well-organized) argumentation and persuasion. Poetry, particularly new or innovative poetry, deliberately defamiliarizes our reading (and sense-making) experience. The poem is on the side of discovery, not on the side of repetition or summary. Unlike writing that can be read for factual consumption, the poem savors its own incompleteness. The ideology of the poem is simple: no reading is final. As Elizabeth Robinson points out in the previous chapter of this book, re-reading is a way of affirming the ongoing malleable nature of reading. The poem and poetic reading anticipate a return to the poem, as in Robert Duncan's "Often I am permitted to return to a meadow" (7). For poetry is at heart—and this is a crucial meaning of the word "verse"—a turning (and thus a re-turning), and poems are built of rooms (which is a key meaning of the word "stanza"). The poem makes room for intensified (and pleasurable) thinking—an engagement and an amplification of an essential human attribute: our peculiar residency in/with language.

There are not difficulties, only opportunities. If we remain aware of the great advantages of reading (and writing) with a beginner's mind, much of the fear or anxiety of reading "difficult" poetry will vanish. In his introduction to Shunryu Suzuki's talks, *Zen Mind, Beginner's Mind*, Roshi Baker tells us: "Beginner's mind was a favorite expression of Dōgen Zenji's. . . . The Zen way of calligraphy is to write in the most straightforward, simple way as if you were a beginner, not trying to make something skillful or beautiful, but simply writing with full attention as if you were discovering what you were writing for the first time; then your full nature will be in your writing" (14).

And so it is for reading as well. Suzuki-roshi explains, "Our 'original mind' includes everything within itself. It is always rich and sufficient within itself. You should not lose your self-sufficient state of mind. This does not mean a closed mind, but actually an empty mind and a ready mind. If your mind is empty, it is always ready for anything; it is open to everything. In the beginner's mind there are many possibilities; in the expert's mind there are few" (21). As Suzuki concludes, "This is also the real secret of the arts: always be a beginner" (22).

What does an advocacy of "beginner's mind" mean for us as readers, particularly as readers of new poetry? It means learning a very difficult discipline, particularly difficult for very bright students who have been rewarded for their quickness of judgment and argumentation: it means learning to set aside our (often unconscious) preconceptions. It means valuing our *lack* of expertise. With the new poem particularly, "correct" ways of reading are not set in stone. The reading of a poem is an opportunity to collaborate with what is written and see and hear what is possible. Reading with a beginner's mind also means noting, valuing, and taking seriously (and playfully) all the questions that come to mind. The questions we have as we read the poem are deeply sufficient. No matter how simple or "ignorant" they may seem to us, these questions become pathways into the kind of attentiveness (without judgment and without a quick reaching after the "theme" or "meaning" of the poem) we seek. It is very much akin to what Keats referred to (in a Dec. 21, 1817, letter to his brothers) as "*Negative Capability*, that is, when a man is capable of being in uncertainties, mysteries, doubts, without any irritable reaching after fact and reason" (277). As Keats suggests, the kind of rapt attention we seek in reading poetry is not a discipline fully aligned with reason. Such reading involves another kind of intelligence and other modes of thinking.

Let us then consider one final example, this from my ongoing *Notebooks (of Being & Time)* project.[3] Here is what N20P61 looks like:

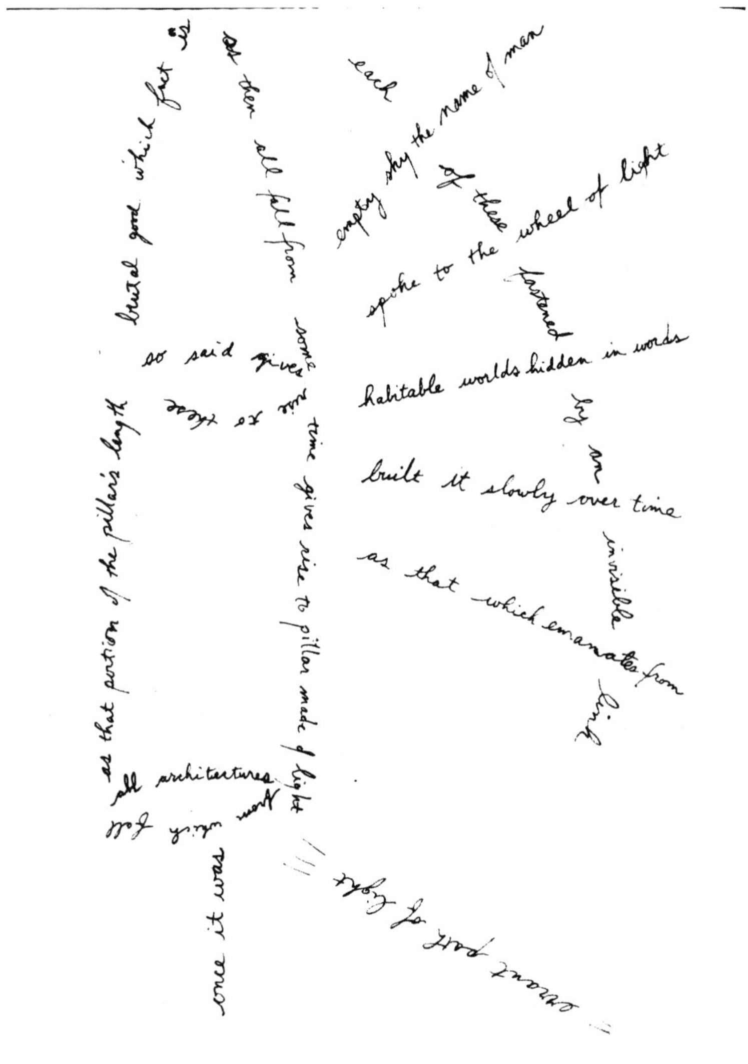

As with "INTER(IR)RUPTIONS 5," there is not an immediate apparent, habitual, or commonly known way to proceed with reading the page/poem (to oneself or aloud). Thus, a first question might be, "where do I begin?" And other questions tumble into place: why don't I know where to begin? Might this lack of an obvious beginning be a critical part of the experience of the poem? How might the shape of the poem on the page be joined to ways of reading the page? Why is the poem handwritten? How does the handwritten appearance affect our sense of the complexity or possible naiveté of the writing? Could we devise ways of reading the poem aloud that might honor or imitate the shape of the writing? Is the shape of the writing itself an element in the poem's meaning? In thinking about how the poem might sound—sounding it out—what would happen if I assumed there were multiple voices participating in the page? As with "INTER(IR)RUPTIONS 5," might some of these voices be spoken simultaneously? When sounding out the poem, what do I do with the upside phrase "errant path of light"? If I begin the poem with the rocket-fuse phrase "once it was" (which does sound a little bit like "once upon a time"), does the reading proceed from left to right—first the rocket-shape (beginning on the left side, then the right), and then the material (the rays with an arched phrase threaded through the rays) on the right? Might these two sections interact with one another and be read simultaneously? Might elements of the page/poem be read as a kind of call and response? Why, or why not? Is it useful if for fun or to see what happens I extract a phrase and explore its resonance for the overall page? For example, does "spoke to the wheel of light" speak to the shape of the right-hand side of the page? Does "habitable worlds hidden in words" suggest a kind of quasi-mystical, spiritual kind of text and reading experience? What kinds of "habitable worlds" might be hidden in words? Why and how are they "hidden"? What do we make of the recurrence of the word "light" throughout the page? What kinds of light are suggested? So much of the page/poem refers to architectures (pillars, built, length)—what is being built here? How is it "habitable"? Are there echoes of other literary texts suggested? For example, does "from which fall all architectures" send us to read Robert Duncan's "Often I am permitted to return to a meadow"? What do such echoes suggest about the building that takes place on this page? What of the Biblical overtones and echoes? Might there be ways of reading the poem that honored or embodied these spiritual or religious elements? If we were to imagine the poem/page as read with music in the background, what music would you choose? How does this process of imagining and choosing an accompanying music help you to dwell in/on the poem? What makes this writing a poem? Is there a difference between a poem and a page? What are the implications if the page itself is a fundamental unit of composition?

Are any of these questions wrong? Of course not. Are there others? Plenty. Notice, too, we have not even begun to engage questions of "theme" or "meaning" (or, truly, indirectly, we have just begun that process as our questions indicate areas of recurring concern). And we have not yet learned that these handwritten poems are improvisations—written without any rough drafts or prior sketches, as in improvisational jazz or calligraphy, a once only composition.

The great pleasure (and for some, anxiety) of the new poem is that it defamiliarizes the process of reading itself. It asks us to think again about how to read relatively simple words on the page. It asks us to think again about something—reading, and, by implication, our residence in language—that we think we already know how to do. The "difficulty" of the poem awakens us again to the depth and variety of our uniquely human relationship to/in/with language—what Heidegger called the house of being.

Perhaps the alleged "difficulties" of poetry are resented by readers because they feel that such difficulty is unreasonable. After all, we already speak and read the language (with complete fluency); surely it is not *our* problem that someone is presenting us with a series of words that we do not understand. The problem at the heart of this experience of frustration is that we have not interrogated our understanding of "understanding," nor have we fully considered the possible *range* of our life in language. Poetry in particular, especially new or innovative (and thus truly contemporary) poetry involves us in an experiment, an extension, an ad-venturing in language. As the philosopher Emmanuel Levinas suggests, perhaps we might wonder "whether language is not based on *a relationship that is prior to understanding*" (4, emphasis mine). Poetry, in its defamiliarization of language and of reading, awakens us to the complex miracle of language. Just as our lives are spent habitually in a state of oblivion to fundamentally mysterious human dimensions—for example, *being* and *time*—so too our utilitarian, non-investigative relationship to language itself calls out for an obstacle that brings us to a temporary halt so that we can reconsider what we are doing. Then, we can begin to read—to see, to hear–one word at a time.

Reading is not about rightness, nor about being right. Rather, reading, like meditation or writing or other forms of art-making, is about intensity of attention: comprehension and passion of engagement. To be moved by reading, and to be moved (and thus to change one's mind), one must have a willingness to set aside preconceptions. As with a taste for wine, or cheese, or single malt scotches, such reading is an acquired appetite and aptitude. (It is also a pleasure.) It is an appetite for otherness; an openness and appreciation for what is not familiar or already known. It involves a passion for possibility. I would suggest too that such an aptitude may prove to be a fundamental survival skill in a profoundly and rapidly changing world, a means for learning to live more fully in the ever-emerging present and for savoring the infinite differences among human beings. Is such an aptitude difficult to develop? It would seem so. Perhaps the reading of poems might be a site for learning and developing such an aptitude. Certainly the allegedly difficult poem is a great place to begin. And to begin again.

Notes

1. My special thanks to instructor Allen Jones and her students over the years in UH 210: The Arts of Tuscaloosa, where many of these ideas in this essay have been tested.

2. See Shunryu Suzuki, *Zen Mind, Beginner's Mind*, especially 21-22.

3. For additional information about the *Notebooks*, see: http://jacket2.org/commentary/furnishings-house-voice-interview-hank-lazer. *N18 (complete)*, a complete handwritten version of the eighteenth notebook, was published by Singing Horse Press in early 2012.

Articulating a Radical and a Secular Jewish Poetics

Walter Benjamin, Charles Bernstein, and the Weak Messiah as Girly Man

Stephen Paul Miller

> The primal world, Kafka's secret present, is the historical-philosophical index that lifts [shame as Kafka's strongest] reaction out of the domain of the private. For the work of the Torah—if we abide by Kafka's account—has been thwarted. And everything that Moses accomplished long ago would have to be reaccomplished in our world's age.
>
> —Walter Benjamin

> The secular Jewish culture that was wiped out in the Second War . . . stranded the correlative developments in America. . . . Imagine European poetry and philosophy by the descendants of Benjamin and Heine. But, to a large extent, this is not to be, or anyway, insofar as it to be, it too must be the task of secular Jewish culture on this side of the Atlantic and of our radical poetry and ambiguating poetics. I think it is difficult to acknowledge this unwanted and perhaps even insufferable task, certainly it has been difficult for me. But perhaps this is what we have been chosen for.
>
> —Charles Bernstein

The above two epigraphs sound more like critical nonstarters than starting points. Charles Bernstein's statement asks for the seemingly impossible. How can one go back through time, total devastation, and languages one might not know and continue someone else's pre-World War II project? Bernstein maintains "to think Benjamin committed suicide is too easy an out for us"; he was more accurately "suicided" (*Radical Poetics* 16). Benjamin reportedly "claimed" that one of his manuscripts was "more important than his own life" (Britt 143). His guide over the Pyrenees when Benjamin fled from France to Spain stated that "what counted was that his manuscript and he were out of the reach of the Gestapo" (*Arcades Project* 952), and it is remotely possible that Benjamin was murdered to suppress that manuscript.[1] Still, if all of this is so, how can one rewrite that manuscript as it was or in some other way account for such a loss?[2]

And what, other than vague generalities, could one add to Walter Benjamin's even more daunting notion that "everything that Moses accomplished long ago would have to be reaccomplished in our world's age"? Would such a notion necessarily imply Benjamin's concept that "the work of the Torah" might have been "thwarted"? Putting these two Benjamin and Bernstein statements together seems even less of a useful place to begin critical exploration. What could it mean to assert that it is a contemporary task to reaccomplish the Torah? And what place would this claim have within this critical anthology of essays examining groundbreaking strategies for reading difficult poetry?

What critical tools might help answer these questions? Alfred Hitchcock said he knew "quite a bit about stuffed animals because it takes one to know one."[3] Similarly, this "chapter" uses its own self-characterized and necessarily fluid (if fixed) status as a work of "poetry-criticism" to identify some of the difficulties offered by the "poetries" of Bernstein and Benjamin by using strategies similar to theirs to model modes for readers to adapt when they both read and write difficult poetry. Everyone's a poet-critic.

However, this text is also an antagonistic model. By observing poetic and critical gaps within Bernstein's and Benjamin's texts, this work contrasts with those essays and poems. This critical mode can be called "cleaving," "since," as Bernstein observes in the *Artifice of Absorption*, "*cleave* means both to divide/ & to hold together" (16). Bernstein uses this notion to describe how a poem can incorporate and be advanced by what in form and in content opposes dominant characteristics of a given poem that are paradoxically aided by that which is seemingly wholly against it.

Although we are here examining Bernstein's critical statement concerning how "secular Jewish culture that was wiped out in the Second War" and not a seeming poem, it should be noted how his inconsistent inclusion of Heinrich Heine within the legacy lost because of the Second World War both serves and furthers Bernstein's argument. Bernstein makes the "difficult" acknowledgment of "the task of secular Jewish culture on this side of the Atlantic and of our radical poetry and ambiguating poetics" to do the work of "European poetry and philosophy by the descendants of Benjamin and Heine" who "to a large extent" were "not to be" (*Radical Poetics* 16). It is curious that Bernstein includes Heine in this formulation. It might have been sufficient to evoke Walter Benjamin alone as a lost "European poetry and philosophy" ancestor because Benjamin himself was biologically "descended" from Heine. Heine and Benjamin were, in the words of Benjamin biographer Momme Brodersen, "related at some (not very great) distance" through Benjamin's maternal grandmother, Brunella Benjamin (née Mayer, 1827-1919)

(14). Benjamin retold his grandmother's stories of Heine rocking her as a little girl upon "his knees" (Brodersen 15). That Benjamin was Heine's descendant is of particular note here since Heine (1797-1856) obviously was not lost in the Second World War, and Benjamin obviously demonstrates that his descendants continued to live in Germany. It would make more sense to say that Heine's *literary* family "line" through Benjamin is discontinued with Benjamin's death in 1940, though it should be noted that Benjamin's son, Stefan (1918–72), together with his former wife Dora Sophie Pollak (née Kellner, 1890–1964), managed to relocate in Great Britain where Benjamin's two granddaughters, Mona Jean and Kim Yvon, were born in the '70s (more than thirty years after Benjamin's death) and raised. In addition, Walter Benjamin had at least one relative, nephew Michael Benjamin, who lived in Germany after the Second World War.

Most importantly, however, is Bernstein's point that Benjamin's work was seriously curtailed by the specter of European genocide, which ultimately led to Benjamin's untimely death and an interruption of the natural avenues through which his literary influence would have proceeded, delaying for many decades the publication, translation, and assimilation of much of Benjamin's work. This explains why comparable European writers who follow Benjamin with similar ideas and forms of writing get credited for them and were for a long time much better known and more influential than Benjamin.

Indeed, Benjamin still does not receive proper credit for innovations in "mythological cultural studies," accomplished a decade or two before Roland Barthes,[4] "synchronic historical studies" done well before Michel Foucault,[5] pre-Derridean deconstructive principles,[6] pre-Marshall McLuhan media studies that include Benjamin's seminal "The Work of Art in the Age of Mechanical Reproduction,"[7] and pre-liberation theology.[8] The sense that most of Benjamin's writings seem "prophetic" in methodological and historical ways (see later in this chapter for discussions of his insightful certainty about European genocide, future media, and archaeological revelations about ancient Israel and how they relate to sustaining Jewish identity) may be the product of confirmatory bias since one would not tend to note the applicability of Benjamin's pioneering methods and the accuracy of his uncanny prognostications. And yet, in an unscientific test, I opened a random volume of Benjamin's *Selected Writing* to a random page and came upon Benjamin's "Painting and Graphic Art." In this essay, Benjamin, probably playing off Prague Rabbi Judah Loew ben Bezalel's (1512-1609) distinction between the dialectical axis between "vertical" divine powers and "horizontal" Renaissance humanistic and secular scientific powers, differentiates "vertical" painterly space from "horizontal" informational space;[9] this stance very closely prefigures by about three decades Leo Steinberg's *Other Criteria* groundbreaking insights into the semiotic nature of painterly space's new orientation toward a desktop-like pictorial space rather than the wall- or window-like space within the artwork of Robert Rauschenberg, Jasper Johns, and later pop artists. And just when I think this paragraph is done, I hear a television football game commentator in the background talking about the difference in reality between a football play as it appears live and how it looks in slow motion "in this high definition super slo-mo world we live in." The commentator believes that the result of the referees' review will be determined by whether the officials watch the play in slow-motion or undoctored speed, echoing Benjamin's mind-bogglingly sensible point in "The Work of Art in the Age of Mechanical Reproduction" that filmic techniques add to and change our sense of reality itself and not merely how we feel that we perceive it. After all, as Benjamin culled from Kafka and contemporary physics alike, the realities of phenomena, contingent on one's perspective, are often inherently fluid. Indeed, as the sensibility of the football announcer's comments show, the extent to which so many of Benjamin's ideas now seem commonplace defy how odd they seemed when he wrote them, and how little of what he said seemed sound or correct, even to his closest friends such as Scholem, Brecht, and Adorno. This speaks to how intuitive and poetic Benjamin was as a writer.

A Hegelian notion of which Benjamin was fond, that quantity affects quality, is pertinent here. The high number of his accurate predictions and methodological innovations call for a reevaluation of the kind of writing Benjamin did. Was he the greatest "philosopher" of his time, as Brecht considered him, or a writer whom even if he were a philosopher wrote outside the discipline of philosophy, as Adorno described Benjamin?

Perhaps Benjamin's "prophet mantle" can be better explained by both Benjamin himself and Bernstein as a trait directly attributable to language and the nature of Benjamin's writing. "Doctrine of the Similar," Benjamin's still unappreciated and relatively recently English-translated 1933 essay, literally accredits prophecy to language: "It is to script and language that clairvoyance has, over the course of history, yielded its old powers" (*Selected Writings* 2 Pt. 2: 698). Benjamin maintains that "in their most transient and delicate substance . . . language now represents the medium in which things encounter and come into relation with one another." Augury is therefore an inherent part of language that replaces "the augur or priest." However this "magical aspect of language" is not "direct" and cannot "develop in isolation" (*Selected Writings* 2 Pt. 2: 697-698).

Fascinatingly, Benjamin theorizes that paradoxically unintended "intention" is contained within most language since "everything mimetic in language is an intention which can appear at all only in connection with something alien as its basis: precisely the semiotic or communicative element of language" (698). In other words, language inherently forecasts the objective world and reality because through its "nonsensuous similarity," language mimics reality; therefore language is the real's predictive laboratory. However, it can only have this effect in relation to "something alien," some strange and new "semiotic or communicative" act that passes through the crucible of a kind of non-, perhaps anti-relation and thereby generates a more profound, truer poetry, whether or not it functions as prophecy. These theoretical underpinnings explain Benjamin's avowed practice of using quotations and references in strange and unexpected contexts that startle one's knowledge bases and forge "a newer kind of reading" with new knowledge "flashing up in an instant." Language offers a direct form of knowing the past, future, and present (aspects particularly addressed by Benjamin's great "On Concepts of History"), bypassing the ancient indirect and triangulating "mediating links" of "stars, entrails, and coincidences" (*Selected Writings* 2 Pt. 2: 697-698).

My point here is not that Benjamin was a prophet but rather that he advances a new kind of poetry intermingling with prophecy and aspects of the Hebrew bible in general. As regards the reading of difficult contemporary poets it must be acknowledged that Bernstein shares both Benjamin's approach to writing and stance as a writer and a poet.

It is extremely telling that one of Benjamin's lesser known essays, "Doctrine of the Similar," which concerns language's role as a modern prophetic form and, in turn, Bernstein puns that he translates "with a similar name" (*Shadowtime* 20)—"Doctrine of Similarity"—is the most prominent Benjamin title in Bernstein's homage to Benjamin. Bernstein calls one of the seven scenes "Doctrine of Similarity." According to Bernstein, Benjamin's "Doctrine of the Similar" concerns how "language echo[es] or mimic[s] the primordial structures of the cosmos" (20). Bernstein calls three of the thirteen short "canons" that compose "Doctrine of Similarity" "Amphibolies," suggesting the crystalline nature of language and the glimmer of recognition through which we glimpse reality through language. However this glimpse requires an alien mode of non-relation: "The leaves turn dark before the trees are shot with light" (Bernstein *Shadowtime* 64). The non-relation is felt as a sorrow that echoes Benjamin's mysterious death at a border he cannot cross: "Find no words/ Cannot cross/ Cannot cross" (66), and "It is never just a matter of recognition as refiguration but redemption through resistance" (67). *Shadowtime*'s "Doctrine of Similarity" seems to have reached a terrible point of no return until the scene dips into Benjamin's similarly titled essay and notes the necessity of language and reading: "This is not a theory of reading/ this is about staying alive" (69). With great tragic resonance, however, Bernstein's "Doctrine of Similarity" rests on a notion of a non-relation and blankness within language itself and ends: "The blank soul of our toil [soil]" (*Shadowtime* 75). And yet this tragic sense is counteracted by the note of binary unity (see the discussion of biblical parallelism below), since "soil" suggests growth.

Bernstein's criticism often describes a process of meaning-making similar to Benjamin's "Doctrine of the Similar." Language, says Bernstein, is of the material world. "There is no escape in writing (or 'elsewhere') structures/forms, they are ever present—'de' forming and 're' forming," maintains Bernstein, "[t]o *see* them—to *hear* them—as inseparable from 'content'" (*Content's Dream* 72). Here Bernstein more forcefully voices arguments implicit in Benjamin's "Doctrine of the Similar" and obliterates our assumption of a divide between form and content. Bernstein asserts Creeley's dictum "Form is never more than the extension of content" and also makes the case that when we acknowledge the material content of language "the world gets revealed" (73). Hence, although Bernstein cites Benjamin's "Doctrine of the Similar" at length, he utilizes Benjamin's concept of a common material constituting signifier and signified, in addition to an implied accompanying diminishment of fixed distinctions separating writing genres, not so much to explain prophecy as to propose "a more reciprocal relationship between political, cultural, and literary theory and contemporary literature" (*Content's Dream* 382). Bernstein also incorporates Benjamin's call for the new and alien semiotic act: "There is no given (set of) structure(s) for all cases; they must always be generated [(re)discovered] anew" (73). And yet a poem "lives" in the same gross and material world we inhabit. In a sense, a poem is part and parcel with a poet's responsibility for a chosen process utilizing non-relation. Bernstein says, "There is no automatic writing. . . . Every phrase I write, every juxtaposition I make is a manifestation of using full-blown language. . . . You're responsible for what turns up. . . . Formal decisions are made and these decisions shape the work" (*Content's Dream* 46-47).

Bernstein postulates that because of the linguistic materiality poetry can offer, we need it as an alternative to "the stale formulas of ideational mimesis" (379). However one describes Benjamin it seems apparent that he thinks and writes poetically, that poetry is an essential part of the genre in which he worked, and that Benjamin's intuitive brand of poetic thinking furthered his philosophical thinking, making possible critical and philosophical advances.

Therefore, given that Benjamin is in a "prophetic line" with the best of post-World War II cultural, political, literary, and artistic criticism and theology, can it be said that Benjamin is in the *poetic* "line of Heine" since, if Benjamin represents Heine's literary lineage, it is not Heine's poetry but rather

Heine's politics that interests Benjamin? On August 11, 1936, about four years before Benjamin's death, Benjamin writes to Werner Kraft about Kraft's *Heine* that "I find only the political material to be at all assailable—not, as I must admit to myself, the poetic material. . . . It would probably be asking the impossible of it to expect it to awaken in me at this time the mood of Heine's poetic voice" (*Correspondence* 531). On January 30, 1936, Benjamin writes that he cannot compare Heine with Brecht due to his "limited knowledge of Heine" (520). In 1936, Benjamin says he is reading Heine, but only reading his "prose insofar as it deals with conditions in [nineteenth-century] France" (521), the subject of Benjamin's *The Arcades Project*. Interestingly, given that a poet, Baudelaire, is a central figure in *The Arcades Project*, Heine's poetry itself does not more immediately interest Benjamin. Indeed, Benjamin asks Kraft to suggest representative Heine poems, though there is no indication that Benjamin receives or follows up on any such suggestions responding to his seemingly polite interest.

Since *Shadowtime* represents figures who indirectly concern Benjamin in a broad cultural context, such as Einstein and Hitler, it makes sense for the opera libretto to also feature Heine and some of his poetry. However, that does mean that Heine's poetry was close to Benjamin. Momme Brodersen's biography of Benjamin speculates that Benjamin's aversion to his ancestor Heine's poetry might have been related to Heine's Christian conversion (15), but this is only speculation.

We do know that in an essay published in 1931, Benjamin, without objection, paraphrases Karl Kraus "denouncing Heine as an ornamentalist, as one who blurred the boundary between journalism and literature, as the creator of the feuilleton in poetry and prose" and a "betrayer of the aphorism to the impression" (*Selected Writings* 2 Pt. 2: 435). Benjamin uses Kraus's observation to attribute "the empty phrase" (for which Kraus blames Heine) and a general dilution or inflation of language to the technology that allows newspapers to put out three editions a day, a reality which demands "inauthentic" news that is not there. This is another instance of Benjamin's prowess as a virtual if not actual seer, or perhaps we might say a new kind of poet, since he foresees similar contemporary critiques of the twenty-four-hour news cycle (*Selected Writings* 2 Pt. 2: 436).

For whatever reason, despite being related to Heine and hearing stories about him from his family, Benjamin was relatively unacquainted with and did not appear very impressed by Heine's poetry, and it therefore does not seem convincing to say that Benjamin, if he had lived out World War II, would have embodied and saved the legacy of Heine's nineteenth-century poetry. Heine may have been censored in Nazi Germany, as were many authors of

Jewish birth. Nonetheless, despite Heine's greatness, the Second World War much more clearly endangered Benjamin's legacy. In short, Bernstein's statement about rectifying the near eradication of Jewish culture by World War II genocide seems more applicable to Benjamin than Heine.[10] And yet how can Benjamin be said to represent a lost *poetic* tradition? What poetry did we lose with Benjamin? Did Benjamin even write poetry?

My point here is that we should consider Bernstein as Benjamin's direct *poetic* descendant in addition to being a critical and philosophic descendant, perhaps giving ascendance to new forms of poetry, criticism, genres, and reading. Does Bernstein assist Benjamin in a new kind of biblical project as relating the two epigraphs at the head of this essay suggests?

These questions seem so overwhelming that it is perhaps better to ask how Benjamin can be read as a poet. Can Walter Benjamin's criticism be read as a new mode of poetry or of poetry criticism? Bernstein seems to include the loss of Heinrich Heine together with Benjamin's loss at least in part because it is difficult to call Benjamin an influential poet. However, we may ask, is Benjamin Bernstein's main poetic influence?

Any argument concerning a poetic characterization of Benjamin's prose is perhaps further confused by Benjamin having written a limited number of very fine "poems" as understood in a more conventional sense. Perhaps through the influence of Brecht's poetry, Benjamin's verse tends slightly toward the Whitmanesque since it is organized by a structure of dynamic biblical parallelism. Indeed, Benjamin's poems are instructive in how they use biblical parallelism and what it will eventually indicate about both Benjamin's and Bernstein's writing.

I use the term "biblical parallelism" in the way Roman Jakobson modified its prevailing sense "of the correspondence," says Adele Berlin, "of one verse, or line, with another." Such a characterization of parallelism had been and perhaps still is usually limited to "semantic and/or grammatical equivalences and to operate only between two or more consecutive lines." Jakobson, however, admits "smaller segments as being parallel—e.g., words, phrases, even sounds—though the lines to which they belong are not parallel" (Berlin *The Dynamics of Biblical Parallelism* 3). In effect, Jakobson uses the mechanism of parallelism, which includes all manner of "figure and field" correspondence, to discover how biblical poetry works. Jakobson's method, says Berlin, "enables us to unify phenomena whose relationships have not been perceived" (*Dynamics* 3).

For instance, the body of Benjamin's "Sad Poem" (Brodersen 201) is primarily happy, but overwhelming sadness is conveyed by the poem's title and last line, resembling the biblical poetic device of the inclusio in which a poem's very beginning and ending are similar and, though in juxtaposition with the rest of the poem, in some manner defining. Five of the ten lines of "Sad Poem" begin with the word *you,* culminating with the contentedness suggested by the line: "You have money." The first three lines of this one-stanza poem's second half play off that monetary "gift from the Dear Lord": "Life is wonderful!/ Your heart beats louder and louder and louder." However, an oppositional biblical parallelism contrasts "louder and louder and louder" with "quieter and quieter and quieter" in the poem's concluding couplet: "The sea grows quieter and quieter and quieter/ To the very depths." A prophetic inkling of universal catastrophe, such as a lull before Noah's storm or the "disturbance in the force" felt during a planet's annihilation in *Star Wars,* is implicit in the sea's "very depths." This impression is reinforced below the poem by the information, "San Antonio 11 April 1933,"[11] which evokes the first few months of growing consolidation of Nazi power that Benjamin cannot help feeling from afar.

Similarly, this wonderfully suggestive and haunting poem skillfully wields many forms of biblical parallelism and yet points toward something else. One senses a magnificent form of articulation emanating from the other end of this poem's silence. If we mix a mental metaphor, we can hear Benjamin's criticism in his depiction of Karl Kraus's writing: "a silence turned inside out" bringing "a precise apparatus of control . . . into play." One relates the poem's "very depths" to Benjamin's notion that "silence is a dam before which the reflecting basin of knowledge is constantly deepened" and Benjamin's description of polemics as "the trinity of silence, knowledge, and alertness" (*Selected Writings* 2 Pt. 2: 436). Benjamin's "Sad Poem" is alertly shaped by a dynamic form of what Robert Alter calls intensification within biblical parallelism, but the pull of such a dynamic points to Benjamin's radically intense prose. It should be noted that biblical parallelism often blurs obvious distinctions between poetry and prose.

Alter links biblical parallelism to the unfolding of biblical content so that "the structure of biblical poems is determined not by any subsurface impulse of narration but rather by a steady progression of image or theme, a sort of mounting semantic pressure, which is to say, a structure of intensification" (73). Certainly, more than any thematic strategy, this mode of intense structure describes Benjamin's criticism.

Since biblical poetry is all we have remaining of the origins of "Jewish poetry," one wonders what connection there could possibly be between Jewish poetry and intensity. Seriously, the Bible only begins to be assembled and codified as a response to the Assyrian and Babylonian threats that culminate in the first exile. This biblical codification starts with a suspicious serendipity concerning a discovery of Moses's writings in the temple. These "found" writings identify the future temple as the only place to sacrifice animals to Yahweh and thus the only avenue to him, giving a rationale for the temple as the only link to divinity and providing an important motivation for fighting for it. (For reasons soon to be given, ancient Israelites were characteristically ambivalent toward a centralized government that the temple bespoke.) However, when the temple is destroyed the Bible itself becomes an indispensable road to divinity. "Text substitutes for land," says Mark S. Smith (194).

The Bible in many ways concerns an unprecedented kind of ethnic survival and, therefore, is nothing if not intense. Similarly, Charles Bernstein employs an ultimate form of intense biblical parallelism by claiming an authority based in sin and ineptitude: "I am as low and befuddled as any man, as fouled and out of touch and self-deluded, that is what gives me a place from which to speak" (*My Way* 98-99). Note that, in the tradition of biblical parallelism, Bernstein paradoxically opposes his moral and authoritative states by placing them in apposition.

This kind of troping between affirmation and negation through the dynamic paralleling of opposing terms is found throughout Bernstein's poetry. For instance, the opening of Bernstein's great poem "Sunsickness" critiques this kind of trope itself: "Blame it on resembling as if it would/ change so easily" (*Dark City* 31). Change negates resemblance, but, since some form of resembling is not actually in the cards, then where is the so-called blame? "Sunsickness" can be read as a slapstick chase after an agent of blame through significations of signification, "rough[ing] up glares" through "avenues" "trace[d]" "by fingertip" (31) until change is accepted blamelessly within, "Worlds/ hourly changing/ sparring with cause to an/ unknowable end./ Asking/ no less, demanding no/ more" (38). Intensity opens to a relaxed form of perceptual exile.

Indeed, a greater examination of Jewish intensity will bring us to the heart of much that Benjamin intuited and held dear about his work involving Jewish tradition and history. In retrospect, there is strong evidence that Benjamin the prognosticator struck again by insisting that Marxism and Judaism were inseparably, one might say, joined at the hip like Jacob and an angel of god. That Judaism and class struggle are inextricably aligned was deemed ludicrous by nearly everyone else, including Benjamin's Marxist friends such as Adorno and Brecht and Jewish friends like Scholem.

However, patterns of archaeological finds since the '80s provide strong evidence for Benjamin's view. "On the basis of shared traits such as pottery and other burial types, language, and other cultural features, scholars have come to the conclusion that the 'Israel' of the highlands in the premonarchic period largely developed out of the local culture," says Mark S. Smith (*Memoirs*

21-22). It has been firmly established that the first ancient Israelites, together with the significant addition of "a motley crew" (Dever 182) of many kinds of outsiders sympathetic with the emerging Israelites, were the same people as the ancient Canaanites that the Israelites claimed to have conquered.[12] Although other suppositions about the ancient Israelites that follow from this archaeological consensus are more speculative, with some evidence open to interpretation, it seems reasonable to strongly suspect that the first ancient Israelites were marginalized, lower-class, and exploited Canaanites, in addition to surrounding peoples joining a slowly evolving revolt against corrupt Canaanite kinglets propped up by the steadily declining Egyptians.[13]

I hypothesize that different cultural qualities might ensue from this first successful agrarian, relatively egalitarian, and more ideologically than tribally based rebellion. These cultural qualities might explain the intense, returning to the topic of intensity, and (for an ancient people) uncharacteristic resolve of the ancient Israelites even hundreds of years later to maintain their culture and at least one of their gods when faced with utter annihilation. Ancient peoples overwhelmingly tend not to value vanquished gods and ethnic identifications so the resolve of at least some ancient Israelites to maintain their culture and a "loser god" is unusual. If the Israelites could not maintain a classless society and a distrust of government as a tool of the powerful, as government was then for the most part understood, there is nonetheless much evidence that these powerful notions initially inform ancient Israel, and, when a centralized government and army become necessary, ancient Israelites are ambivalent toward them.

However, a half century before these archeological finds, Benjamin claims that there is a Jewish tradition that those ready to "hear" can simply hear if they do not "strain" to hear it (*Selected Writings* 3: 326). More than Marx and most others, Benjamin sees Marxism in Judaism. It is remarkable how certain Benjamin is about this aspect of Jewish tradition. None of his friends understand him. Those preoccupied with Marxism do not understand his Judaism and vice versa. And yet Benjamin sees no distinction between the two.

In 1938, before German-initiated genocides are fully implemented, Benjamin wonders how Kafka's writings could have anticipated a world "preparing to do away with considerable segments of the planet's population" (*Selected Writings* 3: 326). (Benjamin himself does not seem to ask for any advance prophetic credit, but he did deserve some. Not everyone was so sure what would happen.) Benjamin reasons that, "The sole basis for [Kafka's] experience was the tradition to which he wholeheartedly subscribed. He was not far-sighted, and had no 'visionary gift.' Kafka listened attentively to tradition—and he who strains to listen does not see" (*Selected Writings* 3: 326).

Jewish tradition is thus perhaps a complementary form of the "nonsensuous similarity" described in "Doctrine of the Similar" wherein prophecy also percolates.

Therefore Benjamin did not require archaeological evidence to know the Jewish tradition found in Exodus, ancient Israel's founding tale of liberation, and running through not only the Bible but also the rhetoric of Hillel and the New Testament's Jesus. Indeed, before these times, around the first Jewish exile, biblical scholars such as Mark S. Smith and archeologists such as William Dever note evidence that the Israelites codifying the Bible might have had collective memories of conditions surrounding their founding revolt.

This might not surprise either Bernstein or Benjamin. *Shadowtime* bespeaks an intuitive need to remember Benjamin's mysterious and unknowable death just as Benjamin's dedication "to the memory of the anonymous" (as "On Concepts of History" puts it [*Selected Writings* 4: 406]) is in line with ancient Israelite and Jewish compulsions to remember the dead since this remembrance seems to keep them in touch with something so special and strangely unique that it ironically can too easily be forgotten. It is no accident remembering is a crucial part of Yom Kippur and Passover, the two most significant Jewish holidays. The wonder must be stressed here that a thinker as secular as Benjamin could so value the past for theological reasons. It is also remarkable that Bernstein can move beyond the great many ideological mines limiting all-time greats such as Adorno, Scholem, and Brecht and be so quick to recognize the staggering power of the resources Benjamin's secular Jewish poetics makes available.

Intuitive Jews such as Benjamin and Bernstein, therefore, paradoxically try with great intensity to remember something they cannot remember. If we had no grasp of the import of Jewish memory fueled by the need to remember lost traces of class struggle Benjamin would seem to take this endeavor over the top. Benjamin says, "Every age must strive anew to wrest tradition away from the conformism that is working to overpower it. The Messiah comes not only as a redeemer; he comes as the victor over the Antichrist. The only historian fanning the spark of hope in the past is the one who is firmly convinced that *even the dead* will not be safe from the enemy if he is victorious" (*Selected Writings* 4: 391). Benjamin argues that the memory of the dead takes precedence over future generations not because he lives in the past but because he owes the past for his bearings. We owe our descendants the memory of our ancestors, completely upsetting the smug assumptions about progress of the powerful: "The concept of man's historical progress cannot be sundered from the concept of its progression through a homogenous, empty time. A critique of the concept of such a progression must underlie any criticism of the concept of progress itself" (394-395). For Benjamin this is why we write. "The origin is the goal," Benjamin quotes Karl Kraus (395). For Benjamin, "criticism and prophecy" are "categories that come together in the redemption of the past" (Benjamin *Selected Writings* 4: 407).

Whether conscious of it or not, no one better expresses and thus comes closer to remembering the probable founding conditions of ancient Israel, and by extension the world we know, than Charles Bernstein: "A bunch of blokes push their way forward. When the real aim is achieved & society is accomplished. As when we find our way in it without thinking in terms of the old. The event itself appears like a bolt from the blue" (*Content's Dream* 33).

The Jewish tradition of class struggle informs Bernstein's and Benjamin's writings, and they both view Marxism through glasses tinged by poetry and theology. Benjamin likens this Marxism to a tangibly messianic force: "The historical materialist who investigates the structure of history performs, in his way, a sort of spectrum of analysis. Just as a physicist determines the presence of ultraviolet light in the solar spectrum, so the historical materialist determines the presence of a messianic force in history" (402). A historian must "brush history against the grain" (Benjamin *Selected Writings* 4: 392) to register its fleeting poetic sparks and encounter oneself by redeeming the dead.

Bernstein is also a secular yet mystical Marxist. "Marx saw as inevitable that a proletariat conscious of its alienation would be able to develop human relations—solidarity—which would be stronger than any other human power," says Bernstein (28). "The promise of the return of the world can (& has always been) fulfilled by poetry. Even before the process of class struggle is complete. Poetry, centered on the condition of its wordness—words of a language not out there but in here, language the place of our commonness—is a momentary restoration of ourselves to ourselves" (Bernstein *Content's Dream* 27-28). Bernstein's "ourselves to ourselves" can be likened to Benjamin's notion finding the meaning of one's time in the past's resurrection within it.

Benjamin's notion of the hybrid nature of time is echoed by the hybrid quality of Benjamin's "poetry-criticism." Robert Christgau notes a similar "hybridity" in the writings and songs of Bob Dylan. In this sense, Benjamin's writing might be said to resemble how Perry Meisel describe Christgau's characterization of "rock and roll's enormous plasticity as a medium. Rock and roll includes everything—the history of world music, the history of world speech, the history of world movement and dress. It even includes Dylan" (Meisel 103).

Although Benjamin's prose is certainly creative, often, in works such as "One-Way Street," "Central Park," "A Berlin Chronicle," and *The Arcades Project*, employing a Surrealist-inspired form of verbal montage, it does not necessarily follow that Benjamin's criticism can be accurately termed poetry or poetry criticism. Cannot, however, the same question be raised concerning much of Bernstein's poetry? Despite the interruptions of what Bernstein terms poetic artifice such as line breaks, many would say that Bernstein's "Artifice of Absorption" reads like a prose essay only nominally written in verse.

And yet "Artifice of Absorption," like Benjamin's and Bernstein's prose, is poetic because of this prose quality. In "Artifice of Absorption," Bernstein says "absorption," which describes an endlessly ongoing process, exists in an essentially shifting "relationship between/ a reader &/ a work." Therefore the ongoing quality of prosaic absorption presupposes a poetic artifice in, as Benjamin puts it, a "textile" quality "woven" into "good prose" that the reader cannot help but combine with associations brought to the text by each reader (*Selected Writings* 1: 455-456).

Both Bernstein's poetry and prose often work as poetry because they have qualities of good prose as Benjamin characterizes it. "Work on good prose," wrote Benjamin, "has three steps: a musical stage when it is composed, an architectonic one when it is built, and a textile one when it is woven" (455-456). Significantly, Benjamin sees prose as a combination of the musical, architectural, and textile arts. "Criticism," said Benjamin, "must speak the language of artists" (*Selected Writings* 1: 460).

It is important to note that Benjamin cautions us about his observation concerning the "three" artistic "steps" to "good prose" with the heading "Caution: Steps." For Benjamin, literature implies possible danger. In 1926, Benjamin reasons that since "the construction of life is at present in the power . . . of fact . . . true literary activity cannot aspire to take place within a literary framework" since Benjamin calls the contemporary mode of facts "the habitual expression of its sterility" (444). Benjamin determines that the world of facts must be challenged, and, in terms of both practical and literary impact, "significant literary effectiveness can come only into being in strict alternation between action and writing; it must nurture the inconspicuous forms that fit its influence in active communities better than does the pretentious, universal gesture of the book" (*Selected Writings* 1: 444).

In other words, despite the love of books that Benjamin describes in "Unpacking my Library" and elsewhere, writing exists within a wider world and the forms in which it is presented are of constant and changing interest. Benjamin calls "leaflets, brochures, articles, and placards . . . prompt language" that are "actively equal to the moment" (*Selected Writings* 1: 444). Of course, for much of Bernstein's career, this describes how he primarily published. Even after he finds publication with major university presses such as the University of Chicago Press, Bernstein is extremely active within the "prompt language forms" of electronic publishing and collaborations with artists in exhibitions and books. It is not surprising, therefore, that Bernstein should say that "[p]oetics is an ethical engagement with the shifting conditions of everyday life" (*Attack* 78). In *The Politics of Poetic Form*, Bernstein speculates that if we need "to found" a "republic" of "letters" or "discourses," "the task requires poetic acts, but not just by poets" (viii).

Poetry insists on unexpected venues. "You might say," Bernstein says, "that several forms of oppression rob a people of its right to poetry—and the crisis for poetry, for the aesthetic, is to create a space for poetry again and again" (*Attack* 35). In a culture in which, as Bernstein says, "American Official Verse Culture operates on the premise that innovation and originality are not criteria of aesthetic value, and while not an absolute barrier to quality, are something to be held against a work" (*Attack* 33), neither a formal or technological center can hold. From a formal perspective, Bernstein's poetry heats up between his poetry and his criticism, and technologically it is not surprising that Bernstein is associated online with PennSound. "There is no poem apart from its material dimension, in typography or in a performance," says Bernstein (*Talking the Boundless Book* 41). Poetry cannot suppress its own manifestation in the world. Benjamin similarly explained the goal of using writing to change the world of objective facts to Martin Buber: "My concept of objective and, at the same time, highly political style and writing is this: to awaken interest in what was denied to the world; only where this sphere of speechlessness reveals itself in unutterably pure power can the magic spark leap between the word and the motivating deed, where the unity of these two equally real entities resides" (*Correspondence* 80).

Benjamin argues that a sense of the world beyond "facts" is a necessary part of writing. Reality, never set, includes the possible, pending, erased, and "speechless." Benjamin writes to Buber that "everything factual already exists in theory" (*Correspondence* 313). Similarly, Bernstein says, "Facts in poetry are primarily/ factitious" (*Artifice* 6). Reality is a process within the greater reality of the poetic, and poems include the real and reality. Essays, associated with reality and sometimes with "creative nonfiction," are in a sense a form of poetry because they necessarily unfold within contexts of subjectively driven and non-value-neutral "inner" interest. After all, essays are a form of discourse, and the word "discourse" is derived from the Latin for "a running to and fro." Keeping this in mind, it seems natural to think of poetry as a kind of river running between the banks of a poetry that looks like poetry and another poetry that is criticism.

Many of Bernstein's difficult poems can be read within the context of how both Benjamin and Bernstein characterize criticism. Indeed, the brilliant last line of "Artifice of Absorption" implies that this is a prime goal of poetry writing. The "fruition" of the poem's speaker's "relationship with readers" is "that the site of reading become a fact of value" (*Artifice* 65). That the poem offers "a fact" suggests that it merges with an objective world rooted in critical analysis. However, that it is "a fact of value" relates this objectivity with what Bernstein has called "language which comes to be in the world as the condition of a specific place, a specific negotiation by a writer that does not appropriate words but invests them. . . . [L]anguage is a living necessity making time and space" (*Content's Dream* 353). And yet it should be noted that this has nothing to do with a politically conservative kind of neoconservative anti-fact-based reality because language encompasses and is not divorced from "reality," whereas such a neoconservative reality by its not fully reasoned premises for actions tends to serve the ulterior motives of those who are anxious to exclude critical analysis that does not support them. Indeed, Benjamin cites Karl Kraus's brilliant jibe against Stefan George's similar conservatism: "he who found the goal before the way/ did not come from the origin" (*Selected Writings* 2 Pt.2: 451).

Benjamin and Bernstein have an opposing methodology. "The site of reading becom[ing] a fact of value" (Bernstein *Artifice* 65) absorbs the function of criticism in poetry. Poetry becomes a tool of criticism. Since even unlearning is a form of learning, we cannot help but learn from poetry. Benjamin and Bernstein teach us to read poetry as the play of important critical faculties.

For instance, the title of Charles Bernstein's great poem, "The Kiwi Bird in the Kiwi Tree" (*All the Whiskey in Heaven* 144), can be read to indicate an essay about a subject that lends itself to an inner life of thought and feeling, that is, the kiwi bird, which finds a corroborating outer reality in an ironically similar internal "site" of, from a New Yorker's perspective, a seemingly imaginary subject, the kiwi tree. "The Kiwi Bird in the Kiwi Tree" plays on this poetically enabling dynamic tension between the inner and the outer, the mind and the world.

The poem starts with a kind of imaginative denial: "I want no paradise." However, this is soon followed by an appositional suggestion of what paradise might be: "only to be/ drenched in the downpour of words, fecund/ with tropicality." "Tropicality" clearly suggests both the paradise of the tropics and fecundity of tropes pouring out of words that are like water. This abundant "tropicality" disarms its opposite number—fundamentalism, which opaquely and unimaginatively follows and clings to interpretations of words that are resistant to being seen as mere interpretations.

Bernstein stresses the ironically fun aspect within fundamentalism while still pointing beyond its severe limits: "Fundament be-/ yond relation." The primary "relation" that fundamentalism is beyond and not enabled through is the dynamic relationship between critical analysis and poetic synthesis. Bernstein here applies the previously quoted Benjamin remark that "everything factual already exists in theory" by saying that fundamentalist truth is "less 'real' than made." Fundamentalism is equated to "arms" that "surround" and apparently suppress "a baby's gurgling." Whereas the alternative of fundamentalism, a secular though perhaps theological tension between poetry and criticism, provides "pinion," fundamentalism can only "pronounce its promise" through the limitations of "encir-/cling mesh." Bernstein demonstrates how his "secular poetics" exists within a discursive continuum with Benjamin's "material dialects" and worldly theology.

However, as in the case of Benjamin's "good prose," "the tailor" enters Bernstein's poem to provide "the seam that binds" and "move on" to more appropriate accompaniments for gurgling such as "toys or talcums, skates & scores." These words are immediately followed by the poetic conclusion that "Only/ the imaginary is real." It is never quite clear whether the poem serves the essay or the essay the poem. The poem's conclusion calls attention to the preceding confusion: "The first fact is the social body,/ one from another, nor needs no other." Although "the social body" might imply the external world, the poem makes a case for its primary existence as linguistic, imaginative, and perhaps subjectively based.

Bernstein's interest in secular Judaism, much like Benjamin's similar interest, indicates the secular and poetic theological alternative both Benjamin and Bernstein provide for fundamentalism. Benjamin's work, like Bernstein's, is best read as several radically new and important manifestations of poetry and poetry criticism. Such a reading invigorates our living poetic traditions and presents possibilities for new and vital poetry. Considering Benjamin as a poet enhances our appreciation of Bernstein's and many other poets' and poet-critics' work.

There had been both great poetic essayists before Benjamin and great poets who were critics before Bernstein. Even in our previous analysis of "The Kiwi-Bird in the Kiwi-Tree," it was difficult not to think of it as related to Wallace Stevens's plays of reality and the poetic and philosophical imaginations within tropical settings. Indeed, Stevens, like Bernstein, does similar work in his poetry and criticism and they play one off the other. We need more studies tracing the continuities and innovations amongst many poet-critics, such as Stevens, Poe, Ashbery, DuPlessis, Whitman, and Damon, to name only a few. There is nonetheless a special need to link Bernstein with Benjamin because of the tremendous poetic work done in their respective prose, the critical work done by Bernstein's poetry, and the synergy at work in the writings of Benjamin and Bernstein. Simply put, there is enough space in this chapter to only treat Bernstein and Benjamin.

Benjamin consciously tried molding his critical discourse into creative poetry. In his autobiographical writing, he interfaced minimal autobiographical vignettes and descriptions with equally minimal analysis, observations, and critical suggestions. As Benjamin put it in "The Coming Philosophy," the goal is to "correspond . . . experience" with "knowledge." Such knowledge becomes a kind of "theological" "teaching"—"theology to the extent that it contains historically philosophical elements" (*Selected Writings* 1: 108). Benjamin's theological perspective, like Bernstein's, is dynamically secular. However, knowledge may be of this world, but it is not close-minded and unnecessarily limited. To the contrary, "Experience," says Benjamin, "is the uniform and continuous multiplicity of knowledge" (*Selected Writings* 1: 108). In "One-Way Street," Benjamin asserts that "[n]ow things press too urgently on human society," and it is no longer "possible to adopt a standpoint." Thus overly dry, limited criticism tending to repress virtually all poetic function becomes less convincing and satisfactory. Therefore, according to Benjamin, only "[f]ools lament the decay of criticism" (*Selected Writings* 1: 476) that does not move beyond strictly contained critical thought and tap poetic thought. New kinds of powerful poetry-criticism, or, at the very least, creative criticism rooted in "the uniform and continuous multiplicity of knowledge" (*Selected Writings* 1: 108) became increasingly necessary and possible. Benjamin's "poetry-criticism" took several forms.

Benjamin has four kinds of poetry criticism: the profane illuminations of critical analysis, the autobiographical writing, *The Arcades Project*, and Benjamin's immortal triple synthesis formed by bottom lining *The Arcades Project* in "Paris, the Capital of the Nineteenth Century," then the bottom lining of his thoughts about the twentieth century in "The Work of Art in the Age of Mechanical Reproduction," and his bottom lining of the future in "On Concepts of History."

Benjamin hoped to become known for his new form of creative nonfiction through works such as "One-Way Street" and "Berlin Childhood around 1900" that weave and juxtapose many thoughts and experiences. "Berlin Childhood around 1900" contains multitudes of richly complex yet startlingly insightful moments. For instance, the final 1938 version of "Berlin Childhood around 1900" (*Selected Writings* 3: 344-386) concludes with a short tale that intermeshes both a theological and sexual coming of age. Entitled "Sexual Awakening," this tale begins and ends evoking an unnamed Berlin street at night wherein "wanderings that know no end" ultimately "awaken" "instincts." The narrator, who can be called Benjamin since the work portends to be autobiographical, feels "an aversion" to "a distant relative" (*Selected Writings* 3: 386), and this oddly corresponds with our prior discussion about Benjamin and Heine. This aversion corresponds with "a suspicion of religious ceremony" because the parents of Benjamin, "whose time had come" for "the awakening of the sex drive," hand him "into the custody of a distant relative" who is to take the young Benjamin to "a ceremony of public worship" since "it was the Jewish New Year."

Benjamin's apprehension about "the virtual stranger to whom [he] had been entrusted" parallels his antipathy about going to "the Reform congregation, with which [his] mother felt some sympathy on account of family tradition" (386). However, this family tradition apparently is contradicted by the unexplained absence of Benjamin's mother herself. We never know why Benjamin is not meeting his parents at the congregation. We do not believe he is because he needs to get his synagogue "admission ticket" from his strange and distant relative. Benjamin implies that he is something like a New Year's gift from his mother to this relative: "For this holiday, I had been given into the custody of a distant relative." The distant nature of the relative equates to the emotionally distant nature with which Benjamin entertains the prospect of going to the Reformed German Jewish service that presumably has been assimilated to the point of being virtually featureless and passionless. For Benjamin, the ceremony "promised only embarrassment." Why? When linked with Benjamin's seeming fear of having a suspicious and morally unproven relative replace the reliability of his parents, there is a hint of an unknown quality of Benjamin's personal orientation toward Judaism. Benjamin likens shame and embarrassment with a kind of theological malpractice since God is perceived to have been improperly approached, that is, approached at times in the tradition of a congregation Benjamin apparently feels is out of touch with Judaism. To feel intimate with the outside world, Benjamin therefore must dodge his distant relative, who is emblematic of something between a distant god and an inconsequential one, and the relative's reformed congregation since they bespeak guarded, non-intimate Judaism.

"Sexual Awakening," as is much of Benjamin's writing, is dynamically structured through pairs and opposites and a kind of poetic though semantic parallelism structurally animating the Hebrew bible. For instance, to contest this unwanted dual "critical distance" separating him from both his sense of familial closeness and his theological bearings, Benjamin matches the endless quality he feels about the Berlin streets at the start of this eerily poetic vignette with the more dire quality of being endlessly lost in the happenstance that "for whatever reason—whether because I had forgotten his address, or because I could not get my bearings in the neighborhood—the hour was getting later and later, and my wandering more hopeless" (386).

However, in keeping with the double structuring of this piece, two emotional waves overcome Benjamin. He is first "overcome by a burning wave of anxiety" since he will "never make it to the synagogue" (386). "But also, at the very same moment, and even before this other feeling had ebbed" he felt "a second wave, this one of other indifference." Hence, Benjamin feels a first wave of shame and hopeless anxiety that is immediately counteracted by a feeling of resignation expressing itself as "So be it—I don't care." Almost magically there is a new synthesis as "these two waves combine" into "a dawning sensation of pleasure." This sexual awakening introduces Benjamin to "awakened instincts" as he takes in the potential pleasures available upon the streets in which he is lost. This new instinctual sense appears to be vital to so much Benjamin values, including sexuality, Judaism, and writing.

Like most of Benjamin's works "Sexual Awakening" operates within a play of poetic "negotiations," as Bernstein terms it (*Content's Dream* 353), and we misread Benjamin's writings if we deny their poetic dimension, or, that is, their reflexively linguistic play, as demonstrated by the poetic parallelism on display in "Sexual Awakening." Although I here consider Benjamin's work in translation, linguistic reflexivity as a poetic function extends to content, audience, speaker, and other language elements consistent with Roman Jakobson's and Adele Berlin's analyses of poetry that corresponds to the tradition of the Hebrew bible. Additionally, micro-elements of language themselves can be considered in translation. Indeed, Benjamin, in his groundbreaking "On the Task of Translation," maintains that a prime virtue of translated work lies in its imaginative and crafty contributions to the language that is the object of the original work's translation.

A crucial facet and power of Benjamin's criticism is lost if we do not read it as imaginative poetry. This is not to say that his criticism should be considered imaginary but rather that Benjamin's readers can apprehend content as it is found within and developed from Benjamin's work when read through imaginative faculties that sometimes employ dynamic biblical parallelism. The critical form of Benjamin's "poetry" renders it more possible for his audience to share in imaginative play through the medium of his work. Clearly, through structure and intensity, Benjamin forges a new sense of the biblical that Bernstein advances. Both writers provide materials for new ways of reading.

Benjamin asks that we "understand direct creativity as a form of communal activity" (*Selected Writings* 1: 42). Benjamin's "The Life of Students" is premised on the folly and impossibility of academia separating the imaginative faculties that develop through learning from all forms of passion. That it is difficult for us to consider Benjamin's criticism as poetry speaks to the crux of much in Benjamin since, according to Benjamin, "the uncompromising hostility of the academy toward the life that art requires can be interpreted as a rejection of every form of direct creativity that is unconnected with bureaucratic office" (42). Benjamin's poetry is formally unconnected with the bureaucratic office of poetry. However, speaking as a poet, it is disheartening to consider a living poetic tradition that cannot read Benjamin as one of our greatest twentieth-century poets, and I cannot imagine a vital twenty-first century poetry or criticism that cannot consider how poetically Benjamin fuses dynamic linguistic, cultural, ethical, spiritual, historical, and aesthetic concerns. This terrible inability would seem to be a triumph of "Official Verse Culture" (*Attack* 33).

Benjamin's "poetry" is quintessentially "difficult" because it is definitively "un-facile" in the sense we now generally use the word "facile." Benjamin's great work can be neither shallow nor superficial because it is shaped by simultaneous critical and creative processes that can, according to his last major work, "On the Concept of History," "blast open the continuum of history" (*Selected Writings* 4: 396). This grand difficulty is implicit in Benjamin's "poetry-criticism" and concerns his writing's multi-dimensionality, which poetically shuttles amongst philosophy, history, and literary criticism. And yet it might be said that Benjamin accomplishes a most difficult poetry-criticism through a relentless yet perceptive ease that recalls Benjamin's appropriation of Baudelaire's flâneur and the flâneur's "propensity that perhaps proves the true efficacy of idleness in human affairs" when walking within the "closed room and airy nature" of "the Jardin d'Hiver, a colossal greenhouse" (*Arcades Project* 422-3). This enclosed yet open space emblematizes much that is central within Benjamin's thinking and writing process: the nineteenth-century Parisian arcades, the modern city, the creative collector and collection, and Benjamin's writing itself. From the time of Benjamin's formative years, inclusiveness is crucially integrated within his subject and method. In "The Life of Students," written in his early twenties, Benjamin asserts that "the creative spirit" requires "the necessary inclusion of women" (*Selected Writings* 1: 44). This observation is in keeping with the creatively critical project Benjamin charts for himself early in his career when "The Life of Students" characterizes a "focus on the system as a whole" as "the exclusive task of criticism" (38). Indeed, one might argue that, in this new sense of criticism, every aspect of a Benjamin work bespeaks the whole. However, Benjamin cognizes the creative, poetic, and critical straightjacket this aesthetic condition can impose, and, in *The Arcades Project*, he insists upon the dissimilarity and "destruction" that facilitates similarity and "construction," thus very literally and specifically anticipating and systematically using deconstruction several decades before its formal inception.

In preliminary fashion, "The Life of Students" prefigures Benjamin's ultimate task of "blast[ing] open the continuum of history" (*Selected Writings* 4: 396). Benjamin's early essay begins by challenging the historian's "faith in the infinite extent of time" and "concern . . . only with the speed or lack of it, with which people and epochs advance along the path of progress, . . . correspond[ing] to a certain absence of coherence and rigor in the demands it makes on the present." Benjamin says that he will instead "delineate a particular condition in which history appears to be concentrated in a single focal point" (*Selected Writings* 1: 37). Benjamin thus brings all history into the purview of something like a textual or poetic tense. History is not to be studied as "details" upon the conveyor belt of linear time. "Rather," says Benjamin, "the task is to group its metaphysical structure, as with the messianic domain of the French Revolution" (*Selected Writings* 1: 37). To contact the sharply pertinent and "messianic domain" of all manner of past phenomena, such as the French Revolution, is perhaps Benjamin's prime poetic and critical goal.

We might not normally consider that poetic "knowledge comes only in lightning flashes," and "the text is the long roll of thunder that follows" (Benjamin *Selected Writings* 1: 456), but it behooves us to read Benjamin's writing as poetry because it advances a tradition for poetry that accomplishes this extraordinary task. In *The Arcades Project*, he speaks candidly about his outrageous compositional system: "What for others are deviations are, for me, the data which determine my course. On the differentials of time (which, for others, disturb the main lines of the inquiry), I base my reckoning" (456). Poetic impact is necessary to history because history can be understood "only through the awakening of a not-yet conscious knowledge of what has been" (464). Conversely, the critical, or as Benjamin also puts it, the "scholastic" can be valued as requisite for art.

"One moment swaggering, and the next scholastic" is how Benjamin positively describes "the Marxist theory of art" (*Selected Writings* 1: 465). "Swaggering" can be likened to poetic in that air-tight proof is not the initial primary concern. Bernstein questions "the academic culture of the humanities," which he says, "places more emphasis on learning its ropes, on professional conformity, than it does on actual research, writing, thinking, or teaching of the people who make up the profession" (*Attack* 16). Bernstein sees a place for his criticism outside accepted rules of evidence and "narrow" "institutional culture" that "deform our thinking to fit its image of rigor" (*Attack* 16).

Bernstein faults academic journals for "permitting the publication of a wide range of ideas—*as long as the ideas are expressed in the dominant style*" (*Attack* 16). For both Bernstein and Benjamin, the style of writing that we might call "poetry-criticism" is in itself of great import. Benjamin calls a similar kind of writing one of "poetic politics" (216), which is fueled by "the true creative overcoming of religious illumination resid[ing] in a *profane illumination,* a materialistic, anthropological inspiration, to which hashish, opium, or whatever else can give an introductory lesson" (*Selected Writings* 2 Pt. 1: 216).[14]

Profane illumination and poetic politics connect writing with an "image field" that makes it much more relevant than the "bad poem on springtime, filled to bursting with metaphors" of "the programme of the bourgeois parties." Writing in 1929, Benjamin equates this bad poetry with the bad politics of the liberal politicians of his time and their unqualified "optimism . . . and unlimited trust only in I. G. Farben and the peaceful perfection of the air force" (*Selected Writings* 2 Pt. 1: 217-218). Benjamin writes here several years before Hitler takes power, the German air force's military buildup, and I. G. Farben's manufacturing of the poisons used in concentration camp gas chambers. The uncannily accurate prophecy within Benjamin's own profane illumination and poetic politics substantiates his methods.

Benjamin, like Bernstein, combines the roles of political and historical analyst, poet, and a kind of "materialist" visionary. For Benjamin "the concept of the present" is theoretical and always in "a transition, but in which time takes a stand [*einsteht*] and has come to a standstill. For this notion defines the very present in which he himself is writing history" (*Selected Writings* 4: 396). Benjamin makes a present or a "now-time, which, as a model of messianic time, comprises the entire history of mankind in a tremendous abbreviation, coincides exactly with the figure which the history of mankind describes in the universe" (396). "A messianic arrest of happening" provides "a revolutionary chance in the fight for the oppressed past." In the past the writer sees a "constellation into which his own era has entered" (397), "(to put it differently) . . . a precious but tasteless seed" of and for "the nourishing fruit of what is historically understood contain[ing] time in its interior" (396). "How much . . . depends on [the past] being made present" (405). Only a "visionary gaze" sees the present, which is hidden to those "who 'keep step' with [the present]" since, "says Turgo . . . 'politics is obliged to foresee the present'" (405). Benjamin prophesizes from a past in the now, unlike optimistic liberal politicians in 1929 who assume I. G. Farben and the German air force will benefit all Germans. Benjamin's more penetrating poetic politics is not fooled so easily. Past horrors shed Benjamin of these illusions. He refuses to rely on notions of an enlightened historical progress to ward off fascism and genocide.

Benjamin's work and life are ever-present anchors within Bernstein's writing. Bernstein's poetry exists in a post-Benjamin world that has absorbed Benjamin and been absorbed by him. Without knowledge of Benjamin, one misses much in Bernstein. For instance, Bernstein's short poem "The Measure" addresses Benjamin's mode of prophecy and warning from a vibrant past. The poem begins paradoxically by noting an "enthrone[ment] on a border," which one would assume is a kind "no man's land" that is not appropriate for a border but rather bespeaks a thin and in some ways non-existent line between past and present. The poem merges "the privacy of a great pain" that is "enthrone[d]" with the more public military sense of the speaker's "borders" and the pain's "command" "to stay at attention" (*All the Whiskey in Heaven* 90). A seemingly past pain has become a present one and "commands": "Be on guard/ Lest the hopeless magic." The pain of the past warns against the truly "hopeless" hope of a private yet apparently political hint of "magic." Bernstein and Benjamin, both working within secular Jewish tradition, eschew the dangers of false political divination. Because "regret" is correlated with a past fashioned into "the/ foggiest avenues," this non-profanely illuminated magic "of unconscious/ Dilemmas grab hold of you" without a more clear apprehension of past pains that political poetry has enthroned. Bernstein, like Benjamin, seems a buffer to progress.

Prefiguring Bernstein's unusual use of "borders," Benjamin alludes to the Romans' borders, called "limes," when he says, "Redemption is the *limes* of progress" (*Selected Writings* 4: 404). Bernstein's poem "Pockets of Lime" also echoes Benjamin. The title "Pockets of Lime" suggests an imaginary space of delimitation, a pocket full of a bordering, or "liming," mechanisms that resists bordering, defining, and narrow limitation so that "Everything has happened, nothing/ possessed" (*All the Whiskey in Heaven* 80). The object/field of "The lawn engages/ Its constituent appraisers," implying that it is more than its appraisers, putting their appraising in question. "Pockets of Lime" is in short a playfully interlinked catalogue of revelation of unreality of overdefinition, of an "end that has no beams" (88).

It might be argued that I am treating Bernstein's great poetry like prose. Indeed, Bernstein's training as a poet was no doubt crucial in honing his prose skills. Nonetheless, if as Benjamin maintains, "great prose is the creative matrix of the various metrical forms" (*Selected Writings* 3: 154), it would follow that the greatest and most concise poetry would paradoxically be written in prose or something like prose, even as that writing made use of a plethora of poetic technique. A sense of traditional poetic metrics and prosody guides the composition of words as they are first thought, written, and shaped. It is telling that Benjamin says that "good prose . . . is composed" in a "musical stage" (*Selected Writings* 1: 455). Such a musical stage presumably corresponds with many poetic techniques. However, such music is not an end in itself and seemingly un-poetic prose can be the most poetic. Benjamin indeed writes that "in the messianic realm . . . language is liberated prose—prose which has burst the fetters of script." Within this "realm," such prose "festively enact[s] history" (*Selected Writings* 5: 404).

This is in keeping with ancient Israelite prosody. Adele Berlin, developing the insights of Roman Jakobson, calls the organizing principle of biblical poetry "dynamic parallelism." Dynamic parallelism juxtaposes syntactic, semantic, and other correspondences of small and large verbal units that are adjacent or far-removed within a poem or narrative. Robert Alter identifies parallelism and poetic intensification as the dynamics of discernible linguistic intensities. In other words, biblical poetry functions by setting up a distinguishing feature or binary opposition of any kind. If, as Ferdinand de Saussure long ago convincingly maintained, language is based on series of oppositions, then Hebrew poetry is an intensification of language itself. Benjamin's "liberated prose" calls attention to the ongoing and non-line-stopped nature of prose in continual opposition to the commodified, pseudo-precious nature of poetry that Benjamin called "bourgeois."

Bernstein realizes the special powers of poetic parallelism. He takes poetic parallelism to an ontological realm. For instance, the entire text of the body of Bernstein's poem "A Poem Is Not a Weapon" is "[THIS POEM IS REMOVED FOR INSPECTION AND VERIFICATION.]" (*Girly Man* 184). This bracketed remark plays upon an implication that the poem itself has a fixed existence that the few words given in the poem paradoxically are not a part of. There is some truth to this since although a poem, or the way we tend to think of it, is composed of language, and language in itself is inherently reproducible, nonetheless poems can be banned from given publications, exhibitions, and performances. Therefore "A Poem Is Not a Weapon" is a poem conveying the surveillance, control, and censuring of poetry, although the "inspection and verification" is presumably not valid since the author and press could have presumably already inspected and verified it.

Bernstein, therefore, demonstrates in poems such as "A Poem Is Not a Weapon" that poetry can be produced independently of any ostensible poetic technique. After all, though, as Adele Berlin puts it, "in a certain sense, parallelism is the essence of poetry," "it is a common feature of all language," and "parallelism is not in and of itself a mark of poetry as opposed to prose, or even of elevated style as opposed to ordinary discourse" (*Dynamics* 4).

In accord with poetic parallelism, by proposing what is not poetry, Bernstein creates a site where anything that is not "not poetry" is potentially poetry. Similarly, later Bernstein poetry often carries ostensible markings of poetry. Poems such as "The Ballad of the Girly Man" rhyme and present perhaps overly understandable and non-difficult poems. This poetic strategy of Bernstein is an analogue of his critical strategy supplied in the essay, "The Attack of the Difficult Poems," which matter-of-factly dismisses all possible stigma involved with being associated with "difficult poems" (*Attack* 3-6). Such poems and essays might seem to eschew "both ends" of poetry-criticism. However, they create a context wherein the noble sentiments they voice—the acceptance of anti-war and non-macho behavior, of, in Benjamin's words, "going against history's grain" and seeing beyond the powers that write it—can paradoxically be voiced through the implied and conceptual context generated by reading these works within the context of Bernstein's oeuvre. In both the verse and prose forms, what must be said can be said, and a certain social function is performed within the context of poetry-criticism. These forms constitute a kind of "Nude Formalism," as Bernstein entitles a booklet. "The Ballad of the Girly Man" is one of Bernstein's crowning achievements. Bernstein presents something that is similar to bad writing, but it functions as, in accord with Benjamin's in "Doctrine of the Similar," an alien basis igniting "intention" (*Selected Writings* 2 Pt. 2: 697), which in this case is a collective notion of poetic prosody. From the perspective of an experimental poet, this is certainly a profane illumination.

"We have been endowed with a *weak* Messianic power, a power to which the past has a claim," Walter Benjamin proclaims (*Selected Writings* 4: 390). One suspects that, if our messianic power were not weak, it would not be messianic. It is therefore fitting for the avatar within Charles Bernstein's oeuvre to be a strong girly man.

Benjamin and Bernstein may not, of course, write a new bible for the same reason Benjamin says Kafka demonstrates our need for a new one: "The consistency of truth has been lost" (*Selected Writings* 3: 326). When, as Benjamin puts it, Kafka hears the tradition, he transcribes parables that can never rest. "To be *more* than parables," says Benjamin, Kafka's parables "must cuff doctrine with a mighty paw" so as paradoxically to generate wisdom without being wise, and, since wisdom is "an attribute of tradition," kindle a tradition of truth that cannot find truth (*Selected Writings* 3: 326). Through nonsensuous similarity, poetic politics, cleaving, a blending of poetry and history with all other language, dynamic biblical parallelism, poetic structures of intensification, modern prophecy, going against the brush of history, material and poetic dialectic and discourse, the flâneur, and profane illumination, Benjamin and Bernstein bring us a much needed radical secular Jewish poetics. Whether or not this poetics is biblical, it is consistent with what Benjamin felt in 1938 as Brecht described fascism's astonishingly far-reaching powers and plans. "While he was talking," wrote Benjamin, "I felt moved by a power that was the equal of that of fascism—one that was no less deeply rooted in the depths of history than fascism's power. It was a very strange feeling, wholly new to me" (*Selected Writings* 3: 340).

Notes

Epigraph. According to Gershom Scholem, Walter Benjamin wrote the last sentence, "And everything that Moses accomplished long ago would have to be re-accomplished in our world's age," as a note to Benjamin's previous passage in Scholem's copy of Benjamin's August 11, 1934, letter to Scholem (*The Correspondence of Walter Benjamin and Gershom Scholem*, 135, note 2).

1. See Lisa Fittko, "The Story of Old Benjamin" in Benjamin, *The Arcades Project*, 946-954, and "Appendix: The Aura of Benjamin's Death: Interview with Lisa Fittko" in Britt, *Walter Benjamin and the Bible.*

2. See Edward Rothstein, "CONNECTIONS; A Daring Theory That Stalin Had Walter Benjamin Murdered," *New York Times*, June 30, 2001, for a contextualization and vetting of Stephen Schwartz's suggestion in a *Weekly Standard* article that Stalin's secret police may have killed Benjamin in Spain at a time when, with the Hitler-Stalin pact still in effect, Soviet operatives were openly working with the Gestapo and Spanish Franco fascists. According to Schwartz's theory, Stalinist forces wished to confiscate a theoretically lost last Benjamin manuscript because it might have been more explicitly anti-Stalinist than Benjamin's 1940 essay, "On Concepts of History." However, even if Benjamin himself might have believed his manuscript lost when he died, the manuscript might have in fact been "On Concepts of History" and *The Arcades Project* since he would have had good reason to doubt that the copies of them that he left in Paris would survive the German occupation as they did due to the efforts of Georges Bataille and good fortune. Therefore, even if revised versions of existing Benjamin works or, as horrible as it is to contemplate, an unknown work were lost, one might still be thankful for the recovery of important Benjamin works that were almost lost.

3. Alfred Hitchcock's portrayal of himself as a "stuffed animal" prefigures Charles Bernstein's notion of "absorption" as a kind of poetic or literary "intention-intensification" (*Artifice of Absorption* 21) that is "central to all reading & writing" (17). Absorption forms a creative poetic synthesis with the formal and/or seemingly verbally resistant element of "artifice" or "impermeability" (21). Adding to Hitchcock's forecasting of Bernstein's work, Hitchcock's self-characterization

as "stuffed" corresponds with Bernstein speaking of a very absorbing poem as a "bloated poem" (17). In addition, Hitchcock's films are perhaps the best examples we have of "absorbing cinema" since possibly no other films better account for the constant flow of their audiences' attention. A more full and precise version of Hitchcock's "stuffed animal" quotation from the May 26, 1957, episode of *Alfred Hitchcock Presents*, "The West Warlock Time Capsule," is:

"Good evening, television watchers. Tonight's masque is entitled, 'The West Warlock Time Capsule,' the tale of a timid taxidermist. This gives me the excuse to exhibit this prize of mine and to discuss taxidermy. I feel I know quite a bit about stuffed animals. After all, it takes one to know one. This, I shot myself. You see, deer poaching is one of my hobbies. It took only two shots. The first one hit a bearded old man wearing a ridiculous red suit and riding in a sleigh. I'm having him stuffed, too. It probably sounds silly to you, but I'm sentimental that way. But enough of this. Here, in a moment, is 'The West Warlock Time Capsule.'"

4. Much like Barthes, Benjamin's *The Arcade Project* isolates and traces the unconscious ideological lives of French and other European "living myths."

5. Benjamin accomplishes much of the theoretical work that Foucault later makes possible by postulating unconscious synchronic cultural relationships absent of direct influence. However, Benjamin goes further by formulating theories and practices, particularly in *The Arcades Project* and "Concepts of History," that assist inter-era relationships and the critical influence of the present moment upon the past. Benjamin, like Foucault, acknowledges how practices of power structure society, but he also accounts for the power of powerlessness and the "weak messiahs" and the "brush[ing] of history against the grain" set up by the accepted historical "document[s] of barbarism" of "On Concepts of History" (*Selected Writings* 4: 392).

6. Startlingly, perhaps even before Derrida is born or certainly when he was a child, Benjamin comes close to formulations not far from the heart of deconstruction, which links construction with destruction: "It is important for the material historian, in the most rigorous way possible, to differentiate the construction of a historical state of affairs from what one customarily calls its 'reconstruction.' The 'reconstruction' in empathy is one-dimensional. 'Construction' presupposes 'destruction'" (*Arcades Project* 470).

7. By analyzing the effects of film and radio as media in themselves completely independent of content, Benjamin anticipates by a couple of decades McLuhan's "medium is the message" manner of media studies, stressing the effects of media when it is collectively and individually assimilated. Interestingly, Benjamin's "The Work of Art in the Age of Mechanical Reproduction" and other writings seem to see beyond McLuhan by seeing beyond film and radio to the Internet, since

the kind of individual-to-collective dialectical participation and self-publication that Benjamin feels film and radio cause make much more sense in terms of the Internet. In addition, one might say that Benjamin anticipates the McLuhan-esque cool participatory quality of television.

8. See Michael Lowi 28-29 for a discussion about Benjamin as a precursor of Catholic liberation theology.

9. "We might say that there are two sections through the substance of the world: the longitudinal section seems representational; it somehow contains the objects. The cross-section seems symbolic; it contains signs" (*Selected Writings* 1: 82).

10. This includes post-World War II "pogroms." Many more Jews, for instance, remain in Poland after World War II than is generally realized. However, decades of postwar pogroms and anti-Semitic harassment exile most of them. See Hoffman's *Lost in Translation: A Life in a New Language.*

11. "1933" still resonates a sense of impending, inescapable disaster. Note Paul Krugman's December 11, 2011, *New York Times* column in which he warns, "High unemployment isn't O.K. just because it hasn't hit 1933 levels; ominous political trends shouldn't be dismissed just because there's no Hitler in sight" ("Depression and Democracy." *New York Times*, A23: 12 December 2011).

12. See for instance Mark S. Smith's *The Origins of Biblical Monotheism*, William G. Dever's *Who Were the Early Israelites and Where Did They Come From?*, and Stephen Paul Miller's *There's Only One God and You're Not It.*

13. See Dever.

14. Benjamin adapts "profane illumination" from Sigfried Kracauer's use of the word "profane" when he says "For today access to the truth is by way of the profane" (see Britt 78). Kracauer considers the profane as a way of using contemporaneous culture to unlock the inspirational power of the Bible. Karkover did not accept Buber's assumption that meditation upon the Bible in itself led to any valuable meditative ends, that there was something in itself sacred about the Bible as we now encounter it.

Reading the Posthuman Subject in *The Alphabet*

Burt Kimmelman

The Alphabet by Ron Silliman, a most remarkable and singular achievement in its great ambition and very presence, might call to mind the Western world's early encyclopedias. These massive undertakings were products of societies that had become markedly literate. Indeed *The Alphabet*, a huge book that is encyclopedic in nature, represents a historical moment in our own time—just as, for example, medieval encyclopedias characterize their era in the eyes of today's historians. Yet Silliman (along with others) has referred to *The Alphabet* as a "longpoem" ("Statement for the Guggenheim," Mack and Rome 740). And in the spirit in which this term has been proffered, I would argue that *The Alphabet*—a literary phenomenon and an event in literary history—is also peculiarly an epic poem. I would also note that the genre of epic poetry, unlike that of the encyclopedia, has its roots in preliterate times. As is true of the encyclopedia, the epic has always been in some respects a historiographico-aesthetic attempt to embrace the world in its entirety; in ancient times and even thereafter it was relied upon to report to its listeners or readers what the world beyond their immediate purview was like. Although Silliman's poem should be acknowledged as a work fitting within the epic tradition, its élan and self-ordering methodology also make it an encyclopedia. It may seem that this generic insistence is not necessary to comprehend Silliman's achievement; yet what I hope to show in this chapter is not only that the basic instinct involved in *The Alphabet*'s creation has everything to do with civilized humanity's encyclopedic activities, but also that this impulse resides at the heart of Silliman's world view, as evinced by this book.

While many a commentator has provided for readers various insights into *The Alphabet*, there is still a need to consider it within the literary-historical context. To be sure, I would want to read it, first and foremost, within a history of ideas, or let's say within our intellectual history. Nevertheless, this book not only helps us to understand what an encyclopedia is all about; it also, in thinking about its encyclopedic nature, both enlarges and deepens our appreciation of one or another literary-critical analysis Silliman's work has already attracted.

The encyclopedic impulse to gather the sum total of all knowledge in the world within the expanse of a book (or a series of books, when the plenitude of knowledge has exceeded the physical limitations of a single volume) has coalesced over time—since human beings first developed the technology of writing. Starting with the beginnings of history as we know it, this impulse has embodied an inevitability. With the emergence of literacy, the motivation to hold the known world within one's grasp, so to speak, found materialization in the artifact of the book, as if it were created for this purpose. Accompanying this apparent achievement was a sense of triumph as people marveled at the record of their own civilization. This was no mere historical record but rather the entire panoply of human expression. Such were the encyclopedias of the Middle Ages in particular which were read by early-literate human beings who felt empowered by their accomplishments. Indeed, the conceptualization of the mirror, which is a key image and symbol in the literature of the medieval era, is most apt in comprehending the role the medieval encyclopedia played within society.

The invention of writing is the most significant technological development in human history. And an encyclopedia—itself a technological artifact distinguishing people of its time from their forbears—is impossible without literacy, due to its very nature and mission (as Walter Ong in *Orality and Literacy: The Technologizing of the Word* and elsewhere, and others, would suggest). In orally based societies a *sceop* or *griot* told stories in part as a way to keep track of who their preliterate people were. Tales of the tribe (thus Ezra Pound's famous coinage *sagetrieb*) imparted to listeners a sense of a past, nebulous as it might be, as well as identity and meaning. These stories were a kind of record keeping (of course *record* might now imply *writing*), though they naturally mutated over time due to a lack of objective documentation that might survive human mortality or contradict changing contemporaneous memory.

This living "memorializing" could also influence the imaginative activities of these poet-"historians"—notwithstanding their exceptional powers of remembrance—who created *word-hoard*s (to borrow the Old English expression) that were not merely collections of "facts" but also matrices comprised of meters, epithets, and other verbal formulations that held the "facts" ready for the poet's retrieval during performance. The matrices later formed the basis for the aesthetics of literate-based poetry. Given the *sceops*' priorities, those who listened to these pre-literate bards' versified poems would seem not to have been disturbed by the transformations one or another story would undergo over time. Yet with the emergence of writing—and in consequence the development of abstract and higher-order thinking—early literate people began to attend to the details and ideas of a fabricated history (i.e., of history proper), the elements of it comprising civilization as we know it.

The first encyclopedists, in striving to preserve knowledge, concerned themselves with the implicit relationships among the *facts* or *truths* of their world. Their concern, given the nature of written text, was unavoidable, and I would maintain that it gave rise to the fetishization of those facts and truths, an experience that was beyond the pale of a preliterate society. Within this fundamentally new milieu, encyclopedic activity became so compelling that we might now speak of the relatively high-tech activities in early literate societies as having effected a transmogrification of human life according to a new set of interests with which people found themselves presented, new priorities that demanded, among other activities, scholarly dedication.

So, what specifically might the history of the encyclopedia have to do with *The Alphabet*? And why does Silliman's postmodern poetical work remind me especially, among all the early encyclopedias (or even those of the eighteenth-century enlightenment), of Isidore of Seville's *Etymologiae*? The *Etymologiae*, one of the first true encyclopedias ever written, was a monumental achievement of the early seventh century. One thing this work discloses to its reader is that it is its own peculiar genre of writing. And in noticing this early-medieval, pointedly writerly genre, we might perhaps come to terms with, to be more precise we are perhaps able *to read*, Silliman's distinctively postmodern work—one that I would argue should be comprehended as such even within the world of Language writing, a world in which writing *per se* is of great consequence and a world that Silliman was instrumental in creating.

Given this brief overview of the history of the encyclopedia as well as of writing, the moment has now come to begin to analyze Silliman's book in some detail. I would begin by observing that, for one thing, *The Alphabet* is gigantic and monumental. In its way, too, though it mostly concerns itself with the details of Silliman's life, including his inner life, it is far ranging in its exploration of how language can be made to do extraordinary and oftentimes surprising things—particularly through his employment of what he has named "the new sentence" as well as through his procedural verse and prose arrangements (which I will discuss at length later in this chapter). In its sheer physical aura and more importantly in the range of writing experiments within it, *The Alphabet* suggests an author's effort to be, in some way, comprehensive—especially once a reader learns it was written over three decades and contains both its author's personal and intellectual history.

This grand poem or epic—or encyclopedia—is made up of a series of long poems, and a reader will sense both implicitly and explicitly within the series the author's need to embrace the artificial order he has imposed upon the poems' creation. This order has resulted in a certain kind of poetry and, more fundamentally, a certain kind of linguistic expression. As Anne Mack commented some years before the poems appeared as a single volume (its individual segments were published over time), Silliman's project imparted "an important sense in which we want to think of *The Alphabet* in terms of a concept of totalization." The fact that the completed work will have exactly twenty-six sections is an unavoidable sign of its commitment to totalization. Indeed, as Mack points out, "there is a sense in which one ought to see the work as already having 'solved' the problem of the American longpoem" (Mack and Rome 746).

In a 1988 statement for a fellowship application (shared with Mack and J. J. Rome), Silliman speaks of his future "longpoem" as "an attempt to reconceive what I take to be the archetypal American poetic genre, something that has come to be known (for want of a better term) as the 'American longpoem'" ("Statement for the Guggenheim," Mack and Rome 740). Silliman has been influenced by a number of *longpoems*, such as Pound's *The Cantos,* the modernist epic that sets the stage for a large number of long poems or otherwise epics to come, as well as Robert Duncan's *Passages*, Charles Olson's *The Maximus Poems*, and Louis Zukofsky's "*A*", the latter of which is arguably the most significant for Silliman in his writing of *The Alphabet*. However, he saw these works as having fallen short of their apparent goals. "When I started *The Alphabet* back in '79," he tells Gary Sullivan in an interview, "my only sense was . . . that I knew any larger writing would have to be structured in such a way as to push my work in different directions. Part of this was simply my perception that what made 'A' work in sharp contrast to the other long poems [*sic*] of the first two-thirds of the last century was that its individual sections were both self-contained and yet logically related."

Yet even "*A*" did not fully succeed. In his Guggenheim application, Silliman also writes:

> Olson's, Duncan's, [Ed] Dorn's [*Gunslinger*] masterworks simply dissolve: [William Carlos] Williams never finished book six of *Paterson*: Zukofsky gave up on closure and tacked on a work of his wife's. From Pound's *Cantos* to the untitled and abandoned 1,000 page work of Clark

> Coolidge in the 1970s, it has been as if the longpoem inherently must be a poem manqué.
>
> My thesis is that such poems have failed because, for reasons that are historical and in fact specific to the history of the U.S., they typically have been constructed upon organicist assumptions about poetry and form in general. ("Statement for the Guggenheim," Mack and Rome 741)

Silliman's solution to what he perceives as this ongoing problem is to create (though at this point he had been at it for almost a decade) a long poem "on other grounds"; he claims that there will be a "unity in *The Alphabet* [that] is phenomenological, the way 'unity' (which I prefer to think of as 'the unity effect') is experienced in the world, as something immediate, apprehended and rendered problematic by investigation. The reader is kept aware of their [*sic*] presence as an active producer of meaning during the consumption of the text" (qtd. in Mack and Rome 741). Before *The Alphabet*'s compilation, he tells Sullivan he came to know that "the sections would have to differ one from the other and fit into a larger intuitive logic. . . . I seem to know where a given section is going to be headed sometimes years in advance, but very little about what it will look like when it gets there."

Here Silliman is establishing similarities that are helpful in comprehending his grand project and perceiving its singularity. That in some respects *The Alphabet* can be viewed as a life's work (especially in terms of the number of years it took him to write it) situates it critically among a number of other such poems. Along with those already mentioned, there are contemporary "longpoems" such as Rachel Blau DuPlessis's *Drafts* and Ronald Johnson's *ARK*. These works, like *The Alphabet*, fall within the "disjunctive poetics" tradition (to borrow the title of Peter Quartermain's landmark study). Certain Modernist poets in this tradition, like Zukofsky and Gertrude Stein, recognized that not only were poems objects, they were also "difficult to read, because they challenge[d] our assumptions about the processes of reading, about what constitutes 'value,' about knowledge and about 'knowing.' [Such a poem is] a decontextualized object [that] creates enormous problems for the reader, and it is the experience of these problems which constitutes that of the poems" (Quartermain 2).

Another long poem that seems to fit Quartermain's definition because of its similar effects on a reader is *The Tablets* by the older Armand Schwerner. This pseudo translation of some of the earliest extant writing poses compelling challenges to efforts at construal. Others of Silliman's generation like DuPlessis, Johnson, and the Language poet Lyn Hejinian in *My Life* may have viewed the twentieth-century American long poems in much the same way as Silliman and sought to write their own poems in part as acts of redress even though they might acknowledge their influences either by declaring them openly or by disclosing them through their poetics.

Yet I would set *The Alphabet* apart from them. As has been suggested, the long poem, the epic poem (since Virgil), and the encyclopedia are all manifestations of what it means when we speak of literate society. They are examples of a civilization's flowering. *The Alphabet* may be aligned with epics, long poems, and encyclopedias not only of recent times but also of the distant past, including the *Etymologiae.* These works differ from much earlier literary works like Homer's epic poem *The Odyssey* that originated in a preliterate society (first written down circa eighth century BCE but begun several centuries earlier). Nevertheless, *The Odyssey* was meant to present to listeners and later readers not only a grand scale of action but also, again, a *summa* of knowledge about the world. How else might someone of this period have found out what existed over the ancient Greek horizon except through word of mouth? Over time the written word, the physical text, came to possess more authority (authorship became increasingly significant as a social and intellectual status) as well as a kind of monumentality (and along with it a psychological heft) until by the time of the Renaissance and printing press the written (and then the printed) word would gradually be considered more reliable and more believable than oral utterance, for instance in business arrangements (Clanchy 230 ff). Yet even writing of a much earlier period possessed an allure (Ong 93) and inspired awe.

A guiding motivation in Homer's *Odyssey* is not that different from that of, say, Thomas Aquinas's *Summa Theologiae* (thirteenth century CE). Silliman and Aquinas share something that only becomes possible with the institution of literacy and, furthermore, with the use of an advanced, abstracted writing system such as the Roman alphabet. The line between encyclopedia and epic poem is blurry at best. Indeed, *The Alphabet* (which appeared in its entirety in 2008) calls our attention to this liminality—just as does a work like Johnson's *ARK* (published in its entirety in 1996, also with portions of it having appeared earlier). There is a crucial difference, however, between Johnson's and Silliman's two huge, nearly contemporaneous tomes. The poetics and concerns of *The Alphabet* are of another order altogether. The difference has to do with an assumption about Silliman's language—especially within the context of his long poem's organization and mode of creation—a necessary assumption that one must bring to its reading.

What is meant by *reading* here requires explanation. First of all, *The Alphabet* is beholden to that sense of awe with which a written text has come to be held. I would argue that Silliman's work depends on this reverence we give to texts (including texts on computer screens). Beyond this, a key motif in *The Alphabet* is that of the actual act of writing. Silliman's identity as this book's author is tied up with that of someone who writes. It is no coincidence that the first words of the book are "If the function of writing is to 'express the world'" (1) and the last words of the book are "The angle of my pen as it brushes this page" (1054).

The work's title sends an obvious signal about Silliman's working praxis in creating this long poem made up of long poems in which each of its segments corresponds to a letter of the writing system its author employs—even though he did not write each of the segments in sequence. Jumping around in the series, he wrote the individual poems that are compiled under the titles of the various segments. Each of these segments belongs to a certain letter of the alphabet. Thus we find the "A" entry, "Albany," most likely an autobiographical narrative of sorts that takes place in Albany, California, where Silliman grew up, and the "S" entry, "Skies," whose rhetoric is quite different from "Albany," a sequence of passages corresponding to a particular day in the year in which a particular passage was written (Green). Yet Silliman's out-of-sequence approach does not mean that he was working outside of the structure of his organizational plan for the eventual larger book. In fact this structure constituted a constraint, one that inflected the respective language and architecture of each of the segments. Aside from the ambition exhibited by Isidore in the *Etymologiae* (he was a great figure in the early Church; his intellectual prowess as Archbishop of Seville was possibly as immense as that of Thomas, also a Church Father), I associate *The Alphabet* with this early medieval encyclopedia and I view Isidore's achievement as a distant yet true source of Silliman's tome (albeit Silliman did not know of it when I mentioned it to him ["Email to Burt Kimmelman"]) because of a foregrounded sense of writtenness in both works. In theme as well as practice, both works contain deictic strategies (more obviously so in Silliman's) meant to call attention to their respective existences as writing *per se*.

Silliman wants us to appreciate his poetry's *textuality*, its very materiality of language. That language jumps out at his reader. Moreover, a reader might realize that Silliman as author—or his poem's persona—is consumed by the palpable materiality of his book's language, and he may wish to disappear into the book itself so that what we ultimately attend to is the supreme presence of the book, that artifact, its objectness (to reprise Quartermain). There is an irony in this dynamic, which will become plain shortly. We are meant to contemplate the book itself, in all its massiveness—1054 pages of text proper, plus author's notes (compare this to *The Cantos*, which is immense even at 815 pages)—most likely in hard copy.

The Alphabet is metapoetical. At times the text not only reveals an awareness of itself as poem and text but also comments on its own rhetorical methodology. Picking up from Silliman's statement of poetics made to the Guggenheim Foundation, Mack describes his "concept of poetry as a scene of 'investigation' [that is] explicit throughout *The Alphabet*" (Mack and Rome 742). She also points out, for instance, these prescriptive lines from the section of the book titled "What":

> End lines precisely
> where it makes least sense, until
> a new order emerges—then examine
> that. Even the one syllable word,
> the simple morpheme (the letter "A")
> contains a caesura. (*The Alphabet* 754)

As for Silliman's notion (in his Guggenheim statement) of a "unity effect," Mack comments that "one of the principal objects of the writing [of *The Alphabet*] seems to lie in casting forward, into consciousness, the many ways that a unity effect can come into being: that the reader should become aware of those effects, and of the limits of the effects." Taking the concept of what Silliman in that Guggenheim proposal calls "narrative," Mack reads this term as "a sign for unity and totality" in *The Alphabet* and argues that "he unfolds an image of his idea of poetic form as it would/might operate in a completable (which is not to say a 'unified') longpoem" (742). Hence, Silliman writes in "What," referring to the very words he's writing (as Mack observes), the following:

> It is not that
> there is no narrative
> here (each sentence
> is a narrative,
> each line *moves*)
> but that there is
> no hierarchy
> of narratives (not even
> the story of the
> poem), no sentence

to which the others
(all the others) defer
and are ranked
(the map is not
built about the city).
(835)

A prior remark, several lines earlier, perhaps sums up the epistemological nature of Silliman's verse methodology: "Typos / or topos, which one? / The pen in my pocket, / cap off, bleeds ink. I / think I write. The poem / is about what, / even it asks" (833). Or note this passage, cited by Mack as comprising what she calls a "textual scene" that serves as "an emblem of Silliman's writing" (Mack and Rome 743): "This sentence points not / to the 'work as a whole' / (no such thing) but to your, / the reader's, life" (*The Alphabet* 768). This kind of paradoxical self-awareness recalls René Magritte's famous painting *Ceci n'est pas une pipe*.

To take issue with Silliman's preaching to and prodding of the reader (i.e., saying in effect "this is how to read my poem that is a nonpoem") is not merely futile but it is also wrongheaded and to miss the point. His nagging has important precedents. At its heart the Judeo-Christian impulse that, theologically, was a product of inscription and was both conceptualized with and through writing—to be more precise *text*—gave rise to a world in which textuality was dramatically prominent in Western existential consciousness. This dynamic had developed well before John proclaims, in writing (i.e., religious texts have at this point become material objects): "at the beginning was the word and the word was God." Later, Augustine in the *Confessions* describes the eternal as the "sky of skies," with the created world "[s]tretched out beneath [it as a] scroll of the firmament, a layer of 'skin' where the primal dictation of creation is dispensed as a written text, as Scripture" (XIII. xv.16; scrolls were made of vellum, therefore Augustine's use of "skin" in his description). The idea of and the term *text* hearken back to preliterate times but later are completely appropriated by a religio-literate tradition. Certainly by the end of the Roman Empire, if not earlier, writing had become the basic metaphor according to which a body of knowledge, or what might now be considered *knowledge* itself, came to be organized and recognized as residing over and against the person who might contemplate and even marvel at it. Hence, a work in writing stood on its own, the product and glory of *homo scribens*. Medieval scribes would, because of a requisite self-effacing humility, sign their manuscripts "*Adamo me fecit*" ("Adam made me")—the words of the text now speaking, as it were, directly to their reader, autonomously. Apparently, Adam not only now wore clothing but kept a pen in hand (as is possibly captured in the phrase "text, texture, textile").

Writing fundamentally altered culture. It also changed humans physically, including alterations to the brain (Ong 29-30). The preliterate brain structure of human beings was not what it became by, possibly, the time of Isidore in the early Middle Ages. Surely by the time of Dante and Aquinas, and possibly earlier, language and text were an enormous presence in people's hearts and minds and could even be seen as the basis for explaining theological as well as natural phenomena (Kimmelman *Poetics* 45, 82). Furthermore, today in hindsight, one might claim that the modern world has acted as a divider between medieval and postmodern worlds, insofar as modernity, with the emergence of modern science, consigned and relegated textuality to the outer bounds of human thought during the five-hundred-year era of the book (commencing with the use of the movable-type printing press), to some far edge of the intellectual and spiritual landscape (see Kimmelman "Text"). Yet in their own way the early encyclopedias, vast and profound accomplishments, were the real precursors for epics of the modern world such as *Paradise Lost*, eventually *The Cantos*, "*A*", *Paterson*, and a spate of other "epics" we tend to call long poems (which may reveal an awareness of ancient and medieval works like *The Aeneid* and *The Divine Comedy*). In all these works the reach is, to say the least, broad, extensive; and if Pound cries out in old age that he "cannot make it cohere" (796) we forgive him for that (even though at one time Silliman would not do so).

Still, *The Alphabet* is another kind of epic—even in comparison with *The Cantos* or "*A*". I would maintain that the roots of Silliman's long poem go back to a work like Isidore's. Thinking about *The Alphabet* in relation to Isidore's *Etymolgiae* places Silliman's achievement into a vivid contrast to those of Pound's and of Zukofsky's. The very title of Isidore's work suggests this filiation; the term *etymologiae* in the early seventh century could denote simply the origins of things, yet there was a special dispensation as concerned language. Isidore was keen on creating a portion of his work that would be devoted exclusively to what we today think of as etymology. In this manner he was being exceptionally sensitive to the issue of language and writing, to a degree matched by Silliman, one of the progenitors and principal theorists of the Language movement. Silliman's title signals not only this orientation but also the book's *modus operandi*. Ironically, however, it makes less sense trying to "read" his huge poem (a book of related verse poems and prose poems) than any of the prior extensive acts of writing (including any encyclopedias produced during the Enlightenment, that second great era of encyclopedic activity, for example Denis Diderot's).

The fundamental difference between *The Alphabet* and all these other works—including, I submit, contemporaneous texts like *Drafts*, *ARK*, and possibly even *My Life*—is that these other works are meant to function under the aegis of a presence/absence intellectual paradigm of the modern world, which had fully evolved by the time of the Enlightenment. In *How We Became Posthuman: Virtual Bodies in Cybernetics, Literature, and Informatics*, N. Katherine Hayles analyzes this paradigm and shows how it helps us better understand contemporary culture, science, and technology. According to Hayles, the focus is no longer what is present in consciousness but how something behaves. Hence, in contrast to the other contemporary literary works I've mentioned, let me suggest that *The Alphabet* (written by someone who would eventually work in the field of computing) is a literary work that, sometimes implicitly and sometimes overtly, reflects and maybe even champions and announces the advent of digital technology. Silliman consistently employs terms, metaphors, and otherwise concepts from the discipline of information theory (what Anne Mack has referred to as his "word processing model" [Mack and Rome 746]). This orientation and point of view are also elements in other writings by Silliman. For example, in *The Chinese Notebook* he says that "[a] poem, like any language, is a vocabulary and a set of rules by which it is processed. . . . [T]he definition of a language [is] also the definition of a poem: a vocabulary plus a set of rules through which to process it" (qtd. in Mack and Rome 744).

What Silliman means by this language takes us back once again to the larger context of literacy and epistemology. Mack explains:

> For Silliman the very existence of an alphabet (any alphabet) declares the existence of a specific language, and it says in addition that that language has both a vocabulary and a set of processing rules. (It does not necessarily tell us whether the language is "dead" or dynamic—we learn such things definitively only in the actual practice of a language, in its "usage.") As a scriptural event in the historical development of language, an alphabet is therefore both the sign and the limit of everything that particular language can do (phonetically, lexically, syntactically). The existence of an alphabet tells one that a specific language has achieved conceptual completion. (Mack and Rome 746)

Therefore *The Alphabet* can also be seen as a work of irony and perhaps sarcasm while, in this postmodern context, it is a throwback to the era of the book. This strategy constitutes for Silliman a gesture, if not a salute, then a smirk, toward the half-millennial period that began with the invention of the printing press and that has ebbed with the advent of digital technologies. The modern era produced unique literary genres, such as the novel, which came to fruition over time, creating a dramatic landscape that moved from exterior road trips to inner voyages that focused on discovering and exploring the self or personhood in all its psychological fullness. This evolved ego that the novel at least helped to create came about through the indirect agency of the artifact of the book, which served as its objective correlative. Between the covers of that book there was a complete story, or rather a world whose narrative achieved closure, in fact a unique and independent human being. Is it wrongheaded to think of the highly evolved nineteenth-century novel as having provided a ground for psychoanalysis in the late 1800s? Is it incorrect to think individual human personality first came into existence in literature, a literature shaped by the technologies of literacy?

Another possibly unavoidable question to be asked when reading *The Alphabet* is if the interiority so glaringly absent in an early epic like *The Odyssey* has been repudiated in the post-book era and if *The Alphabet* represents the quintessential example of this literary and intellectual shift in our society—a society in which, as Hayles has asserted, the vital guiding duality has been transformed from presence/absence to "pattern/randomness." In the conclusion to her book, Hayles writes:

> When the self is envisioned as grounded in presence, identified with originary guarantees and teleological trajectories, associated with solid foundations and logical coherence, the posthuman is likely to be seen as antihuman. . . . But the posthuman does not really mean the end of humanity. It signals instead the end of a certain conception of the human, a conception that may have applied, at best, to that fraction of humanity who had the wealth, power, and leisure to conceptualize themselves as autonomous beings exercising their will through individual agency and choice. What is lethal is . . . the grafting of the posthuman onto a liberal humanist view of the self. . . . the posthuman need not be recuperated back into liberal humanism, nor need it be construed as anti-human. Located within the dialectic of pattern/randomness and grounded in embodied actuality rather than disembodied information, the posthuman offers resources for rethinking the articulation of humans with intelligent machines. (286-87)

Hayles has come along at the end of a dialectical trajectory that originates in tandem with the waning of the modern era. And while she does not address the ideas of someone like Roland Barthes, her near contemporary, who is of great interest to Language poets, it is possible to see his thinking as a forerunner to hers (although she comes to her conceptualization of the posthuman through her study of cybernetics and information technologies while Barthes concerns himself with other matters that can be partially viewed as proto versions of hers).

In any event, the relatively recent thinking of someone like Barthes—arguably Silliman's intellectual father—must be taken into account to understand *The Alphabet*.[1] In the posthumously published *The Responsibility of Forms* (1985), Barthes's ideas (to borrow from Steve McCaffery) reflect "the precarious entente between letter and word" (McCaffrey xix), such as when Barthes speaks of "the alphabet's power: to rediscover a kind of natural state of the letter. For the letter, if it is alone, is innocent: the Fall begins when we align letters to make them into words" (Barthes 119; McCaffery xix). There is a "prodigious desire invested everywhere in [Barthes's] oeuvre," Steve Evans has written, "to the search for exceptions to the rule of naturalized forms." It is with Barthes's contemporary Jean Baudrillard, however, that this fiercely uncompromising view of language, thought, and reality is fully developed, especially in his theorizing of the *simulacrum*, which finally equips us to grasp Silliman's project completely.

Along with the notion of the simulacrum, there is Baudrillard's formulation of the hyperreal, which provides the context within which Silliman's work holds together, especially if we contrast it to a "real" residing within the presence/absence paradigm (such as Hayles discusses in her study). What may confuse many readers who attempt to comprehend a work like *The Alphabet* is their supposition that the poetry in this book is meant to signify things in a real, actual world. The personal references in the book do indeed invite this kind of reading of the poem, but they are also a trap. Baudrillard's simulacrum has, paradoxically, become the only real thing. In the premodern world, according to Baudrillard, an image of an actual thing was viewed as a copy, and in the modern world, by the time of the industrial revolution, mass-produced copies threatened to overwhelm the actual or real. (In this formulation, the invention of the movable type printing press looks ahead to the factory assembly lines of the nineteenth and twentieth centuries).

In the postmodern world, however, there is no longer, as Baudrillard has argued, what he has called "the map, the double, the mirror or the concept" (*Simulacra and Simulation* 1). Reference abolished, simulation has become "the generation by models of a real without origin or reality: a hyperreal." Within a grand reordering, the "territory no longer precedes the map"; on the other hand, it does not "survive it." Still, within this historical evolution, it is "the map that precedes the territory—*precession of simulacra*—that engenders the territory, and if one must return to fable, today it is the territory whose shreds slowly rot across the extent of the map" (1). Hence for Baudrillard, within the new order, "[i]t is the real, and not the map, whose vestiges persist here and there in the deserts that are no longer those of the Empire, but ours. *The desert of the real itself*" (1).

Reading this rather poetic passage of Baudrillard's, we might recall Silliman's use of "map" in "What." Silliman writes: "no sentence / to which the others / (all the others) defer / and are ranked / (the map is not / built about the city)" (835). This segment's title embodies an ontological query that corresponds and may allude to a key comment by Baudrillard—particularly when he writes "[i]t is the real, and not the map, whose vestiges persist."

The *example par excellence* of the postmodern simulacrum, for Baudrillard, is Disneyland. Likewise, the text of Silliman's self-reflexive poem, signaled by its title *The Alphabet* as well as by its organizational structure and rhetoric, is a simulacrum in which language—text that exists only for itself, that glories in its own material existence and signifies only that rather than a world beyond it—provides the reader with an overabundance of details from Silliman's personal life: his observations, thoughts, events in his life, and so on. These details, though, are not finally meant to be interpreted as, and finally do not put forth, an autobiographical narrative. The only way really to comprehend Silliman's language in *The Alphabet* is to posit it conceptually within the pattern/randomness paradigm Hayles finds as key to what she calls the post-Enlightenment, post-human, and I would add post-book era.

The principal irony in this construct is that Silliman, who anticipated but perhaps not necessarily with full recognition the significance of what he was writing, has not ultimately realized the problem he encounters as he struggles to explain the very poetics he has developed intuitively. For instance, despite his outsized intellect, which is perhaps on a par with that of someone like Isidore, he proposes the notion that each particle of language possesses "presence." In his essay "Who Speaks" Silliman is not ready intellectually to jettison "presence" (though this is what he's doing in his poetry), such as Hayles as critic has done. While discussing specifically Barthes and Roman Jakobson's respective attempts to disaggregate utterance (for example, "Jakobson's six functions of language—contact, code, signifier, signified, addresser, addressee" [Silliman "Who Speaks" 365]), Silliman asks whether their analyses account for presence. He answers this question: "Absolutely not! Like the ghost in the machine, presence persists in the signifier" (366). Of course what Silliman wants to do is to lay bare that signifier for all of us to see and appreciate. Yet it should not be concluded here that Silliman's work resembles that of a typical poet from what Silliman derisively calls the "School of Quietude," in other words mainstream poetry. In Silliman's poetry, as Marjorie Perloff has noted, "the distinction between inside and outside has been eroded. For Silliman . . . there are no ideas or facts outside the language that names them. . . . Rather—and here the difference in epistemology is profound—language constructs the 'reality' perceived" ("Language Poetry and the Lyric Subject" 432).

One of the methodologies in a lot of Language poetry—a way of working central to a number of the sections of *The Alphabet*—is the practice of proceduralism, through which the signifier comes to reside in the foreground of the reading consciousness, in contrast to what occurs in "traditional metrics." In this regard Perloff provides probably the most succinct and focused exposition of proceduralism:

> What has been called constraint or procedurality is not equivalent to the concept of rule in traditional metrics, where the choice of, say, ottava rima sends a definite signal to the audience that every stanza will have eight lines of iambic pentameter, rhyming abababcc. Rather, a procedural poetics, which can, incidentally, apply equally well to "prose" and "verse" (the distinction between them being much less important than the concern for language as a site of paragrammatic play, of the sedimentation of verbal, phonemic, and graphic traces in interaction), is primarily generative, the constraint determining, not what is already fixed as a property of the text, but how the writer will proceed with his composition. (*Radical Artifice* 139)

The reader, then, as well as the poet (who might create a metapoetical text at times—that is to say, a poetry aware of itself as poetry and more basically as text), are to be attentive to the operational value of the procedural poem. Elsewhere Perloff has said that proceduralism establishes "a *generative device* [that] creates a formal structure whose rules of composition are internalized so that the constraint in question is not only a rule but a thematic property of the poem as well" (*Differentials* 208). Nevertheless, as William Watkin comments:

> In addition to being generative, [procedural] constraints differ from traditional prosodic conventions in terms of their frequency (most procedural poems are the result of the procedure taking place only once),

> the origins of their rules (primarily from fields other than poetry using very different vocabularies), and their aims (which are nearly always a form of critique of the conventions of poetry). Thus a procedural constraint can be defined as dissimilar to a conventional prosodic rule by its being generative, not proscriptive; strictly limited in use so that it can never become a convention; based on rules that do not stem from the vocabulary of the poetic community; and critical of conventional rule-governance in intent. ("Systematic" 503-04)

The ultimate reward of proceduralism, it seems to me, is its ability to make evident otherwise unnoticed tendencies of language as well as the textures and inherent *thisness* of words and phrases, even in their disjunctive states. A procedural poet is forcing language out of its syntactically grounded referential propensity and out of a typical reader's comfort zone.

David Huntsberger concludes that—especially in light of the neoMarxist theoretical basis Silliman and other Language poets have established for their writing—"[t]he procedural poem . . . requires an examination of the 'mechanism' behind its production. And what one finds, of course, is that the 'mechanism' is the labor of the individual herself, producing an artifact that is at once a product and critique of the society in which it is produced" (27). I would quibble with Huntsberger here inasmuch as the "mechanism" he speaks of, while it might lead a reader to consider the poet's role as creator, it need not do so; and the very purpose of the procedural poem—more largely of Language writing—is to dwell within the contemplation of and the experience of the language itself as embodied within this mechanism. Furthermore, to extrapolate the notion that the language poem wishes to draw attention to an author (*pace*, Barthes) or even a self seems to me to run counter to the abundant prose theorizing on the part of the Language poets variously as well as, on occasion, in their poems proper.[2] Most Language poets believe that the self, or at least speech or voice, is either non existent or is subsumed within the language of the poem. In any event, the attempt to identify a self is to move "outside" of the poem to a counterreality of the sort Perloff and others have identified, which is the world outside the poem, the very world with which mainstream poetry wishes to involve itself.

The case is much more like what Kristin Prevallet has suggested: the reader is to be put into the position of being able "to appreciate the games and experimentation of such processes as a pushing forward of form and a necessary shattering of the expectations of what a poem, or poetry, is or should be" (124). Yet what is interesting here is that this proceduralism is meant to defer or completely disable any sort of close reading, any *explication de texte* a reader might attempt to bring to bear on the poem. (We may see a forerunner of this practice in some of Zukofsky's procedural work, and the case might be made that we can see how some of Gertrude Stein's writing provides a fertile ground out of which this poetics can emerge.)

There is also an important relationship between Silliman's proceduralism and his use of what he calls "the new sentence." In his essay by this name, he lists the requisite "qualities" of the new sentence.[3] Addressing them as a group, I would say that they are for Silliman a response to what he has seen as the problematic nature of syllogistic rhetoric. Too, they are collectively a prescription for a kind of writing that is in fact *writing* rather than a mimicking of oral utterance or writing in which the language itself (a language or rhetoric that may indirectly have been affected over time by a regularization or rationalization imposed by printing) is subsumed within, and so disappears within, the logical flow of a discourse when sentences collectively contain interrelationships of subordinate nature, and/or when sentences are syntagmatically whole. Silliman's reading of Ferdinand de Saussure, Tzvetan Todorov, Viktor Schlovsky, Jacobson, Barthes, and others concerned with language and writing leads him to taking a position that for him must lead to the creation of *the new sentence*. He also sketches the historical backdrop for his innovation, and reasons that if "the sentence, as distinct from the utterance of speech, is a unit of prose, and if prose as literature and the rise of printing are inextricably interwoven, then the impact of printing on literature, not just with the presentation of literature, but on how the writing itself is written, needs to be addressed" (73).

The essential concept contained in this argument is fleshed out later in Silliman's essay; it should be noted that the essay also serves as a *raison d'etre* for the development of his materialist poetics:

> The sentence is a unit of writing. Yet the utterance exists as a unit of speech prior to the acquisition of writing, for both individuals and societies. The utterances of *Gilgamesh* or the Homeric epics would appear to have been translated without great difficulty into written sentence form long before the advent of creative or aesthetic prose. Nonetheless, it is the hypotactic logic of the prose sentence, prose paragraph and expository essay which is most completely the model through which the sentence is communicated in Western societies by means of the organized process of education. . . . Accordingly, the function of this unit within creative prose proves essential to our understanding of how a sentence might become "new." (78-79)

"New sentences" tend to suspend meaning or message in favor of their larger paragraphs or even the entire poem created by them. In other words, Silliman would wish to create paragraphs or whole poems containing new sentences, which in themselves individually defer meaning to some larger unit of expression, such as the paragraph or entire poem. In this rhetorical practice (is it better to call it anti-rhetorical?), the materiality of the written text comes to the fore, no longer masked by syllogistic rhetoric.

Such a practice of writing can lead to a radical extreme in which, as in "Ketjak2: Caravan of Affect," the portion of *The Alphabet* Silliman has called its "secret spine" ("Interview [with Gary Sullivan]"), both fragmented and syntactically ordered units of expression make up not only a single paragraph but a greater expression comprised of this one paragraph. Here is how the poem starts:

> Revolving door. Revolving odor. Slivers or sofa, splinters or couch. Curious as that face (your own) in the old photo (no sense of recognition whatsoever). The deer swim in the clear lake. Begin again, in again. The east is rad, the west is rotting. I didn't say that. In a hang glider, hovering, suspended over farm fields, watching workers, silent bending. Grease spots on the train window. (139)

These are the first few of a large number of "lines" on the first page of this segment of *The Alphabet*, which continues for another eighty-four pages.

Remarkably, however—as fragmented as some of the "sentences" are, and as skittering or elliptical as the narrative voice turns out to be—a story, and the creation of a world, one in which the materiality of the text begins to be noticed less, emerges. Yet to say this is not to discount what Silliman's program has been; instead it highlights how difficult it is to achieve fully such a program. To read this kind of "poetry," nevertheless, requires not only an enormously focused attention but also a great degree of alacrity.

Surely poetry can demand at least this much from its reader. It is interesting to speculate how much more popular Stein has become for many readers in recent years, maybe because they have been confronted with the work of someone like Silliman. On the other hand how really, deeply, different is this work from some of what we find being produced from within the "School of Quietude"? A concession Silliman seems to make as he concludes his essay "The New Sentence" helps us answer this question. After quoting a portion of "For She" by the Language poet Carla Harryman, which is made up of *new sentences*, Silliman concedes that "what endows Harryman's piece with precisely the intensity or power that makes it worthy of our consideration are the many ways in which individual sentences are *not* 'in free-standing isolation'" (92).[4]

The Alphabet, however, does want us to appreciate its language (something like this may be said as regards Harryman's "For She")—language in, of, and for itself; and to a very great extent Silliman's poem especially succeeds in doing so. In this sense Silliman has read into Barthes's notion of the *pleasure of the text*, of *the rustle of language*, and seen it as an inevitable next step, one Barthes has not foreseen but for which he established the ground. *The Alphabet* does aim to be, like Baudrillard's famous example of Disneyland, a simulation of a non-existent real, and it pretty much achieves its goal. There is no exaggeration in saying that Silliman's work is language itself, but language removed from the actual.

It is within this world of language, in a world where language's playfulness (perhaps we could rather, à la Barthes, use the term *jouissance* in this respect) is meant to spur a reader's contemplation of utterance itself, that we find once again the literate human being's impulse to comprehend the totality of knowledge. It is just that for Silliman knowledge has become the language proper within a supreme act of *sui generis* inscription. What is so extraordinary about *The Alphabet* is that it bespeaks the supremely humanizing phenomenon of humanity since the creation of history, which comes about through the agency of writing. Therefore we can appreciate Silliman's work as an homage, in its own way, to that most ennobling of human endeavors: the act of writing. What then might follow is that, insofar as it is a body of ordered knowledge, the encyclopedia as a genre of writing is not completely different from that of procedural poetics. The world is understood according to the way the encyclopedist orders the work.

Isidore's *Etymologiae*, undoubtedly the greatest of the early encyclopedias, held immense intellectual sway through its categorizations; these categories were conceptualizations that instructed readers as to how the entire world's knowledge was to be approached and comprehended; in this manner they represented an arrangement of the world. Yet only one of the categories within the larger work of the *Etymologiae* was organized according to alphabetical order. It might seem obvious to us—we who with almost straight faces speak of carbon-based versus silicon-based life forms, we who live in a world of codes, be they genetic, digital, or whatever—that a work attempting to hold all knowledge together, such as an encyclopedia, should be organized alphabetically. Writing came to provide that basic arrangement for us. In fact the fundamental irony of Isidore's work—which might readily have been viewed by scholars in his time as having achieved the epitome of writing, and by us today as typifying humanity's arrival at the pinnacle of early literacy—is that only a small portion of the *Etymologiae* (the actual book, of the twenty books in the encyclopedia, on the origins of words) was arranged according to the alphabet, in fact according to any system of inscription. (The greatest part of the encyclopedia was arranged as per the typical scholarly classifications of the time, such as what were called the topical, educational, conversational orders, and so on.)

It took time to think of alphabetizing records (just as it did for reading silently and using books rather than scrolls). The technology of the book (beginning in the late first century and gradually growing in popularity through the fourth century) has yet to be surpassed, as evinced by computer hard drives arranged in sectors. Silliman's work, which covers not only an expanse of time but also of place, over-full as it is with his daily thoughts and the details of his daily life, makes the inevitable "correction." It is aware of itself within an evolutionary intellectual and literary continuum as it seeks to make the fact of the writing the central focus of his life.

While Silliman's work (of which *The Alphabet* is emblematic) has been praised by some readers, it has also garnered its detractors. Michael Heller, for instance, in discussing Silliman, suggests that he must "envision a reader without history or memory, a reader who won't resist the presence of the text" ("Avant-Garde Propellants," *Uncertain Poetries,* 216). Heller deplores Language poetry's "flight from content—or, at least, an inscribing of a Saussaurian [*sic*] bar between sign and signified. If mimetics were not the point of the activity," he continues, "it would be presumptuous to infer reality behind the words; the words would have to stand by themselves" (Heller 214). For Heller the problem ultimately has to do when the reader is "*severed* from even considering the social meaning of freedom by being delivered into the polymorphic pleasures of the non-referential—*plaisirs du texte* indeed [a reference to Barthes's 1973 book *Le Plaisir du texte*], but privatized and unavailable for the social agenda many of the language poets claim" (217).

Of course this non-referentiality emerges out of Silliman's poetics of "the new sentence" as well as through his employment of procedural practices of others. We can think again of Zukofsky, an important influence on Heller's own poetry, and, arguably, the sense of the materiality of language is a key in the work of all the Objectivist poets (Heller's *Conviction's Net of Branches* is the first book on them). I would suggest, though, that the distinction between the poetics of proceduralism and the poetics of the new sentence is merely partial; for a poet to commit to writing in the new sentence mode is in fact to write within a procedural constraint, for in such a mode of writing the writer has to avoid subordination and syllogistic aspects of discourse. It may be the case that Heller is not interested in providing a full account of what can happen when normal language is constrained in one or another radically artificial way (or it may be that he sees the virtues of proceduralism, such as, for instance, Zukofsky's use of a five-word line, as possessing virtues but also inherently limited in trying to achieve eloquence).

Another detractor, Stephen Rodefer, addresses this matter head-on, and seems to be in sympathy with Heller. He comments that "Silliman's writing thrives, [but] then is in danger of getting stuck, on varying mathematics that threaten to become the theme of the writing. [Robert] Creeley counts syllables, Silliman counts sentences (actually really only dots, in, for instance, [the section of *The Alphabet* titled] "Carbon"—all 7s and 3s, etc. etc. etc.). After you notice it for a second, it's of secondary interest" (54). Then there is this deeply perceptive comment by Mack, who seems to think highly of *The Alphabet* in some respects, which may comprehend all of these criticisms: "Silliman's whole effort has been to oppose the imagination of transcendental orders. . . . His project means to substitute a poetic 'activity' for a poetic 'form': poem as 'study group' instead of poem as 'thing of beauty'" (Mack and Rome 745).

I might sum up these complaints by asking, when standing back and taking in Silliman's achievement as a whole, why there is always the need to live with writing in all its raw purity placed before one, in contemplation of it, such as we see addressed in *The Alphabet*. It is as if there can be no cognizant life, or at least no human life, in the sense that people might only be truly self-fulfilled through the act of writing—that supremely, peculiarly self-determining and self-articulating undertaking. The question then becomes: is Silliman in his creating the perfect instantiation of the postmodern simulacrum parting company with not only Isidore but also Zukofsky, Pound, Duncan, Johnson, DuPlessis, and others who have constructed long poems in recent times? In other words, by demonstrating what I'd like to call posthuman writing (à la Hayles), is he implicitly declaring an end to both selfhood and poetry through the most civilizing act of inscription?

Jed Rasula has commented that "Silliman's work may be read as a grand refusal of the chronic strategies of authorial domination" (qtd in Perloff "Portrait" 6). Grand indeed. Silliman's grand intellect, relentlessly brought to bear upon his testing of the powers and limits of statement, has given rise to a rethinking of what poetry is and can be. Nevertheless, in its own way *The Alphabet* is a product of its time and may, in its *modus operandi*, be viewed as addressing what is often glibly referred to as the postmodern condition. Still, we are no longer living in the modern world, however we may wish to talk about our present moment.

Ultimately, does *The Alphabet* see a way forward? Baudrillard has often been taken to task for his pessimism (cf. among others Raffel). I wonder if Silliman, whose trenchant and creative intelligence cannot be denied, means to write the ending to poetry and in a sense the end of writing and human civilization. I suspect not. Yet his work is utterly confounding, while being equally compelling. It belongs in anyone's literary history.

In discussing a passage from the section of *The Alphabet* titled "Paradise," Keith Tuma possibly captures the essence of this long poem as a whole and more broadly Silliman's contribution to poetry and letters. Tuma tells us that a reader "might be tempted to call" a typical Silliman "poem a kind of 'collective text' for the way it assembles and refuses to order hierarchically a wide range of cultural discourses, resisting meaning as it might be constituted by an individual" (45). As I think Tuma would agree, *The Alphabet* is not a collage. This is surely Silliman's point, as evident in his aesthetic or cognitive approach to structure.

As Tuma also states, however, "Silliman himself is the master of this ceremonial mimicry of all seriousness" (45). This said, let us not overlook the fact that, in large, Silliman's writing constitutes a historical step in Western letters. Whether this is a fact readers should feel pessimistic about is another matter. Like the posthuman condition Hayles describes, we should understand Silliman's work as a reality of sorts, and furthermore we should recognize that the still-to-be-cherished selfhood, which emerges first in the modern era, may indeed live on in the form of the posthuman subject.

Notes

1. See among other sources Silliman's "*Who Speaks*: Ventriloquism and the Self in the Poetry Reading" and Huntsberger (especially 113 ff.).

2. See "Aesthetic Tendency and the Politics of Poetry: A Manifesto" by Silliman, Carla Harryman, Hejinian, Steve Benson, Bob Perelman, and Barrett Watten (1988), which is remarkable for its vehemence. Among other early theorizing, see particularly *In the American Tree*.

3. Silliman lists the "qualities" of "The New Sentence" as follows:

(1) The paragraph [rather than the stanza] organizes the sentences;
(2) The paragraph is a unit of quantity, not logic or argument;
(3) Sentence length [rather than the line] is a unit of measure;
(4) Sentence structure is altered for torque, or increased polysemy/ambiguity;
(5) Syllogistic movement is (a) limited (b) controlled;
(6) Primary syllogistic movement is toward the paragraph as a whole, or the total work;

(7) Secondary syllogistic movement is toward the paragraph as a whole, or the total work;

(8) The limiting of syllogistic movement keeps the reader's attention at or very close to the level of language, the sentence level or below. (91)

4. Silliman's comment comes right after a pertinent remark from Frederic Jameson discussing "the postmodern cultural text" (Silliman 92), which refers to "the isolated Signifier." Silliman quotes from this, replicating Jameson's phrase "in free-standing isolation" (Jameson 73; Silliman 92).

Cooking a Book with Low-Level Durational Energy; or, How to Read Tan Lin's *Seven Controlled Vocabularies*

Kristen Gallagher

Reviewers of Tan Lin's *Seven Controlled Vocabularies* (7CV) have produced some interesting misreadings. Some mistake the story of someone ("I") meeting his wife at a Macy's event for straight autobiography; others regard the reproduction of Laura (Riding) Jackson's Foreword to *Rational Meaning* as a statement of affinity between Lin's book and her theory of intrinsic meaning; still others compare the book to Theodor Adorno's aesthetic theory or treat it as a manifesto. Each of these misreadings presents its own problems. Taken together, they show us exactly what the style of the book does—tempts us to lapse into certain habits of reading (focusing on what is most recognizable to us, projecting our own desires and interests into places they aren't, etc.). The stylistic play of 7CV is only the latest variation on a way to perform something Lin has sought in all his projects: to create reading environments that get the reader thinking about how various texts trigger certain kinds of reading.

Yes, 7CV teases at being both a book of aesthetic theory and straightforward stylized autobiography. It is certainly concerned with the meanings of words. And while it concerns topics such as beauty, art, and society, and contains elements of both theory and story, very little of the content is what it seems at first reading. The book does not go after these issues directly, "with hammer and tongs," as it were. Whenever you think you're reading in one framework, you're often actually reading in several others.

This book is unlike most of its contemporaries. It doesn't isolate blocks of sampled text and leave them for the reader to work with, as in much of Conceptual poetry. And it doesn't employ the typical strategies of post-Language poetry. Most post-Language poetry takes up structures of utterance or idiolects as they are commonly used and places them in relief through juxtaposition or shreds them so that meaning is compromised for the purposes of social critique. Lin's work doesn't do this. Instead, Lin works text as a molecular gastronomist engages in "recombinant cooking based on the analysis of the structure and behavior of molecules" (This 2). Or think of a book written by a literary botanist who uses style to cross-pollinate the standard vocabulary systems for organizing information, and in doing so opens new ground for thinking through the reading environments established by those "vocabularies." This new style of writing produces in the reader a less clear sense of where one vocabulary begins and another ends. It's not merely about the relationships between things and ideas, but about how we read, and are always reading, often according to methods and guidelines we are not entirely conscious of.

Lin has published four books to date, including 7CV. His more recent books have emerged out of sourced or "marginally authorial" writing processes such as collages of material plagiarized from the Internet (*Heath Plagiarism/Outsource*) and riffs on ambient and electronic music (*Blipsoak01*). Like *Heath* and *Blipsoak01*, the work of 7CV is sampled and written-through, collaborative and democratic, but it does not register as polyvocal. As Roland Barthes says, "The text, in its mass, is comparable to a sky, at once flat and smooth, deep, without edges and without landmarks" (*S/Z* 14). The style of 7CV, on the level of sentence and paragraph, is glassy and seamless, insinuating the warmth of statement. It pulls its sources together with results that resemble more airport muzak than hip-hop, less post-Langpo and more something we haven't seen before. Any interruption or seam-rending happens more at the level of the book—between chapters and pages, between the cover, which displays the "front matter" usually consigned to an inside left-hand page and the back of the book, which looks like a front cover.

In discussions of his turn toward this kind of work, Lin often talks about wanting to make reading easier, more relaxing, by creating a smoother textual surface than what his readership had become accustomed to with Language poetry. 7CV is his smoothest attempt yet. While this smoothness often induces reading strategies appropriate to popular forms such as the novel, autobiography, or restaurant review, the subject headings of the "Library of Congress Cataloging-in-Publication Data"—descriptors whose job it is to locate the book within American library databases—inform us that it is to be categorized in ways that don't seem apparent on first glance: poetry, engagements with mass media, cookbooks, book design, and the product standards of the publishing industry, "Literary form—data processing," among other topics. Lin seems to want us to attend to this right away, foregrounding these headings by moving them to the cover of the book, away from their usual place in the unreaderly front matter. These moves are clues for how to read the book. They activate its poetics. A reading framed by these descriptors reveals a text less concerned with the truth-value of any statements and more concerned with blurring the lines between the vocabularies and genres.

Lin has come to be known for what he calls "ambient stylistics," a style he has described in a few interviews, but whose greatest articulation yet may be 7CV. In a 2005 "Close Listening" interview with Charles Bernstein, discussing ambient stylistics in his flash video poem-films, Lin provides us with a key insight into the concept of ambient writing when he expresses interest in Stein's idea that a reader cannot help but create meaning when faced with any combination of words (Lin and Bernstein). He asks, "Can three words that appear together be made into a narrative?" Lin tested this idea in his poem-film experiments, which bring words together in various combinations of three on the screen. In the animations, there are always three words and no other images. The program sequence allots each word the same amount of time on screen, and all the words fade out at the end simultaneously. The question is how far apart in meaning can the three words be and still produce a narrative?

When Lin came to read and talk at CUNY-LaGuardia Community College in May 2009, we watched one of his poem-films. He asked students to talk about how they processed the language during viewing. Beforehand, he told students he intended the video to be soothing, yogic, and he invited them to view the film meditatively. After we watched for a few minutes, he asked them to discuss connections they made between the words. Students volunteered associations, and what we discovered was that they tended to either be narratives or flashes of scenes involving the meaning of each word. One student saw the same woman doing various things associated with the words on the screen.

7CV builds on this experiment, moving it from film to the realm of the book—though it is useful to think of the book as working like a film, employing the dissolve as a way of moving across discourses. It takes combinations of discrete words and turns them into explorations of "controlled vocabularies," many from the publishing industry: poetry, fiction, autobiography, theory, art book, and so on. How many generic terms and reproductions of images are required to trigger a reading response of "art book"? How many references does it take to positions in the structure of the family (wife, father) before the assumption "autobiography" begins to creep into the reading? In this sense, Lin's work is genuinely experimental, recalling not only Gertrude Stein but the early-twentieth-century psychophysical studies of Hermann Ebbinghaus. Ebbinghaus, whose experiments were designed to test memory through the memorization and recitation of randomly chosen syllables, noted that, at least initially, his subjects tended to produce meaning involuntarily, forming narrative chains through the association of the test syllables with known words. (It is worth noting that Stein took part in comparable "dissociative" language experiments during her student years at Harvard University.)

Lin says in his *BOMB Magazine* interview with Katherine Sanders, "[s]tyle is what is statistically likely to induce a reading." In other words, a statistically significant showing of lexical elements and other features associated with a specific controlled vocabulary, say poetry, tends to produce, involuntarily, particular forms of reading. One reads differently when there are line breaks. One reads a certain way when it seems the text is guiding the reader through a recipe. Anyone might lapse into certain reading habits by way of textual cues or even as a result of the marketing strategies used to sell the book. With this realization in place, Lin's book playfully cues, samples from, and surfs around specific structures and vocabularies, mixing and echoing and reversing throughout. The vocabularies of painting, architecture, autobiography, design, shopping, etc., slowly shift and blend.

When asked about the connection of 7CV to ambient stylistics, Lin described the book as "a piece of low-level durational energy" that emphasizes a long-time concern of his to create reading environments—but in this one, according to Lin, "distinctions between recipe, novel, etc. are dissolved" ("Close Listening"). He compares this to visual artists like Jorge Pardo who renovated a house, presented it as art, and had an "opening" there, thereby blurring the line between art, carpentry, and gallery. Works like Pardo's make Lin wonder about the possibilities for a generic poetic work for today. He realizes that "it would be metadata/controlled vocabularies." Using these generic terms, he says, he wanted to create a reading environment where "a novel . . . could be confused with or blurred with airport or architecture."

This blurring of vocabularies across the book creates a peculiar sensation of drifting and floating—a haziness—while reading, as the surface of the text shifts laterally across the reader's expectations; this makes it quite a different reading experience/environment than any other I know of. So the scan (about two-thirds of the way through 7CV) of the 1986 preface to Laura (Riding) Jackson's *Rational Meaning* should not be taken to mean that Lin has an affinity with her theory of radical meaning. 7CV performs mostly in opposition to Riding's theory; this is perhaps the one binary remaining in the book. Where radical meaning posits that a word has rigid intrinsic meaning that must be preserved, Lin's ambient stylistics moves against that toward the edges of meanings. In 7CV there is no rigidity of aesthetic terminology, no ultimate truth to our vocabulary. Lin wants to soften meaning, as opposed to Riding's hardening it; he chooses drift where Riding chose focus.

The vocabularies Lin works with, pulled together by a bland elliptical style that seems to hold them in solution, will often suggest a specific genre to the reader, setting up certain expectations for what will be covered—but the text subverts those expectations as often as it sets them up. The play with vocabulary creates a reading game for the audience to think around the limits of both genre and the construction of books, treating those constructs as material bases to draw from. The game consists of playing on a series of vocabulary markers as they are encoded in readers; the book is more concerned with playing on those codes than saying anything directly from within them. Further, the suggestive nature of the content not only plays on our habits of reading but consistently tempts us to lapse into those habits. In the end, questions of agency arise as the reader contends with the alternating experiences of suggestiveness, relaxation, and drift. The text plays with readers, acts on them subconsciously, but it also provides opportunities for them to arrive at a self-conscious awareness of its operations. Questions of how to read and also how much to "read into" the text become primary.

Because of this playful drifting between vocabularies, the text of 7CV cannot be taken at face value; and here we can see why the misreadings of Lin's reviewers are so instructive. One cannot say "Lin asserts" or "Lin thinks" and then take a sentence or phrase from the text because the text consists primarily of lexical cues drawn from the vocabularies in play. (This makes the text difficult to quote well.)

The best example of this play of lexical cues may be the section that offers a first-person account of meeting one's wife at a flash mob event at Macy's. The story reads as autobiographical and even contains the name of Lin's wife, Clare Churchouse. But this narrative is called into question when the wife enters the story, reports that this is not where they met, and offers her own journal as evidence that they met two-and-a-half years earlier. With such a time difference, one already has to question the degree to which the reading "autobiography" can be applied. It may be that Lin has a poor memory, but the date and description Lin gives for the flash mob event match the description of the first flash mob ever in the Wikipedia entry for "flash mob." This strongly suggests that he borrowed the flash mob description and mixed it with names and a point of view that suggests the "autobiographical" in order to place those categories in relief. (Of course, it is also possible that Lin edited the Wikipedia entry to match his book, but we'll leave that for another essay.)

The romantic personal story available in the flash mob section of 7CV is easy to believe if you don't want to see the evidence that it is likely (at least in part) a falsification. Invited to "read" autobiography, to lapse into that comfortable pleasure, the reader is also given the opportunity to begin thinking about the triggers that evoke "autobiography" and why even the most trained readers are so susceptible to its codes. It is also worth noting that the flash mob in question involved a critique of shopping. Combining these issues in this segment also creates space for readers to consider the relationship between the forces that produce shopping, the autobiography, and the subject that desires autobiography.

Every chapter is an example of this kind of category blurring. In the chapter titled "Field Guide to American Landscape Painting," a reader might find himself expecting everything to be about American landscape painting, but the text instead concerns itself with topics that seem marginal to that discourse. Rather the text deals with various forms of sequencing, primarily as found in media outside painting, such as: A-side vs. B-side, top vs. bottom, the number of things the human brain can remember at once, the convention of numbering plates to display paintings in a book about painting, the way a poem can instigate looking more than reading, that the way a novel is most often ordered according to what will make it most hypnotic and mesmerizing. All of these concerns seem to come down to how "everyone says 'cogito'" (22). Reading between the categories of "field guide," "landscape," "painting," "sequence," "narrative," "cogito," and others reveals that each category already contains elements of the other. On one hand, the controlled vocabulary system for landscape painting is the mediatory apparatus that allows one to speak about painting and also for painting to exist as a function of particular discursive practices. On the other hand, that vocabulary system, at its margins, can be used to re-orient the way we think of other media, and vice-versa. This opens up an opportunity to think about how we define thinking itself: the way we have been trained by narrative discourses to think of novels or even our own personal stories, or the way we have been influenced by landscape painting and books about the subject to think of certain landscapes as beautiful. What is the difference between a frame and a fence? How do those discourses influence our conceptions of thinking or art or nature?

Reading this way, one can see that the chapter title already suggests a network of relations between words whose opposition and reconciliation lead one toward the central concern of the book: dissolving controlled vocabularies. A painting is a two-dimensional representation; a field guide suggests preparing for experience in a three-dimensional landscape where one might want to identify wildlife or rocks or minerals. One has field guides for birding and for recognizing flora and fauna but not for painting. Moreover, field guides help users *distinguish* animals and plants that may be similar in appearance, but 7CV forces the reader to think about similarities between categories and explore their fuzzy boundaries. In this respect, 7CV is more of an "unfieldguide," or a unified field guide. It helps us formulate questions such as: Can we look at paintings the way we look at wildlife or study them as emerging forms in environments? What is the environment for painting and how has it determined what survives?

Surprisingly, there are no photographic reproductions of paintings in this chapter. Instead several pages have the language typically used to catalog paintings when they appear in a book— "plate 1," "plate 2," and so on. This focuses the reader's attention more on the production of a book about painting than on the painting itself. In that spirit, reading this chapter one might ask: How much text does it take to instigate the reproduction of an image, and how much reproduction of an image instigates a book? And, crazier yet, in the context of a book partially titled *The Joy of Cooking*, the word "plate" begins to accrue meaning that would otherwise be considered quite marginal to any consideration of painting. But then again, any viewer of "Top Chef" knows that presentation matters; a few seasons ago the winner was called the "Picasso of Presentation." This line of connection gets reinforced later in a section describing painter Bruce Pearson, at home, attempting to reproduce a recipe from a high-end New York restaurant.

The third chapter, titled "American Architecture Meta Data Containers," also does not approach architecture directly in the traditional sense but explores the paratexts of books (back covers, barcodes, etc.) and their construction, blurred with more marginal reading contexts such as designer clothes, product tags, and credit card bills. Here the vocabulary for "architecture" and related concerns of space, territory, etc., dissolve into considerations of reading: American Written English (AWE) is "a series of spaces" (62); the page is "a quadrant filled with various codes that resemble flags" (64); "literature should function as a pattern with a label on it" (66); a Louis Vuitton bag has scrambled letters all over its surface "in order to be read" (66); cineplexes function like pastoral poetry (73). And here we find the following sentence repeated twice: "Literature as Space with Language Attached to It" (74, 76). But what does this all mean for how we define/categorize literature? What would we learn if we defined literature by its spatial relations first, treating language as an accessory? Most of us are not trained to attend to books or text in this way, and yet Lin's work here suggests that so much that is happening, including the shape of things inside and outside the space of the book, unconsciously affects how we read.

In this chapter, the vocabulary of architecture helps to frame a consideration of reading as a spatial experience: "reading is generic and immaterial like most of the buildings we pass through [ ] and the streets we happen to be on. [As anyone] [who has spent time on the Las Vegas strip] can tell you" (78). The use of brackets in the second sentence suggests we take seriously the contents of the brackets in the first, that the brackets are both meaningful and have essential information inside them. So the empty space in sentence one is pregnant. It seems to invite us to compare buildings and brackets, and what comes to mind immediately are *things treated as parenthetical, aside from the matter*. This suggests that we pass through buildings as we read [and don't read] brackets and bracketed information.

In a context—such as difficult or experimental poetry—where we are asked to think of whatever triggers us to lapse into habits of reading, we might think of a parenthesis as a representation of the unconscious, a kind of space of repression. We know we are unconscious of a great deal of what is affecting us when we read. Why not also the spaces in which we read? The physical places where reading takes place—parks, libraries, cafés—are generally considered "outside" the book, but they influence it nonetheless. Buildings may be thought of as the brackets in which we read. Reading happens within, between, and alongside a variety of structures, but how much are we aware of the physical during any given act of reading? Likewise, a book and its readership are in part created by the generic and metadata structures ostensibly "outside" of it. Furthermore, feelings and expectations often seek fulfillment "inside" a book, as when I buy a book marketed as an autobiography of Andre Bréton, hoping for literary gossip in biographical form, only to find out that it too is constructed according to surrealist principles and will not deliver the reading experience I wanted.

The section "2 Identical Novels" plays out these concerns further. Where, based on the title, one might expect a story or comparison of stories or the way they appear, one instead finds oneself immersed in a discussion of cooking and recipes as "typologies for those feelings we have forgotten were inside us" (106). Some questions might arise: How are novels (and their similarity or identicalness to each other) also typologies for forgotten emotions? How are novels like recipes for cooking? Where a novel is designed to induce particular feelings or habits of reading, or draw on the desires of someone seeking empathy, the recipe produces a flavor profile that persons with culinary experience can recognize. Where a novel has a fundamental reproducible form, a recipe is also endlessly reproducible.

This chapter gives way to a brief discourse on potentiality: "An emotion, like a recipe, is always waiting to become the thing that it already is. . . .

People who think they have their own emotions are incapable of empathy or cooking" (106). Feelings, like genres, can be difficult to identify, but we learn to identify them and are often uncomfortable when we can't. Many people enjoy or even need a certain amount of coherence in the handling of literary genre as well as in the use of spices. Experimenting with either can produce a number of effects, from "this has X influence" to "those two flavors/approaches do not work together." The question in 7CV is whether "the novel" has about as many options as there are flavor principles, ways material can be combined to create recognizable effects and connections, pleasure or displeasure, identification or dysidentification in the reader/eater. Overwhelmingly, the novel—especially the popular novel—like a recipe, formulaically induces target results in the form of certain emotional responses, which author/cook can assume are shared among consumers to a more or less statistically significant degree, and the degree to which a product fails to please a mass of consumers is a matter of (preferably) calculated risk. These assumptions of "shared experience" should not, however, be assumed to occur "naturally," as if coming from "within" human individuals, but rather should be attributed to the influence of the cultural institutions of reading and eating. Those responses tell us how "Everyone says cogito," that is, how a certain tendency to trust experience can restrict future risk. 7CV raises questions that suggest the relationship between what we are willing to read and what is marketed as a novel is not unlike the relationship between the kinds of foods we are willing to eat and those foods we have always eaten.

Categories aren't blurred only within but across the chapters of 7CV. For example, in the field guide/landscape painting chapter we consider how a poem might be sequenced to instigate looking or skimming instead of the intensive reading practices traditionally associated with poetry, and in the architecture/metadata chapter we consider the relationship between reading and appearance, how "the most powerful texts function like logos, a code wherein words and reading are synthesized into looking and staring" or how "a logo-like text is text and reading instructions as one" (70). Should this be read to mean Lin wants texts that are logo-like? I wouldn't force the text to choose, but instead consider what can be learned from evaluating the reading of logos.

The Louis Vuitton logo works because it requires a certain amount of reading for anyone to get it. Then a moment of recognition occurs, after which the logo has claimed a small bit of real estate in one's brain. (That's branding.) On one hand, Naomi Klein has popularized an analysis that says such occurrences are a manipulative invasion of daily life and experience and a transformation of bodies into brand carriers. On the other hand, the logo induces reading and, as 7CV suggests, it may teach us something about how we read other texts, like poems.

When one looks at a long, thin piece of writing with line breaks, one "knows" it is a poem before one reads the words. The line-break writing announces itself as "poem" from afar like a giant Chanel logo on a t-shirt worn by a stranger on the subway. When one does finally read the language, certain assumptions about what a poem is or does will influence how it is received. If expectations are not met, a reader might question whether such a piece meets the standards for the genre and claim false advertising. If readers are bringing traditional, or very rigid, practices to the act of reading, they may have difficulty engaging a poem that subverts what they see as the standards of the genre. Some contemporaries continue to dismiss Language poetry because the language is too disjunctive or has no clear voice; some may look at books like Lin's *Heath* and see huge chunks of plagiarized prose text and images of advertising and numerical codes and say "that's not poetry or even writing." But texts like *Heath* offer us an opportunity to learn something about both genre and the act of reading. Any time something unfamiliar begins happening within a genre, some readers may want to push the material out and say the descriptor "poetry" cannot contain it. Often, however, these challengers to the genre are redefining it, re-branding it, and teaching us as they do.

7CV occupies the limit space between generic terms: How is a blouse like a poem? How is a strip mall like a film? If we observe these forms in terms of how they instigate reading, we ask other questions: What instigates a reading and what codes do people respond to in the same way across a wide variety of objects? And how are the various forms of non-reading also the products of systems of reading? Is there anything that is not instigating reading? Lin does not blur these categories for the sake of playing with signifiers; the process of softening these categories—feeling their edges and experiencing content as a statistical aggregate—ultimately opens out onto a much larger question of cultural production and the role of metadata in it. Metadata and controlled vocabularies play a large role in how we read. Not only is any object of art or literature defined by the multitudinous descriptors and frameworks that cue our responses to them; these works are artifacts of production or moments in a work-flow that does not stop with the consumer but carries through in the production of scripted responses. In this sense the content of designer clothes, like the content of the book, is identical with its frameworks.

Metadata emerges as one of the central concerns of 7CV not only through its ability to dissolve controlled vocabularies but also through its consistent reference to the manufacture of goods and services and the tracking of sales. Images of or reference to bar codes, backs of books, clothing tags, credit card bills, shopping, restaurant matchboxes, and the like appear throughout. The text becomes less about the genres themselves and more about how texts and objects are positioned within flows and systems. This emphasis, in the context of thinking about reading, ultimately defines "literature" in terms of work-flows and mechanisms of exchange. But just as this book cannot be separated from its marketing and American library database categorization, it also cannot be separated from the work at the compositional phase of production.

Both the exposed raw information of the cover image and the full title, *Seven Controlled Vocabularies and Obituary 2004 The Joy of Cooking*, play with descriptors in unusual ways that point to things ostensibly "outside" the book. You will find this questioning of genre and response throughout the book. For example, when I first read the subject heading "poetry—therapeutic use" I assumed it was ironic. My own somewhat anti-confessional training surely influenced this reaction. But in the context of thinking through the book in terms of work-flows and the false inside/outside division of the book, it occurred to me that my own bracketing off of "poetry as therapeutic" may be yet another of the categorical limitations that this book challenges. Who is to say the author wasn't experiencing personal difficulty during the production of this book? Who is to say struggles with attention and memory are not behind the new form of writing we find here? Perhaps creation of the book and personal difficulty re-frame each other throughout, and to therapeutic effect. Perhaps every blurring of vocabulary marks an important event in the life lived ostensibly "outside" the book. Perhaps 7CV is autobiographical in ways that are submerged but everywhere, and lived events are generic driving forces in the composition phase of the book.

The parts that read most immediately as autobiographical, like Lin's story of meeting his wife, are clearly partially plagiarized, but perhaps some parts that do not register as autobiographical also contain personal elements. In his interview with Bernstein, Lin talks about his Chinese family learning about American cuisine from *The Joy of Cooking*. There isn't much directly related to that story in 7CV, but the title memorializes that fact, and cooking, cookbooks, and restaurant reviews are referenced throughout.

It is possible that the backs of books displayed in the metadata chapter refer to texts that influenced 7CV. For instance, Gary Sullivan's *How to Proceed in the Arts*—a register of frustration with the "business" of poetry that broke from the disjunctive poetic style of its time—may have influenced the desire for smoother surface apparent in 7CV as well as its appropriation from other genres of ideas about reading. And while some of the autobiographical elements may be Lin's own, it is anyone's story, found on the Internet, shared by so many that it had become everyone's story. It also may reflect to what degree we learn to tell stories in the same ways we have heard them told. In the end, Lin has produced a text that appears fairly seamless in its writing but also suggests that an abundance of stories and processes are rendered invisible in any book.

Although, upon first reading, I sensed that autobiography was part of the project, I was hesitant to take that at face value because of prior knowledge of Lin's work. But after many rereadings, autobiography has re-emerged for me as central to this project. Like Breton's *Nadja*, 7CV views autobiography not so much as a straight story of a life but as a catalog of important moments, somewhat disjunctive from each other, but recognizable as containing pivotal problems and questions in one person's coming to be who they are as an artist. Whereas, for Breton, the stories create a picture of his most important surrealist influences and experiences, Lin's autobiography is a series of ambient constructions built around the vocabularies and codes that have influenced his life and practice, with each of these constructions organized to alternately trigger or diffuse its reading as "autobiography." This raises the question: where does the construction of the book begin and the life lived outside it end? In the *BOMB* interview, Lin suggests that the distinction itself is false: "Context is more important than content. There is a lot of personal and extra-personal communal history (errors of attribution: death, tragedy, etc.) beyond a book's covers. . . . Every book is an abbreviation/revision that erects some sort of false distinction or difference between reading and non-reading, between the life lived inside and the life outside the book. I wanted to exteriorize the ecosystem of reading as much as possible."

I have come to understand 7CV as an ambient autobiography of a book about ambient autobiography. Lin created a book out of his life, which is largely made up of what he reads, how he reads, and his relationships to food, friends, and art, and the ways all these things inform each other.

Engaging with (the Content of) John Bloomberg-Rissman's *2nd NOTICE OF MODIFICATIONS TO TEXT OF PROPOSED REGULATIONS*

Eileen R. Tabios

In response to interviewer Tom Beckett's question, "Where did/does poetry begin for you?" John Bloomberg-Rissman replies: "It begins for me in a constraint-based making of new texts out of a chorus of other voices/writings, other others, other sames, in a *voyage of discovery*. . . . [But] I don't approach language only in terms of its materiality. I don't think Wittgensteinian language games are purposeless (after all, the builder wants to be handed that brick, and wants to do something with it), or that Snyder was wrong when he wrote, '[t]he moral imperative in this yuga is to communicate.' So, yeah, I am trying to 'say' something."

In the same interview, Bloomberg-Rissman speaks of his process of "writing *beyond* [him]self": "for the last five years or so [his texts] have always involved appropriating/ sampling/ collaging/ assembling/ mangling other texts." He regards "this assemblage-work" as "the opposite of a tight corner. It ties me to, opens up for me, opens me up to, the human universe." Bloomberg-Rissman's *2nd NOTICE OF MODIFICATIONS TO TEXT OF PROPOSED REGULATIONS, REGULATION AND POLICY MANAGEMENT BRANCH, CALIFORNIA DEPARTMENT OF CORRECTIONS AND REHABILITATION* is a document that the poet unexpectedly received as a PDF. Its text addresses modifications to regulations for how the death penalty is administered in the state of California. Bloomberg-Rissman decided to print it out. He then created a cover to be folded around this print-out and, voila, a "poem" was born.

Bloomberg-Rissman says that *2nd NOTICE* was partly inspired by a similarly-conceived project, *Tragodía 1: Statement of Facts* by Vanessa Place, a poet, conceptual artist, and lawyer. A note from the publisher, Blanc Press, explains that "[a] statement of facts is a legal document which sets forward factual information without argument. These documents are used in a variety of legal settings, ranging from appeals to filing vehicle registration paperwork. The goal of a statement of facts is not to put forward an argument, but rather to present factual information in a clear, easy to understand way."

Tragodía is composed of the three parts of an appellate brief: "Statement of Facts," which sets forth, in narrative form, the evidence of the crime as presented at trial; "Statement of the Case," which sets forth the procedural history of the case; and "Argument," which are the claims of error and (for the defense) the arguments for reversing the judgment. Place's *Statement of Facts* project involves reproducing statements of facts from some of her appellate briefs and representing them as poetry.

Later, I will suggest that Bloomberg-Rissman's use of thorough appropriation differs significantly from Flarf poets, who "mine the Internet with odd search terms then distill the results into often hilarious and sometimes disturbing poems." I will also argue that Bloomberg-Rissman's work differs from conceptual work such as Place's *Tragodía* and Kenneth Goldsmith's *Sports* (Make Now, 2008), *Traffic* (2007), and *The Weather* (2005), which consist of "a transcribed broadcast of a baseball game, of traffic patterns, and of the weather, respectively," as well as *Day* (2003), which Goldsmith created by retyping "the entirety of the *New York Times* newspaper from Friday, September 1, 2000, resulting in an 836-page tome" (Kenneth Goldsmith, Academy of American Poets). I will also compare Bloomberg-Rissman's use of found text to my own poetic practice as found in my book *The Light Sang As It Left Your Eyes: Our Autobiography.*

Bloomberg-Rissman's source text for *2nd NOTICE* was an edited document that contained various editing formats, like underlines that indicate added or deleted text. These edits offer much of what's poetic—or can be poetic—about the document (poem). For example, at one point, "person" was deleted and replaced with "inmate" (1). "Inmate" allows for a distancing effect from the "person" soon to be killed. When the word "warden" was edited to reflect the capitalization of the first letter into "Warden," that capitalization gives additional weight to the role of said Warden.

However, one doesn't have to rely on the edited parts of the text for instances of poetic or political irony. For example, the following sentence—copied from the original text without any ornamentation—bludgeons the reader: "Inmates sentenced to death shall have the opportunity to choose to have the punishment imposed by lethal gas or lethal injection" (1). Throughout the poem, many effects are generated without the need of the author's additional textual aids. Allowing *the thing to speak for itself* can maximize the effect on the reader. For instance, legalese or bureaucracy-speak serves to elide the horror of the matter at hand. Some sentences serve to eliminate the reference to "Condemned Row" within the document. There is also the section: "(t) Lethal Injection Room means the room where the inmate is executed" (3). Why use the euphemism "Lethal Injection Room"? Why not use "Execution Room," which would be a more powerful reference to what the poet calls "judicial murder" (5)? Who is doing the spinning—the massaging of language—and how is it being done? Who is being protected and not?

One of the exhibits features a "SERVICE OF EXECUTION WARRANT-WARDEN'S INITIAL INTERVIEW." The inmate is supposed to sign this document to acknowledge receipt of the Warrant of Execution issued by a Country Superior Court as well as to acknowledge that he understands he is entitled to choose either lethal gas or lethal injection. Why is it necessary to force the inmate to address the means of execution? Why could not the more humane option simply be applied? Forcing the inmate to address this issue can only serve to heighten suffering. Given the fact that he's already being executed and it's often not the inmate's choice, it seems an unnecessary potential source of mental torture.

Numerous other passages in *2nd NOTICE* stand alone and accomplish the poet's goal of drawing attention to death penalty proceedings without having to insert his own words. For example, in "Administration of Lethal Injection Chemicals," the following sentence needs no further commentary: "If the inmate continues to refuse to comply with orders, an emergency cell extraction will be authorized" (21). Similarly, on the same page, there is a passage about precautions that the staff is supposed to take while administering lethal injections that could certainly be a list poem:

Disposable gown
Facehead protection
Rubber gloves
Padded gloves
Leg protection. (21)

Like a poem, what's described here is a different world, but this world is ours, even those of us who may resemble that proverbial nuclear family sitting cozily in a warm living room. There is recognition that we are all implicated—that we are all part of a world where executions do not simply occur but are continually finessed for effectiveness or to address other issues that Bloomberg-Rissman says do not concern bureaucrats but, as he said to me in an email, may concern non-bureaucrats, for example "moral" issues. The recognition of this shared burden is presented more powerfully to the reader precisely because of the lack of authorial ornamentation to the found text. When the reader goes beyond the conceptual format of the project to read all of the words, one realizes that the content is significant precisely for its particular presentation of concerns.

2nd NOTICE suggests that poetry exists all around us, and that it is the poet's role to recognize what already exists rather than to engage in a more interventionist authorial act. It should be noted, though, that Bloomberg-Rissman seems to suggest that *2nd NOTICE* extends this genre of found conceptual poetry. The cover of *2nd NOTICE* presents and strikes through statements from Immanuel Kant, Robert Fitterman, Vanessa Place, and Gary Sullivan and replaces them with a sentence labeled as Bloomberg-Rissman's: "TO THOSE WHO SAY, 'THIS ISN'T WRITING, IT'S TYPING', I SAY, 'NO, NO, NO, THIS ISN'T TYPING, IT'S JUST DIGIMECHANICAL REPRODUCTION; ITS NOT EVEN CUT N PASTE.'" Bloomberg-Rissman is certainly correct. Whereas Goldsmith and other conceptualists copy or type a text from a source, Bloomberg-Rissman merely printed out the emailed PDF and the manuscript was born.

The relevance of a concept like Bloomberg-Rissman's depends on what is done with it. For instance, the choice of which text to "find" and present as a poem is an authorial decision, and this decision matters. One of poetry's many possibilities, after all, is to raise attention. The subject of *2nd NOTICE* is how the death penalty is applied. The reader learns, for example, that the process of execution is broken up so that no individual takes responsibility for the actual death. Bloomberg-Rissman says the text was "revelatory" to him in "how the whole process is so broken into pieces that no single person, except the warden, maybe, has to take any actual responsibility for the act." Different individuals are in charge of preparing the chemicals and saline solutions for the lethal injection.

Interestingly, the form of the document, with its occasional broken-up narrative, metaphorically matches the piece-meal execution process. For example, Section 3349.1.3, "Lethal Team Injection Team Duties," notes a list of steps which, at one point, states that intravenous catheters should be inserted into the inmate's veins "as set forth in section 3349.4.5" (5). It is common in legal documents to unfold a narrative with various references to sections elsewhere in the document. Such a legalistic format, though, interrupts the flow of the narrative and, by doing so, can dilute the horror of the content's impact. Bloomberg-Rissman's observation of how the execution process is broken up so that "no single person" bears responsibility demonstrates that *form matches content.*

Such dilution of individual responsibility for the execution poses interesting implications about morality. This evasion of responsibility is as moral an issue as the question of whether death penalties should be applied. And

Bloomberg-Rissman poeticized this document because, as regards this matter (and related issues), he "thought people should know" (email from author). By seeking to inform people through a found text presented matter-of-factly rather than more didactic or biased or impassioned analytical accompaniments, Bloomberg-Rissman makes his project more effective. Here, the horror is enlarged when the horror speaks for itself.

While the concepts of found and/or repurposed texts are not new, *2nd NOTICE* introduces a new dimension to how a text may be "found." The poet did not search the Internet or specifically look at other people's words to create *2nd NOTICE;* rather the source was a document emailed to him unexpectedly one day. Bloomberg-Rissman believes that he received the document as a result of his online activities. In the past, as he told me in an email, he has signed many online petitions on a variety of topics. Significantly, those who use the Internet to harvest information about individual proclivities came to identify Bloomberg-Rissman as someone likely to be interested in the death penalty and other matters addressed in the document. The author is no longer, in other words, the finder of text. The text found its author! Bloomberg-Rissman's online activities evidently facilitated the creation of a profile—an avatar?—which may now attract the attention of other parties, be they advocates on some political issue or commercial marketers.

This effect poses certain implications. To the extent, for example, that our actions speak louder than our words, it may be that material that comes to the poet in the manner in which *2nd NOTICE* did may be more focused, i.e., more directly related to the poet's true concerns (based on his actions), than material he is lightly curious about and researches in order to create a poem. In this sense, *2nd NOTICE* may rely on found material but clearly reflects a stronger authorial presence and investment than, for example, my approach to found material in *The Light Sang As It Left Your Eyes: Our Autobiography* (2006). In this work I copied the text of responses to mail-order bride/sweetheart notices and reconfigured them into couplets to show how ridiculous some of the men dabbling in mail-order sites were. The plight of mail-order brides interested me enough to write poems about the subject but it is otherwise not a matter in which I'm politically engaged (through advocacy such as petition-signing). In contrast, the *2nd NOTICE* text found its author and thus forcefully presents the author's proclivities as part of the work's conceptual underpinnings.

The poet didn't create *2nd NOTICE* to reflect on poetic form as a function of what's "found" or to manifest collage or to explore whether art can be plagiarized. *2nd NOTICE* came into existence precisely because the poet was already involved in public discussions regarding the death penalty. Thus, the book is the result of political involvement and action, and not purely an exploration of aesthetic style, a mode that has come to characterize some quarters of the contemporary avant-garde. After being so "informed" about the death penalty issue, will readers who oppose the penalty decide, in turn, to get involved personally or politically in the matter?

The back cover of *2nd NOTICE* reproduces a drawing by the poet's daughter Rebekah May. This drawing shows what Bloomberg-Rissman describes as "a child's version of an execution." The root of this illustration is the description from *2nd NOTICE* of the trays that contain chemicals and salines:

> (1) Two identical trays shall be prepared.
> (A) Tray A shall be color-coded red and will be the primary tray used for the lethal injection process.
> (B) Tray B shall be colored-coded (sic) blue and will be the backup tray.
> (2) Each tray shall have eight color-coded syringes to match the tray and be labeled by content and sequence of administration as follows:
> #1 60cc syringe 1.5 grams sodium thiopental
> #2 60cc syringe 1.5 grams sodium thiopental
> #3 60cc syringe 50cc saline flush
> #4 60cc syringe 50 milligrams pancuronium bromide
> #5 60cc syringe 50cc saline flush
> #6 60cc syringe 100 milliequivalents potassium chloride
> #7 60cc syringe 100 milliequivalents potassium chloride
> #8 60cc syringe 50 cc saline flush. (19)

Although May visually represents the A and B trays, the labeling of these trays with the letters "A" and "B" implies that the text is being injected into the author's (writing) arm. This effect fits the project's underlying concept.

Done with markers, the drawing helps make the project more than another instance of "found poetry." It helps us better see the presence of the artist's *hand* (pun intended) than, say, a photocopied image or a collage of photocopies. And it reminds the viewer/reader that conceptualism is only one way to create poetry, and that the one conceptual failure in art-making is the insistence that its way is the only path.

Bursting at the Seams

Exploding the Confines of Reification with Creative Constraints in *Sleeping with the Dictionary*

Carrie Conners

Harryette Mullen's poems in *Sleeping with the Dictionary* are playful, yet mysterious. They seem to toy with the reader:

> More than a woman's name. Her traditional shape. Rapidly
> spread and rubbed with a wedge. Straight drunk with a
> crooked lick. A brief suck on time. Diminutive. Promptly popular
> still on the border. As one version of stamina went. A great show of
> suffering in order to arouse. There were sweet ones. Frozen ones and
> fruity ones. Her little resemblance to the original. Shake her one key
> part. Control her ice. Shake her poor stem. Her rim rubbed. Slice
> juice and pour control out with dusty salt. Or to taste if desired.
> (*Sleeping with the Dictionary* 18)

The opening line of "Daisy Pearl" above reads like a riddle, challenging the reader to look closer for clues to figure it all out. By the time one reaches "Frozen / ones and fruity ones," the reader will most likely think of margaritas. As it turns out, "margarita" is a woman's name, the Latin word for "pearl," and the Spanish word for "daisy." As soon as the poem's subject and organizing principle are discovered, puns abound. For example, "diminutive" is punning on the Spanish suffix *-ita*, which can indicate that something is small; "stamina" puns on the stamen of a flower, in this case a daisy, as well as the effect that one too many margaritas can have on sexual stamina; the reference to "on the border" puns on the border between the United States and Mexico. At some point in the ludic reverie, the reader will probably wonder why Mullen is playing games with her audience. One answer to that question, I suggest, may be found in yet another game: the crossword puzzle.

The crossword puzzle, according to *The Oxford Guide to Word Games*, "developed from the acrostic and the word square, but gained its popularity by combining elements of these games with cryptic clues which are similar to riddles" (57). The cryptic clues often rely upon word games and linguistic structures, such as anagrams, puns, and homophones (Augarde 67-9). These characteristics of crosswords can also be found in Harryette Mullen's *Sleeping with the Dictionary*. The poems employ creative constraints based upon the same chuckle- and/or groan-worthy word games, and the cryptic nature of the constraints invites, if not challenges, the reader to discover the structural principle with investigative skills not unlike those used to solve a clue's riddle.

The parallels between crosswords and Mullen's poems do not end with these shared linguistic features, though. When describing the types of clues commonly found in cryptic crosswords, Tony Augarde claims: "[p]erhaps the best clues in cryptic crosswords are those that ingeniously use lateral thinking to devise new ways of looking at familiar words and phrases" (69). Mullen's poems, then, are similar to the best clues because, through the investigative process engendered by linguistic humor and covert creative constraints, words and phrases are relearned (and sometimes unlearned), and thus provoke in the reader a more complex understanding of the language that constructs his or her world. Readers learn to "avoid taking clues" and language "at face value," and they are able to explore socio-political ramifications of American English.

However, significant differences emerge between crosswords and Mullen's poetry. A crossword puzzle has a strict, determined structure and one fixed solution. Although each poem in *Sleeping with the Dictionary* has a creative constraint that helps to determine the poem's form, Mullen frequently bends rules, as her prose poem "sonnets" and flexible employment of Oulipian techniques demonstrate. (Oulipo or *Ouvroir de littérature potentielle*, is a group formed in 1960 by writers, mathematicians, and other intellectuals dedicated to researching and inventing literary forms.) In addition, the poems do not have a singular or neat solution. While discovering a poem's covert constraint can provide the reader with a richer understanding of that text, the discovery often leads to multiple, complicated readings; this explodes the arbitrary constraint's confines and thus demonstrates the impossibility of containing language and the possibility of transcending imposed limits through innovation, both at the level of the word and the world.

Mullen's poems, though undoubtedly—at times indulgently—ludic, are staunchly socially engaged. They repeatedly invoke, enact, and lament the struggles of those who are oppressed in U.S. society, especially women and African Americans. More importantly, though, Mullen's work explores the potential causes of this subjugation, including American capitalism. Specifically, many of Mullen's poems critique reification, a term first thoroughly explored by Georg Lukacs in *History and Class Consciousness* and aptly glossed by Timothy Bewes in his work *Reification, or the Anxiety of Late Capitalism*:

> Reification refers to the moment that a process or relation is generalized into an abstraction, and thereby turned into a "thing." In Marxist theories of labour, reification is what happens when workers are installed in a place within the capitalist mode of production, and thus reduced to the status of a machine part. It is closely allied to the processes of alienation, objectification, and the fetishism of commodities, in which "the definite social relation between men themselves [assumes] the fantastic form of a relation between things. . . . In the broader sociopolitical sphere, reification is what happens in every instance of racism and sexism, where the objects of prejudice are perceived not as human beings but as things or "types." (3-4)

In my analysis of Mullen's work, I use reification to refer to the mental habits fueled by consumer culture that lead to the formation of static conceptions of the world and detachment from that world. Creating a reified relationship between people and the things they consume, consumer culture also facilitates a tendency for individuals to perceive each other (and their relationships) as things.

At times Mullen experiments with and alters received forms, which, as Jessica Lewis Luck notes, enables her "to revel in the ludic pleasures of Oulipian constructions while maintaining at the same time an accessible, often political, theme" (365). Further, Mullen's creative constraints demonstrate that inventiveness can spring from constraint, which in turn becomes a metaphor for the situation of oppressed peoples. Though constraints are imposed upon people because of their race, gender, religion, and sexual orientation, Mullen shows that constraint need not equal control or containment through the way that her formal constraints yield seemingly innumerable, uncontainable meanings. Mullen's use of humor helps to expose the absurd, skewed values of American society and the warped logic of reified thought. The different types and structures of humor and disruption that Mullen employs promote readers' awareness of reification's negative effects. The game-like poems in *Sleeping with the Dictionary* and the lateral thinking they demand make the process of reification visible, enabling the reader to recognize and critique it.

In this chapter I will examine four poems from *Sleeping with the Dictionary* to demonstrate the varied ways Mullen uses formal constraints and humor to expose the damaging effects that the process of reification has on oppressed peoples and to interrogate and critique the language that sustains their oppression. The poems reveal how reified thought affects such disparate and fundamental areas of life as gender and race relations, religion, and romantic love.

Throughout *Sleeping with the Dictionary* one can see Mullen's diverse poetic influences. Elisabeth Frost, Cynthia Hogue, and Juliana Spahr have convincingly traced Gertrude Stein's influence on Mullen's work, and Mullen claims Umbra poet Lorenzo Thomas as a major influence (Mullen, "Poetry and Identity" 88).[1] Her linguistic experimentation and questioning of subjectivity align her work with Language writers (Frost "Interview"), and her interest in African American voices resonates with writers of the Black Arts Movement. Aldon Lynn Nielsen attaches Mullen to a critically underrepresented and underappreciated tradition of African American experimentalist poets (Nielsen 35). These diverse influences make Mullen's work highly complex and highly resistant to labels, as it foregrounds both "speakerly" and "writerly" aspects of language (Frost "Interview").[2]

This fusion of "speakerly" and "writerly" language can be seen in Mullen's Oulipian influenced, cryptographic writing. In an article on Sandra Cisneros's work, Mullen claims:

> Cryptic encodings of names and secret messages in the literary text privilege the literate over the illiterate, since they have no oral equivalent outside of literate discourses. Yet other encodings, while included in a literary discourse, refer to the "experience of the other" (Freire and Macado 12). This discourse of the other included illiteracy and orality, superstition and folk culture, ignorance and resistance. (Mullen, "Silence" 3)

Mullen's use of covert constraints in her own poems is akin to these encodings. These constraints often produce the unsettling "experience of the other," causing the reader to feel like an outsider until he or she cracks the poem's proceduralist code. This code-cracking process demands a high level of engagement and awareness. Mullen creates an atmosphere of interrogation. This type of poetry turns out to be an effective vehicle for encouraging empathy for oppressed peoples and questioning political conditions.

These experiences of feeling like an insider or outsider are related to Mullen's concerns with subjectivity, which can be seen in the alphabetical arrangement of poems in *Sleeping with the Dictionary*. All the letters of the alphabet are represented by entries with the exceptions of *y*, *u*, and *i*. The homophones of the letters create the question, "Why you and I?" Mullen does not allow her poetic persona to be limited to a single subjectivity and recognizes that her readership, composed of individuals, is not easily reducible to a generic "you." (For a detailed discussion of Mullen's concern for her audience and inclusivity, see her piece "Imagining the Unimagined Reader: Writing to the Unborn and Including the Excluded.") This refusal to limit subjectivity opposes tendencies to reify notions of identity.[3]

These deliberate alphabetic exclusions can also be read as a comment on how the dictionary encourages a more scientific or detached relationship with language. Words are collected, organized, and defined but the dictionary does not address how words affect individuals in their cultural contexts. Words become mere tools with defined functions, and their relationship to subjectivity and individual or group identity is abstracted. As Juliana Spahr claims:

> [R]ace is made absolute in linguistic reality in a way that it can never be in bodily reality. It is grammar that grants subjectivity. The "I" with its place as subject of the sentence can claim as a result of grammar's authorizing powers a substantive existence. This is not to deny the very real nonlinguistic results of oppression—bodily pain, for instance—but rather to suggest that attempts to counter oppression must also concentrate on claims made by linguistic authority. (Spahr 91)

Spahr rightly asserts that Mullen's work illustrates how "the difficult and necessary work of challenging limiting subjectivities requires also that one challenge the strictures of grammar and rigorous narrative" (92). In *Sleeping with the Dictionary* Mullen's elaborate word play focuses this challenge on individual words to question the ideas that words, the building blocks for grammar and narrative, are static objects bound by strict rules removed from one's subjective makeup. In order to challenge reified thought processes, Mullen starts at the foundation with the building blocks of language.

Mullen's lengthy poem "Jinglejangle" is a prime example of how she underscores the functions of words by highlighting non-semantic properties of language. The poem revels in the pleasure that the sounds of language create. It is composed of the jingles, or the background noise that our American culture produces daily, those words and phrases that jangle around in our minds. The poem is an abcedarian, a form determined by the alphabet (Preminger and Brogan 3), and a further constraint involves arranging the entries, which are alliterative or rhyming words and phrases, in alphabetical order (with a few exceptions). Note the letter *d* section:

date rape deadhead deep sleep dikes on bikes dilly-dally
    ding-a-ling ding-dang dingle-dangle
ding-dong dirty birdy Dizzy Lizzie dog log Don Juan
    Donut Hut double trouble downtown dramarama
    drape shape dream team Dress for Success drill & kill
drip-drop drunk skunk dry eye. (*Sleeping* 35)

In *Puns* Walter Redfern explains that puns work "on the most passive level," of "'pleasure in phonetic free association not unlike the joys of daydreaming.' The associative rhyme clearly revels in similarities, recurrences, echoes, reminders, assonances and rhymes. Perhaps we revel so much because we are not supposed to" (11). Taking pleasure in the sounds of words detracts from the way that we are "supposed" to use language, i.e. for communication. As Warren F. Motte observes about Oulipian work, "serious and playful intent are not mutually exclusive" (21). In Mullen's work, I argue, "they are, on the contrary, insistently and reciprocally implicative" (Motte 21). Many terms in "Jingle Jangle" are gleaned from the advertisements that inundate our consciousness ("Osh Kosh B'Gosh"). Others are gleaned from slang: "fried, dyed, laid to the side." Some entries seem merely empty and senseless, like children's rhymes ("dingle-dangle"), yet many of the entries are politically charged. Several terms denote violence ("date rape") and others are discriminatory and as such enact a kind of violence (for example: "Jew Canoe," "hairy fairy," "dikes on bikes," "nig nog," and "jig rig"). When these terms are placed in a silly sounding poem, their violence is even more troubling as their phonetic qualities contribute to the fun.

Mullen's poem emphasizes that language and the way it can be "packaged" fuel and facilitate consumerism. It shows how the humorous, non-semantic aspects help to sell products—in fact, more effectively than accurate descriptions. Language in effect becomes reified, a product that is bought and sold. Although this packaging of language may be used in relatively innocuous tasks, such as marketing food, the poem shows that this packaging is also used for such damaging ends as objectifying women and disseminating cultural stereotypes.

As Mullen's jingles in "Jinglejangle" demonstrate, the packaging of the product's name is as essential for successful marketing as its physical packaging. The poem's title contains a "jingle" that, though it denotes sound in an onomatopoetic way (as in the song "Jingle Bells"), also references the catchy slogan of an advertising campaign, often set to music. Phrases from ads or product names include "Ronald McDonald," "Chubby Hubby," "Chunky Monkey," "Kit Kat," "Crunch and Munch," "Mac Attack," "Shake 'n Bake," and "Shedd's Spread." Indeed, these examples illustrate that the sounds of language are appealing to consumers. Also, these rhyming and alliterative names and slogans are more likely to be remembered by consumers. This phenomenon is explained by the term "bathtub effect," which is used in psycholinguistics "to indicate that the beginning and end of a word have a naturally salient status" (Attardo 91). Additionally, some product names conjure up humorous images. Images of an overweight primate and a portly spouse generated by "Chunky Monkey" and "Chubby Hubby" undoubtedly elicit chuckles from many consumers, attracting their attention and encouraging them to add the product to their shopping cart. Advertisers often persuade people to consume by the product's name, not its inherent merit. After all, "Chunky Monkey" and "Crunch and Munch" do not identify what the product actually is. In addition, these marketing jingles reference food or restaurants and thus emphasize the link between cultural consumption, physical consumption, and language.

Other terms in the poem illustrate how reification encourages the objectification of women. Several slang terms, such as "fur burger," demean, objectify, and mock a woman's body or body parts. Other terms, like "hump & dump" and "pump & dump," refer to having sex with a woman and tossing her aside like trash, which makes women seem like disposable products that are essentially the same and easily replaceable. Although such actions are harmful and heartless, the funny sounding terms, while crass, function like euphemisms in that they distract from the gravity of the actions. These examples of objectification of women give way to terms for more violent acts, such as "date rape" and "gang bang." The process of reifying women's bodies is associated with sexually violent crimes against women because this portrays women as sex objects and such objectification helps legitimize the abuse.

Strikingly, the violent term "gang bang" follows directly after the innocent "gal pal." As Mullen stated in an interview when speaking of her book *Muse & Drudge*: "You can also heighten paradox and contradiction when you compress together things that come from very different registers or lexicons; they jostle each other so there's more tension. Yet there's more elasticity in the utterance" (Bedient 656-57). This idea of heightening contradiction via compression is equally applicable to "Jinglejangle." The proximity of terms from differing lexicons—a result of the form's constraints—invites comparison and connection. One can surmise that the process of reification facilitates someone's "gal pal" becoming the victim of a "gang bang," or rape by multiple men, since she may be viewed primarily as a sexual object by the perpetrators. In other words, the violence of "gang bang" is heightened by the proximity of "gal pal" because of the latter term's connotations of personal intimacy.

Mullen's poem, by emphasizing the phonetic qualities of language, indicates that derogatory terms may be perpetuated because of the way they sound and are "packaged." Just like the rhyming and alliterative product names and slogans, humorous aspects of language are also used to "sell" racism and sexism. Among the many discriminatory terms in American English, some terms that Mullen selects are particularly harmful because their humor allows people to gloss over the violence embedded in these terms in ways that other derogatory expressions that do not rhyme or sound silly cannot. "Jangle," the second part of the poem's title, has connotations of being snarled or mixed up. The collection of words and phrases from disparate lexicons (slang, advertisements, etc.) is a "jangle," and the sounds of language can draw our attention away from the literal meaning of something. Analyzing "Jinglejangle" and other poems from *Sleeping with the Dictionary* with similar forms, Alan Gilbert argues: "[I]n the extreme form of leveling that these pieces perform (where "multi-culti" is the same as "mumbo jumbo"), linguistic—and, by implication, social—hierarchies are assailed" (59). Although the poem enacts a form of social leveling through juxtaposition of different registers of language, I think that Mullen is also indicating how language can be manipulated to perpetuate and sustain social hierarchies.

If one exclusively focuses on and revels in the fun and funny sounds of the poem's language he or she would ignore the meaning of the terms used. A racial slur in humorous packaging can seem less offensive. Such packaging dangerously encourages people to tolerate these terms and, by extension, the derogatory ideas underneath the attractive wrapping. In "Race and Ethnicity and Popular Humor," Howitt and Owusu-Bempah argue "that jokes are bound by social rules which, when not followed, can cause problematic social exchanges" (46). Refusing to laugh at or accept a racist joke breaks these rules (47). Therefore, the rules make jokes and humorous phrases effective vehicles for spreading discrimination. Howitt and Owusu-Bempah consider "jokes . . . a medium through which society disseminates and generationally transmits its dominant attitudes towards outgroups," and so "racist jokes . . . act as propaganda in support of racist ideology" (49). Similarly, I argue that Mullen's poem enacts the way that the dominant culture, by manipulating humorous or phonetic properties of language, can disseminate stereotypes and cultural myths via supposedly playful language. For example, the phrases "Jew canoe" and "jig rig," located next to one another in the poem, stereotype the kinds of cars that Jewish Americans and African Americans drive.

A "Jew canoe" is slang for a long car, such as a Cadillac, that Jewish Americans supposedly drive, while a "jig rig" describes a dilapidated car that an African American, especially one who is poor, drives (*The New American Substandard Politically Incorrect Dictionary Online*). "Jig" is a racial slur against African Americans, and "rig" implies that something was put together in a haphazard manner. Other harmful phrases that contribute to the fun of the poem are "nig-nog" and "fag hag," the former a racial slur against African Americans and the latter a slur against homosexuals, especially homosexual men, and women who befriend them (*Oxford Dictionary of Modern Slang*).

By emphasizing the phonetic properties of language and using juxtaposition, Mullen exposes how damaging phrases and ideas packaged in humorous sounds can be disseminated in a way that other derogatory terms without these phonetic properties cannot. Howitt and Owusu-Bempah argue that racist jokes "continually reinforce the use of race categories in our thinking" (62). Humorous-sounding derogatory terms such as those cited above—whether racist, sexist, homophobic, etc.—reify derogatory ideas about groups, and thereby place people into artificial categories.

Although abcedarians like "Jinglejangle" have been written by many serious poets, they have also been used as a mnemonic device to teach children the alphabet and properties of language. In a sense, Mullen is using this abcedarian to instruct (or at least remind) her readers about the potentially damaging properties of language, too. Abcedarians have a long tradition and have been seen as powerful "since in the a[bcedarian] the master code of the lang[uage] is made the constitutive device of the form" (Preminger and Brogan 3). Mullen harnesses this power to show readers the pervasiveness of violence in American English. The poem includes some type of slur or derogatory term for nearly every letter of the alphabet. In addition, the poem's restrictions and compression allow for surprising, and often disturbing, juxtapositions of terms and ideas, which give the humor an uncomfortable valence and encourage the interrogation of the poem's language and a critique of the culture constructed and sustained by that language.

While "Jinglejangle" demonstrates how words' phonetic qualities can be manipulated to sustain oppression, Mullen's "The Lunar Lutheran" uses anagrams to expose the constructedness of religious identities and the violence and corruption, especially economic corruption, often accompanying religion. Through reified thought, institutionalized religion has become commodified, and many religions have histories of commodifying others. Anagrams highlight the materiality of language. By interchanging the letters of words, Mullen connects different religions linguistically in "Lunar Lutheran." This linguistic connection implies that these religions are made from the same material and, to an extent, are interchangeable, perhaps because of their widespread economic corruption. The religions all appear to be for sale. The humor is generated in part by the seeming oddity of grouping sex, yoga, and Mormonism or Buddhism and Hollywood.[4] The fact that these associations are humorous due to their seeming incongruity might demonstrate that religions function as static structures removed from the system of capitalism, but actually Mullen is showing that capitalism and religious institutions are not separable but in fact are interdependent.

Mullen alters or adopts conventional uses of the anagram. In "On the Anagram and Its Functions," a detailed study of the anagram and its history, Karel Bares notes that the anagram, which owes its existence to graphics, classically involves a complete inversion of the sequence of letters of the base word (141). Bares claims that the diverse reasons for using anagrams throughout history include: demonstrating one's good education, conveying praise, displaying wit or peculiarity, offering an attack, gallant flattery, cryptic coding, tomb inscription, political allusion, and providing name brands of products and advertising (an example of which is the Camry car commercial that rearranges the words "MY CAR" into "CAMRY") (Bares 144-147). According to *The Oxford Guide to Word Games*, Cabbalists believed that there were magical properties in the Hebrew alphabet and that the letters used in sacred Jewish writing could be rearranged to work miracles and reveal truth (Augarde 80). Anagrams of names often were believed to foretell one's future (Augarde 81). These diverse examples all involve the repossession and refiguring of language in order to achieve a desired end.

The anagram helps Mullen foreground the graphic nature of language in her poems' encodings. The anagram's long association with naming resonates in Mullen's concerns with language and identity and with the constructed and prescribed nature of both. As Bares asserts, "in an anagram the thoughts of discovering and disclosing something hidden, on the one hand, and of veiling and hiding something one the other hand, are dialectically combined" (151). Mullen utilizes these properties of the anagram to address issues of identity, especially the notion of "mongrel" identity, which she discussed in an interview with Calvin Bedient about her earlier work *Muse and Drudge*:

> A lot has been said of how American culture is a miscegenated culture, how it is a product of a mixing and a mingling of diverse races and cultures and languages, and I would agree with that. I would say that, yes, my text is deliberately a multi-voiced text, a text that tries to express the actual diversity of my own experience living here, exposed to different cultures. "Mongrel" comes from "among." Among others. We are among; we are not alone. We are all mongrels. (Bedient 652)

Mullen's anagrams demonstrate the interconnectedness of words and of those who use them. Just as anagrams allow us to see words as mongrels, as constructions made from a mixture of letters and languages, so too do they enable us to see people as mongrels who influence one another. This anti-essentialist conception of identity helps to combat racist, sexist, and other reductive reified thought in which "the objects of prejudice are perceived not as human beings but as things or 'types'" (Bewes 4).

Mullen's anagrams demonstrate that a word may contain and be constructed from other words; these other words are coded into the words we encounter, and their presence can and should affect the way we read and interpret the world. Although Mullen's process may be similar to the way etymology demonstrates relationships between words, it is not as restrictive because it allows for phonetic and visual connections between words. While reader and, presumably, writer glean a great deal of enjoyment from language play and making humorous connections, the principles of fracture, rearrangement, and reconstruction inherent to the anagram represent both the violence and the redeeming power that language possesses. In *Sleeping with the Dictionary*, the poems that utilize the anagram do not adhere to a definite structure, and they do not explicitly declare that anagrams are a structural device. Instead, Mullen's anagrammatic play encourages the investigation of organizational forces at work behind the poems and language in general. Mullen's language play is empowering; it is a repossession of language that allows her to examine identity as it is constructed in the world and in the poem. Although her covert linguistic coding can also make the reader feel marginalized and manipulated by the poems' cryptographic nature, these coded poems encourage readers to adopt new reading techniques. Therefore, a reader is granted the freedom to explore the many levels of meaning in the poem's language as well as its accompanying pleasures and challenges. This sense of exclusion and empowerment point to both the limitations that prescribed identities place upon an individual and the available liberation of self-exploration and self-definition.[5]

In "The Lunar Lutheran," Mullen uses humor and anagrams to show the constructedness of religious identities as well as similarities and differences between religious groups. She verbally slides one religion into another, encouraging a more fluid rather than denominational understanding of spirituality. In addition, Mullen humorously weaves in images from popular culture to show how religion and capitalist society overlap and conflict:

> In chapels of opals and spice, O Pisces pal, your social pep makes you a friend to all Episcopals. Brush off lint, gentile, but it's not intelligent to beshrew the faith of Hebrews. I heard this from a goy who taught

> yoga in the home of Goya. His Buddhist robe hid this budding D bust in the B movie dud. If Ryan bites a rep, a Presbyterian is best in prayer. Oh tears oxen trod! To catch oil, or a man born to the manor, you need a Catholic, Roman. On Mon. morn, Mom hums "Om" with no other man but Norm or Ron. A Mormon son would gladly leave a gas slave in Las Vegas for a hut in Utah. These slums I'm from, I'm leaving, Miss Lum, with a slim sum donated by some Muslims. What would it cost to gain the soul of an agnostic? Where the atheist is at, God only knows! 'Tis hate, he is at the heist. A Baptist was able to stab a pit bull when the sun hid behind some Hindus. To fan a mess, I write manifestos. So said the lunar Lutheran. (*Sleeping* 48)

Sentences like "I heard this from a goy who taught yoga in the home of a Goya" create surprising yet deliberate overlaps of religious groups and spiritual beliefs. The opening lines declare that a "Pisces pal" is "a friend to all Episcopals." Mullen's anagrams linguistically connect these figures but also imply that those who believe in astrology associate with or may even identify themselves as Episcopalian. In lines six through ten, the fact that Roman Catholics and Mormons are linked anagrammatically and thematically by a description of a woman engaging in a more Eastern, meditative spiritual activity—saying "Om"—troubles essentialist religious identification. Mullen's humor also encourages readers to interpret this meditative practice of humming "'Om'" as a sexual act since Mullen writes, "Mom hums 'Om' with no other man than Norm or Ron." The anagrammatic association between "Mom" and *Roman* Catholics and *Mormons* connects Mom's sexual activity to members of both religions, thus reminding readers that people who consider themselves to be devout followers may also transgress the rules of those religions. The seemingly nonsensical anagram of "Oh tears oxen trod!" scrambles "orthodox" and hence the notion of orthodoxy itself. Mullen's anagrams also connect Hollywood to established religious groups: "His Buddhist robe hid this budding D bust in this B movie dud." Hollywood stands as its own type of religion replete with millions of devout followers; its influence on the public may be as powerful as that of any religion.

The tensions created by the blending of one faith into another via anagrammatic play also have a grim side. Images of violence as well as references to money lead the reader to think of the corruption of institutions of faith, as well as violence between different faiths. Economically inflected diction makes the question about the "cost" of gaining "the soul of an agnostic" bitingly funny. The mention of soul-purchase indicates how the history of many religious institutions is riddled with economic corruption, one that persists to this day, but, more importantly, the purchase of a soul turns it into a thing, a commodity. In *Reification* Timothy Bewes states, "Christian redemption is the promise of a non-worldly, thus, non-reified existence; it is structurally analogous to the Marxist promise of revolution, but projected in a metaphysical form that is categorically removed from the worldly activity of politics" (Bewes 5). However, Mullen's question and its undertone of buying and selling souls indicates that, in actuality, religious redemption is anything but "categorically removed" from the secular market economy. Thus, the economic corruption of religious institutions corrupts the beliefs and promises that those institutions represent. The poem's closing lines allude to these issues of money and violence most explicitly with the words "hate" and "heist," and the image of "stab[bing] a pit bull." Although the groups mentioned are Muslims, agnostics, atheists, Baptists, and Hindus, the reader has the sense that other groups might be associated with corruption.

In addition, recalling the Cabbalist notions that anagrams can lead to revelation of truths, Mullen's anagrams re-envision relations between religious groups. This language play could also be a critique of those religions that treat religious texts as static objects or artifacts, and thus limit personal interpretation and spiritual exploration and enforce agreement about spiritual beliefs. Her reprocessing of language questions essentialist notions of religious identity and difference.

Mullen explores more secular concerns about modern love through her rewrites of the traditional love sonnet. In both "Variation on a Theme Park" and "Dim Lady" she uses the Oulipian technique of S+7 to rewrite Shakespeare's "Sonnet 130" in order to critique how reified thought, encouraged and sustained by consumer culture, facilitates views of women and romantic love as objects or commodities. The humor, generated, in part, by the difference between the linguistic registers of Shakespeare's poem and Mullen's poems, serves to indicate how capitalist values have corrupted love. The form itself emphasizes words as replaceable objects. As Raymond Queneau describes, S+7 is predicated upon "taking a text and replacing each substantive with the seventh following it in the dictionary" (qtd. in Motte 61), and Mullen's substituted words describe the processes of economic exchange and objects that can be bought and sold. This act of replacement implies that the subject of Shakespeare's poem, no longer a unique, cherished individual, becomes replaceable in contemporary commodity culture; again, reification has negative effects on relationships between people.

Mullen's rewriting of Shakespeare's "Sonnet 130," "Variation on a Theme Park," suggests that contemporary American capitalism overshadows love, the subject of Shakespeare's sonnet. The poem replaces Shakespeare's famous first line "My mistress' eyes are nothing like the sun" (1867) with "My Mickey Mouse ears are nothing like sonar" (*Sleeping* 75). Immediately, aided by her adaptation of the S+7 technique, Mullen transforms this love poem into a poem about a commercialized image. As Motte writes:

> The efficacy of translations of this sort depends largely on the shock they produce as they run into the original: that is, the reader must ideally "hear" the original and the transformation simultaneously, and the latter must jar the former (this is also true of the S+7 Method). To produce this effect, the *untransformed* part of the new text . . . must follow the original faithfully. (189)

Although some of Mullen's substitutions seem to be chosen rather than mathematically discovered, central to the poem's critique and humor is the principle associated with the S+7 technique that the reader should "hear" the original text and that "the latter must jar the former." The substitution of the cartoon mouse is immediately humorous due to the incongruity inherent in the bizarre contrast with the original.

Mullen's rewriting of the first line also plays with the blazon, which is "a poetic genre devoted to the praise or blame of something" (Preminger and Brogan 141-42). The blazon has been indicted as violently dismembering women into body parts (141-42), and Mullen's "Mickey Mouse ears" play on that critique as the ears, sold at Disney theme parks, "dismember" Mickey. The word "her" in Shakespeare's sonnet is replaced with "Walt's," as if Walt Disney is the possessive pronoun form of Mickey Mouse. In this formation the man and the character that catalyzed his empire seem almost interchangeable and also associate Walt Disney, a paragon of capitalism, with ownership and possession. This emphasis on ownership is present in Mullen's economically inflected substitutions: "Wonder Bras" for "wires," "checkbook" for "cheeks," "purchases" for "perfumes," "bargains" for "breath," "bought" for "belied," and "coupons" for "compare" (*Sleeping* 75). Mullen's version replaces substance with superficiality and love with consumerism. She even replaces "heav'n" with "halogen-light," indicating that religious faith has been replaced by commercialism. Most importantly, "love" has been transformed into a "loneliness" generated by a societal obsession with material goods.

Several critics of Shakespeare's "Sonnet 130," such as Stephen Booth in his edited version of *The Sonnets* and Helen Vendler in *The Art of Shakespeare's Sonnets*, critique the blazon and its tendency to objectify women, and while Mullen's "Dim Lady" seemingly tries to echo Shakespeare's version, it actually reinforces the commodification of women and, by extension, shows how consumerism encourages that commodification. This poem is much closer to the original than "Variation on a Theme Park." Keeping the poem's sense, it replaces the original words with more modern interpretations. In this example, "mistress" is replaced by slang terms for a lover, such as "honeybunch," "main squeeze," and "ball and chain" (*Sleeping* 20). Most interesting are the substitutions Mullen makes for the words used to compare the mistress' body parts: "Today's special at Red Lobster" for "coral," "Liquid Paper" for "snow," "Slinkys" for "wires," "tablecloths in Shakey's Pizza Parlors" for "roses," "minty-fresh mouthwashes" for "perfumes," "Muzak" for "music," "Marilyn Monroes" for "goddess," and "lanky model or platinum movie idol" for the implied woman in Shakespeare's closing lines "I think my love as rare/ As any she belied with false compare." The natural imagery in Shakespeare's poem has been replaced with name-brand products or commercialized phrases and images, and this highlights the pervasiveness and primacy of consumerism in Americans' daily lives. These substitutions recall the original in specific ways (e.g., Liquid Paper and snow are both white). By substituting the natural imagery for commercialized objects, Mullen suggests that women are commodified. Even though Mullen's poem retains the sense of the original, the closing of each poem sends a very different message.

Shakespeare's poem of false compare critiques the poetic conventions of the blazon that make unrealistic evaluations of women's beauty. There are two major types of blazon: blason satirique and blason medallon. The purpose of the former is satiric while the purpose of the latter is to describe briefly a single object. Historically, blason medallon celebrated some part of the female body (Preminger and Brogan 141-42). In a sense, Shakespeare's sonnet blends the two types of blazon since it uses the conventional structure of a blazon medallon to satirize the genre. In the last line, the speaker calls his mistress "as rare" as any woman compared in such hyperbolic terms as can be found in many blazon medallons. Although this rarity undoubtedly speaks to the mistress' beauty, it could also refer to nonphysical attributes, such as her character or intelligence. In Mullen's version the final lines send a different message: "my scrumptious Twinkie has as much sex appeal for me as any lanky model or platinum movie idol who's hyped beyond belief" (*Sleeping* 20). Here, the rarity in Shakespeare's poem is translated into "sex appeal," which indicates that the woman in this poem is seen primarily as a sexual object, and the phrase "for me" shows that the speaker sees the woman as an object that can fulfill his or her own desires. That Mullen's poem repeatedly compares the woman to commodities and ultimately evaluates her as a sex object shows the connection between a society's obsession with consumerism and the objectification of women.

Just as Mullen critiques the negative effects that reification has on gender and race relations, religion, and love, she develops creative constraints and humor that can serve as models for oppressed peoples. The playfulness in the poetry undermines static structures of thought, revealing them to be pliable, and thus opening up the possibility for change. Bars that are largely constructed by language can be loosened, as well, by language.

Notes

1. See Hogue's "Beyond the Frame of Whiteness: Harryette Mullen's Revisionary Border Work" in *We Who Love to Be Astonished*, Spahr's *Everybody's Autonomy*, and Frost's "Signifyin(g) on Stein: The Revisionist Poetics of Harryette Mullen and Leslie Scalapino."

2. In *S/Z* Roland Barthes coined the terms "readerly" and "writerly" texts to describe texts that did not challenge the reader to become part of the writing process ("readerly") or texts that did challenge the reader to "write" ("writerly"). Henry Louis Gates in *The Signifying Monkey* coined the term "speakerly" to describe texts that privilege orality.

3. For a nuanced discussion of Mullen's complication of the lyric "I" and her relationship to Language poetics, see Jessica Lewis Luck's article "Entries on a Post-Language Poetics in Harryette Mullen's *Dictionary*."

4. See Elliott Oring's *Engaging Humor* for a thorough discussion of incongruity theories of humor.

5. For an alternative reading of Mullen's anagrams see Mitchum Huels's "Spun Puns (and Anagrams): Exchange Economies, Subjectivity, and History in Harryette Mullen's *Muse & Drudge*."

The Game of Self-Forgetting: Reading Innovative Poetry Reading Gadamer

Judith Halden-Sullivan

> All encounter with the language of art is an encounter with an unfinished event and is itself part of this event.
>
> —Hans-Georg Gadamer

The poem—in this case the "difficult" contemporary American innovative poem—is an event that opens possibilities for *more* events. With each reading, the poem offers a deliberate, unique presence. The poem is play that invites play. The poem makes possible a self-forgetting that opens for thinkers a transitory glimmer of what we daily obscure: our immersion in the language of being. I want to locate language that both grounds these claims and lets innovative American poetry speak—lets it *be*.

I recall how grateful I was for poet Ann Lauterbach's clarity in defining the poem as an "experience," an "event, in and of language" (qtd. in D. Kane 110). Like many of the contributors to this anthology, I teach contemporary American poetry and poetics; once in a graduate seminar I shared with my students Lauterbach's purpose in composing her own verse: "to give people permission to think for themselves, on the one hand, and to be deeply responsive, on the other" (qtd. in Kane 111). Lauterbach suggests that poetry invites self-reflective observations about poetic "experiences" not through traditional questions like "What is the poem's theme?" but through inquiries such as "What kind of event happened to you when you read this poem?" (qtd. in Kane 110). She asks her students to examine the feelings, ideas, and memories these "events" evoked. Charles Bernstein echoes Lauterbach, asserting that, in engaging with innovative poetry, "What is called for is not so much analysis as responsiveness" (*Attack* 80). So I invited my graduate students to think hard, and they were clearly up to the challenge, open to possibilities, eager, and mindful. But, despite my efforts, they remained unconvinced of the character of poems as events. They had such an ingrained vision of poetry as historical artifacts that they hungered for the patterned particulates that construed each difficult poem: what did the word choices say about the poet's life and her or his historical milieu and political stance?

How did the images or symbols add up? What purpose did the verse form serve? Was it original or a parody of some established structure? These are not unimportant or uninteresting questions, but they continue to relegate the poem to the beautiful thing that atom-smashers must explode to know. Some of my students were more distanced observers than engaged "experiencers" of poetic texts. In his chapter in this anthology, Hank Lazer points out how innovative poetry makes transparent the difficulty of understanding *understanding*—understanding that, in turn, permits readers to negotiate with poems to pursue possibilities for thinking. I want to speculate about the nature of such collaboration. This chapter will offer two interconnected parts: first, a preamble in which I define terms central to Hans-Georg Gadamer's aesthetics, such as *energeia*, "play," and the "game," and then demonstrations of these concepts in select works of two quite different innovative "event-planners": the overt poetic festivals of Stephen Ratcliffe and the piercing, implosive moments made possible by Myung Mi Kim. How do these poets show that the "difficult" poem is an event? And what good is a poem that is really an experience?

To describe innovative verse's temporal fluidity, I need to first establish firm ground. The hermeneutic phenomenology of Hans-Georg Gadamer offers a context for the event of reading innovative poetry in all its diverse poetics and modes of composition. But my application of Gadamer's aesthetics in this chapter is in no way a primer for innovative reading strategies nor a totalizing response to "difficult" verse. Instead, in his examination of artworks, poetry in particular, Gadamer fully describes the experience of innovative verse and the event of its understanding in a lexicon that directly accounts for the work's temporality—its distinct temporal identities. Gadamer's *ethos* complements the project of contemporary innovative poetics. As John Arthos claims, Gadamer exhibits a "hermeneutic sensibility" more so than just a perspective: Gadamer's sense of the world and human beings reveals "a commitment to dialogic openness" and "a refusal to separate the ethical, aesthetic, and epistemic" (xiii). These same descriptors capture the intentions of a contemporary American literary critic who also ventures boldly into defining the experience of texts, affective experiences: Charles Altieri, one of the most cogent commentators on innovative verse.

In *The Particulars of Rapture: An Aesthetics of the Affects*, Altieri in many ways permits my forthcoming discussion of poetic events, declaring that "the arts inspire accounts that make affective experience not just something we understand, but something that we pursue as a fundamental value" (4). *The Particulars of Rapture* is a rigorous, meticulously detailed phenomenology of emotional responses to literature and painting—accounting for feelings, moods, emotions, and passions—for all that is possible when we think about our reception of art. Altieri asserts that "responsiveness to aesthetic emotions serves as an end in itself" (268), noting three affective states that constitute such valuable ends: subjectivity modified by intensity, that "involvedness" we feel when our boundaries expand, and the psyche's "plasticity" (186). Altieri even states that the art object establishes "a distinctive experience," describing what is possible for readers as "a sense of transport" (268). While this is only a brief note acknowledging Altieri's contributions, I offer it at this early juncture because, first, Altieri sets the stage for Gadamer's own concerns—although Gadamer defined them in the 1960s and '70s—and, second, Altieri demonstrates in his own work that reading the event of texts is central to contemporary critical pursuits.

Reading is a thinking of the text. And, like all aspects of the human mode of being, hermeneutic phenomenologist Hans-Georg Gadamer grounds his analyses of thinking in the all-encompassing experience of language. Language, Gadamer asserts, "is the reservoir of tradition and the medium in and through which we exist and perceive our world" ("The Scope and Function of Hermeneutical Reflection" 29). Speaking of the "situatedness," the mediated character of language, Gadamer explains:

> Learning to speak does not mean learning to use a preexistent tool for designating a world already somehow familiar to us; it means acquiring a familiarity and acquaintance with the world itself and how it confronts us . . . our very enclosedness in the linguistic world in which we live. In truth we are always already at home in language, just as much as we are in the world. ("Man and Language" 63)

As a matter of principle, the task of hermeneutic phenomenology is dynamically linguistic. Gadamer defines its exploration as:

> the opening up of the hermeneutical dimension in its full scope . . . from interhuman communication to manipulation of society; from personal experience by the individual in society to the way in which he encounters society; and from the tradition as it is built of religion and law, art and philosophy, to the revolutionary consciousness that unhinges the tradition through emancipatory reflection. ("On the Scope and Function of Hermeneutical Reflection" 18)

The work of philosophical hermeneutics, as Gadamer describes it here, reveals the play of human thinking situated in a temporal, historical world:

"There would be no speaker and no art of speaking if understanding and consent were not in question, were not underlying [hermeneutical] elements; there would be no hermeneutical task if there were no mutual understanding that has been disturbed and that those involved in a conversation must search for and find again together" ("On the Scope and Function of Hermeneutical Reflection" 25). Being "at home in language"—remaining open to possibilities for meaning and being—are hermeneutical acts. They are what the experienced thinker—the experienced reader—does best.

The key to staying open is the question. Gadamer states in *Truth and Method* that, "As the art of asking questions, dialectic proves its value because only the person who knows how to ask questions is able to persist in his questioning, which involves being able to preserve his orientation toward openness. The art of questioning is the art of questioning even further—i.e., the art of thinking" (1990 ed. 367). To reflect well demands the ability to pose questions. "When a question arises," Gadamer claims, "it breaks open the being of the object, as it were. . . . To ask a question means to bring into the open" (*Truth and Method* 1990 ed. 362, 363). Gadamer does not refer here to questions with simple, apparent answers but instead to those that bring a subject into a "state of indeterminacy, so that there is an equilibrium between pro and contra" (*Truth and Method* 1990 ed. 363). Such persistent questioning, openness to possibilities, and deliberate indeterminacy characterize a mode of reading best-suited to innovative poetry. In my own teaching, I invite students to be open readers in this dialectic because "[e]very true question," as Gadamer concludes, "requires this openness" (*Truth and Method* 1990 ed. 363). In Gadamer's words, "We cannot have experiences without asking questions" (*Truth and Method* 1990 ed. 362): "the dialectic of question and answer always precedes the dialectic of interpretation. It is what determines understanding as an event" (*Truth and Method* 2004 ed. 467).

For Gadamer, understanding is not just an activity of consciousness but "is itself a mode of the event of being" ("On the Problem of Self-Understanding" 50), so powerful that it "'happens' to us . . . we are 'taken up' and 'transformed'" (Malpas 218). Readers familiar with the existential phenomenology of Martin Heidegger will recall the term *Ereignis*, which is often translated as "the event" or "the happening of truth." Jeff Malpas in *Heidegger's Topology* identifies three qualities that define *Ereignis*: "the idea of event/happening" of truth, the "'happening of belonging' in the sense of a gathering or bringing of things into what is their own," and a "disclosing/revealing" or "coming to sight" of truth (215-216). The happening of the truth in language and the disclosing—and concealing—of being are foundational to Heidegger's concept of truth as revealment. The "belonging" concomitant with *Ereignis*, as Malpas explains, is a dynamic unity arising in the event, a belonging "through the *interaction* of elements rather than through their mere 'standing near' to one another" (215, italics mine)—a connection happening in a moment of time. An articulation, the "saying" of the event, whether by philosophers, poets, or anyone else, Malpas notes, must be able to be "experienced" (218). Such events also occur in the process of interpreting poetry, the experience of the text.

For Gadamer, the poetic text is alive in a way. He attributes to poetry *energeia*: "a motion" that is "without path or goal, something like life itself, like being aware, seeing, or thinking"—a kind of presentness in itself ("The Artwork in Word" 213). He quotes Goethe's notion of art as its being "so true, so full of being" ("The Artwork in Word" 214). With the poem, a kind of living energy is proffered to readers. But what *is* the experience of the text? Gadamer offers two brief enigmatic encapsulations: "It comes forth" and "[t]here is something in the work"; the "it" and the "something" are revealed in the "event of appearing" ("The Artwork in Word" 216). Verse, Gadamer contends, is the "event of emerging" ("The Artwork in Word" 218). In turn, "[t]he event of emerging as experienced by the . . . reader, that is, the performance as experienced . . . is the interpretation" and the interpreter "in truth is the fulfiller" of the poem "in such a way that it comes forth" ("The Artwork in Word" 218). This interaction has a distinct temporal identity that Gadamer defines in a perhaps surprising way: as *play*.

Play, as Gadamer explains, enjoys a "fundamental givenness" in the human mode of being; it is unquestionably part of being in the world. Play is non-purposive, extra, surplus activity; however, human nature imposes upon it self-discipline and order, and our reason sets up the rules ("Relevance of the Beautiful" 23). In its simplest form, play is like bouncing a ball; it does not necessarily involve a particular end but is instead "movement as movement," "a living self-representation." In common parlance, *it is what it is.* "The artwork," he explains, "is there for itself" ("The Artwork in Word" 220).

For Gadamer works of art, like play, reinvigorate traditional notions of presence: verse sets forth a dynamic, performative, autonomous self-presentation. Gadamer claims that "the work of art does not simply refer to something, because what it refers to is actually there" ("The Relevance of the Beautiful" 35). The language of poetry in particular "does not intend something, but rather is the existence of what it intends" ("On the contribution of poetry" 113). As a matter of fact, for Gadamer, the text's autonomy becomes apparent not when representation becomes transparent but only when a "disruption in communication provides a motive for reaching back to the text as the 'given'" ("Text and Interpretation" 34). In other words, the text is received not when matters are simple but when they are problematic, as in innovative verse. As a matter of fact, Gadamer asserts that understanding begins "when one comes up against something that is strange, challenging, disorienting . . . . [T]his experience of not being able to go any further with the pre-schematized expectations of our orientation to the world . . . beckons to *thinking*" ("Language and Understanding" 93; italics mine). Such a movement brings us more in touch with our being at play in the world.

Play as a context for the temporal experience of innovative verse becomes more palpable in the definition of the spectator. Gadamer claims that play "does not really acknowledge the distance separating the one who plays and the one who watches the play. The spectator is manifestly more than just an observer who sees what is happening . . . but rather one who is part of it insofar as he literally 'takes part'" ("Relevance of the Beautiful" 24). As engaged spectators, we choose to give ourselves over to the event; in reading, thinkers are one with the text, immersed, if only for instances of time. In regard to the "play of art," Gadamer asserts "there is in principle no radical separation between the work of art and the person who experiences it" ("Relevance of the Beautiful" 28). "The participant," Gadamer explains, "belongs to the play" ("Relevance of the Beautiful" 26).

But *why* do we play? For Gadamer, it's about time. Innovative poetry can transform readers' experience of time. Gadamer offers the following description of the poem, one that I would argue particularly accounts for the disorienting experience of innovative verse. Such texts have a unique relationship to time: they are temporal events that in themselves can slow the transience of time by engaging readers in thought. Gadamer believes that such texts allow us

> to experience "nearness" in such a way that this nearness is held in and through the linguistic form. . . . What is the nearness that is held there? Whenever we have to hold something, it is because it is transient and threatens to escape our grasp. In fact, our fundamental experience as beings subject to time is that all things escape us, that all the events of our lives fade more and more, so that at best they glow with an almost unreal shimmer in the most distant recollection. But the poem does not fade, for the poetic word brings the transience of time to a standstill. ("On the contribution of poetry" 114)

According to Gadamer, in the face of transience, the human being's task in life is to slow down, "to make ourselves at home" amid the profusion of impressions the world affords us (Gadamer "On the contribution of poetry" 114). However, the poem as an event "stands over and against this process like a mirror held up to it," showing us not so much the world but our immersion in the moment of thought—"this nearness in which we stand for a while" (115). Innovative poetry slows transience to awaken us from our enchantment with the "fallen" world; it surprises us with our own condition. It demands that we tarry: "a tarrying that waits and preserves in such a way" that the poem is allowed to speak. But such tarrying "is not to lose time. Being in the mode of tarrying is like an intensive back-and-forth conversation that is not cut off but lasts until it is ended" ("The Artwork in Word" 211). Gadamer attributes to the poem a special temporal status: it is distinguished by "an immediate presentness in time and at the same time by a rising above time" (The Artwork in Word" 196). The special character of "rising above" leads to Gadamer's final term in the lexicon of the artwork's temporality: the game.

In the "game of interpretation," Gadamer explains, "nobody is above and before all others; everybody is at the center, is 'it' in this game" ("On the Scope and Function of Hermeneutical Reflection" 32). In addition, "[s]omething that obeys its own set of laws gains ascendancy in the game," he notes. Most games have a back-and-forth motion, "a peculiar freedom and buoyancy that determines the consciousness of the player," and each player "conforms to the game or subjects himself to it, that is, he relinquishes the autonomy of his own will" ("On the Problem of Self-Understanding" 53). The "individual self, including his activity and his understanding of himself, is taken up into a higher determination that is the really decisive factor" ("On the Problem of Self-Understanding" 54). We give ourselves over to the game; we forget ourselves. And the result is overwhelming: "an absorption into the game is an ecstatic self-forgetting that is experienced not as a *loss* of self-possession, but as the free buoyancy of an elevation above oneself" ("On the Problem of Self-Understanding" 55). Gadamer likens the game to the give-and-take exchanges of dialogue. An effective conversation with another person, Gadamer asserts, has the same "character of accident, favor, and surprise—and in the end, of buoyancy, indeed, of elevation—that belongs to the nature of the game," and this elevation "will not be experienced as a loss of self-possession, but rather as an *enrichment* of our self, but without us thereby becoming aware of ourselves" ("On the Problem of Self-Understanding" 57). In the game of interpretation, we move beyond ourselves to experience an instant of being—akin perhaps to a flash of insight, a heightened awareness of thinking the world. Texts invite readers to slow down in such moments—to immerse ourselves in play. But despite such tarrying, Gadamer asserts that poetry "always transcends both poet and interpreter. Both of them pursue a meaning that points toward an open realm" ("Composition and Interpretation" 72). New possible interpretations always await each reader among each historical generation.

What critical questions, then, does Gadamer's experiential aesthetics invite? I offer a few starters: If the poem "happens" to us as readers, what unfolds? What emerges? What distinguishes the "lifeforce" of the poem—its voltage, its *energeia*—that special "something like life itself" (Gadamer "The Artwork in Word" 213)? What comes forth to me as a reader? What emerges for a community of readers, such as the classroom of diverse student interpreters that Elizabeth Robinson describes in the first chapter of this anthology? What accounts for differences among witnesses to poetic events? With readers as spectators, if not participants, in the unfolding, what characterizes the interplay of the poem and the reader—their special dance? What sort of *partner* is the verse? The analogy to dance spurs this question: how can one avoid going through the motions as enactors of choreography and instead lose oneself in the event of the poem to the same extent that the best of dancers *become* the dance? Or what might make readers resist such participation in the event of reading? How long might I tarry? Please note that such inquiry demands responding from the interior of our own experiences with poetic texts—from our own contexts, whose constraints Thomas Fink describes in this anthology. Readers poetize texts as participants *within* them. Such interpretation is never fixed, finite, or "correct." Gadamer's aesthetics asks readers to stretch continually toward, with, and in language—in an elastic dialogue with what is possible.

At this juncture, I want to extend these questions to the sites of two very different poetic events to provide, amidst their distinctive temporality, my own reportage of self-forgetting. Poet Stephen Ratcliffe, editor of Avenue B books and director of the Creative Writing Program at Mills College in Oakland, California, is renowned for his detailed attention to temporality and the constellation of his experience in discrete blocks of time. In 2007, he published *Real*, a collection of 474 days' worth of poems—a poem per day—each one composed as 17 lines written as a double-spaced paragraph. He explains in a brief interview in a 2002 issue of the journal *Double Room* his commitment to "writing that transcribes actual things/actions/events in the world as they were, or seemed to be in that present moment of seeing/noting them. The writing in REAL tries to do something of this 'translation' of world into words . . . because I'm trying to give a 'shape' to things (the lines) on the page (among other things)" ("Bio & Response"). Ratcliffe continued this approach in his anthology *Cloud Ridge*, which covers each day from July 2, 2001, to October 18, 2002. But it is his work *human/nature* that fully embodies Gadamer's sense of *event*.

Ratcliffe's *human/nature* is a thousand-poem document responding to a thousand days of observations. In his campus flyer for the performance of *human/nature*, Ratcliffe notes that this text "extends his investigations into the integration of human beings and natural landscape" and also "the relation between things seen/observed in the world and how such things might be made (transcribed/transformed) as works of written (or visual) art" (*human/nature* flyer). What is particularly distinctive about this text is its unfolding: "The reading of the poem will accompany sound, light, movement and sculpture in an open dialogue with the architecture of the surrounding space. Audience will be free to move between an activated courtyard area and a more focused interior environment, creating a dialogue between reception, memory and stimulus" (*human/nature* flyer). Ratcliffe choreographed the *human/nature* poems to be accompanied by music, dance, and charcoal drawings sketched by an artist present at the reading. He notes in his performance's announcement that the presentation might be lengthy, extending to eight or more hours; the actual recording of the event is over twelve hours long. A one-hour segment of the performance is available online at *PennSound*. The play of the text, set in an aesthetic garden of possibilities, is manifold. In the game of self-forgetting, Ratcliffe's *human/nature* is a generous partner.

The performance, of course, is grounded in the print text of *human/nature*. Here is the poem that opens the collection and sets the structural pattern for the 999 others, this one dated October 19th and available online at Ubu.com:

> streaked sparrow landing on lower left perch of feeder,
> another pecking at copper rim of the birdbath below it,
> sound of jet fading away overhead
>
> man in green shirt
> asking if heavily stressed monosyllabic nouns are things
> themselves, Emerson thinking "every word once a poem"
> Whitman's "Crossing Brooklyn Ferry" wanting to empathize
> with what he sees, man on the left opening Kenneth Koch's
> *A Possible World*, in which what you don't remember passes
>
> silver circle of sun in grey plane of clouds above ridge,
> horizontal grey plane to the left of point across from it
> (*human/nature*)

Each poem opens with particular attention to a natural scene and closes with an evocative and often lyrical topographic description. In between these brackets of reflection are philosophic or aesthetic commentary such as: a remark about Vermeer's use of variations of orange and pink, a recollection of choreographic genius George Balanchine's about Igor Stravinsky, and another recollection by Maxim Gorky about his mother's apron. In addition, distinctive and often quirky bits of information are revealed about the man or woman who persistently appears in each poem, always engaged in some sort of dialogue after the opening reflection. In one poem, the man is a World War I veteran who formerly played the flute in the Paris opera. Both the ontic and ontological dispositions of experience are explored. There is a great deal of repetition of key images: the sun, moon, clouds, and a ridge within the poet's view in cyclic procession; colors—in particular white and silver—also appear throughout the remainder of the collection. Movements in the play of thinking also distinguish Ratcliffe's daily poems, such as: an attuned appreciation of the physical landscape, philosophical questioning, a puzzling over absurd non sequiturs, aesthetic debate, and an evocation of lyrical transcendence through *all* of these investigations. Throughout the thousand days, the life force is pitched but also diffuse—pulsations mediated by sharply contrasting domains of thought.

Ratcliffe further complicates the game into which he invites the "experiencers" of this text. As the hour-long excerpt of *human/nature* demonstrates, Ratcliffe employs a female dancer who apparently improvises her choreography in response to Ratcliffe's reading aloud of the collection's text. Freeform, modern in styling, and resembling tai chi movements, the choreography seems to be in a physically expressive dialogue with Ratcliffe's own utterances: the dancer approaches Ratcliffe and gestures, sometimes inviting closeness and other times not. Often the two appear to be moving either elegantly in tandem, like square-dance partners, or in defined opposition, slinking away from one another. At times, the dancer seems to tarry, to hang on Ratcliffe's every evocation and to physically respond to them. This choreography makes possible a dialogue between one variety of articulated experience—the voiced, similarly patterned, balanced wordplay of each of the 1,000 poems—and another, the silent succession of dance moves drawn from a repertoire of steps. Verbal and physical—both evocative—these are two forms of Ratcliffe's "transcription" of the world in the event of *human/nature*.

At the same time, a male artist dressed in black—in contrast to both the light-colored garb of the female dancer and references to white and silver in the print text—sketches in charcoal on large sheets of paper glued to the walls natural scenes and landscapes that suggest places about which Ratcliffe poetizes. His sketches are not painterly or narrative reproductions of Ratcliffe's words but more the artist's own imagistic associations in response to Ratcliffe's language. Like the dancer, the artist is *part* of the text and simultaneously *responding to it*—Gadamer's spectator. The dancer often rubs and rolls between the drawings, thus improvising a dialogue, much like dancing with an artist's composition.

In terms of spatial relations, the action of *human/nature* centers always on Ratcliffe reading from his script, though the recitation shifts fluidly from a second-floor studio decorated at precise increments with what looks like tall wheat sheaves down a staircase to a narrow downstairs room that exits to a garden-courtyard overflowing with plants. The natural world is bright and lush at the doorway's threshold, an invitation to see the unfolding experience of being in the context of nature: breezes, the breathing of flora, and the fading light.

Ratcliffe's elaborate production moves beyond the play of an event and better enacts a term that Gadamer also uses to characterize the temporality of the poem: the festival. Gadamer explains: "It is the nature of the festival that it should proffer time, arresting it and allowing it to tarry. That is what festive celebration means. The calculating way in which we normally manage and dispose of our time is, as it were, brought to a standstill" ("Relevance of the Beautiful" 42). In terms of absorption or immersion in this celebration of aesthetic possibilities—that is, becoming caught up in *human/nature's* many moments of being—self-forgetting is not difficult. However, tarrying with Ratcliffe's text requires patience. In the one-hour video, the audience shuffles—very close to the action of the performance—coughs, rustles, and wanders; actors accent Ratcliffe's reading with thudding rocks; musicians accompany him with a flute, a guitar, and a gong. The *energeia* possible in Ratcliffe's *human/nature* is variegated and abundant, a dynamic interplay of language, movement, visuals, lighting, and the wild card: the participatory audience, who punctuates Ratcliffe's reading with sneezes and whispers but also supports his focal role with rapt attention. While the audience appearing in the video may have been comprised of only about 15 people—some of whom were young children—they appeared completely enthralled with the performance. The audience did not speak or respond to Ratcliffe, the dancer, or the artist, but they followed all three pied pipers quite literally, traversing from space to space.

At a distance in time and space, at my computer screen in Pennsylvania in 2011, I felt absorbed in Ratcliffe's spectacle. Even with the poetic texts at hand, I had no idea where this event would take me. The improvisational character of the dancer's and artist's movements suggested that *each* event of poetic performance would be distinct despite being grounded in the same print text. I think this is Ratcliffe's achievement. His *human/nature* amplifies both the event of artistic production *and* its spontaneous, strategic, dialogic, and surprising being in the world. Ultimately, however, the event is *finite*: our tarrying with this festival must end. Our memories may preserve the event, but Ratcliffe's elaborate text, to paraphrase Gadamer, speaks itself and then retreats. The poet, the dancer, and the artist must go home.

The spare print texts of Myung Mi Kim, however, may endure in our thinking and questioning beyond the time constraints of any festival if we choose to tarry. A minimalist in styling, Kim seems the complete opposite of Ratcliffe's ready poetic surplus; she appears a reserved partner in the poetic dance. Emigrating to the United States from Korea at the age of nine and now a professor of creative writing at the State University of New York at Buffalo, Kim is sometimes labeled an innovator and other times grouped with Asian American writers who articulate "an irreducible alterity that resists assimilation" and write to destabilize "ethnic and national identities" (Xiaojing). While certainly embodying her distinctive, gendered ethnic identity in her verse, Kim also asserts her sense of the poem "coming forth" as an autonomous, temporal event in a 1997 interview with Yedda Morrison: "Once you start working on the notion of the poem emerging, the poem that's being pushed through to the surface, not a poem which you compose—once you make an allegiance to pay attention to that kind of process, there is tremendous release. . . . [T]he poem is what is in fact emerging at that very moment of encounter, with your ear, with your psyche, with your body, with your historical conditions" ("Generosity as Method"). The temporal unfolding available in her verse has been acclaimed by commentators such as Sueyeun Juliette Lee, who focuses on Kim's interests "in enunciation and address, the way we mark time, what we know and how we come to know it, and how language intersects with, shapes, and is shaped by these concerns" (10)—all of which are Gadamerian concerns. Kim herself describes her poetic emphasis on world-relatedness: "I think there is always some kind of invisible, constant, millisecond-by-millisecond negotiation between the form and its divestment, between the poem and the world" ("Generosity as Method"). Kim goes on to claim that "[p]oetry is simply how you participate in language, and we all do that." Kim's participation presents a challenge for the reader's own attention.

Kim's 2009 collection of poems entitled *Penury* provides her "millisecond-by-millisecond negotiation" between the poem and being, a being that emerges as disjunctive in its traversal of time, space, and subjectivities. As Kim's reader, I often felt at a loss for words in my responses to what unfolded in *Penury*, given, as the title would imply, the paucity of declarative or narrative expression in her verse. Sometimes I heard an immigrant struggling to learn a new language:

arri

sway

avri

someone teaches | "topic sentence"

allegiance garland (70)

While the student here perhaps delineates between similar sounding, perhaps hard-to-pronounce root words—*arri* and *avri*—she also wryly identifies the over-determined "topic sentence"—a Western European construct often considered rude and presumptuous in Asian rhetorics—taught by a nameless "someone," as an affect or an "allegiance garland" worn as a reward for her assimilation.

Many pages of *Penury*—such as pages 41, 45, 46, 99—appear as though they are textbook language exercises or word memorization lists—again the studied texts of an immigrant—but the juxtaposition of terms evokes a bleak collage, as this brief section demonstrates:

accumulation of land	maintain household bear	labor of house child
cooking reserve line	belonging to	elaborate isolation
familias implements (45)	enemies captured in war	bearing child rearing

These lines and the full passage—which can be read across the page or in vertical block groupings—suggest land held and lost and the labors of preserving a family—or losing it—in "elaborate isolation."

At other moments in *Penury*, I detected an ironic voice establishing the emptiness of human sounds:

mp
lm
ks
nc
lk
lp
nh

gy
td
nc

you speak English so well transcript (29)

The repetition of the term "transcript" throughout *Penury* made me self-consciousness about the projection of thought in writing—or the anxious distance between utterance and text. The repetition of this term seems to operate as a sometimes painful visible record of the persona's attempts to mean something where meaning is absent. But how should we read lines that end with "transcript"? For example, the italicized, piercing words "*One Arrow transcript*" reappear mysteriously on both pages 69 and 85. Should the term be "One Arrow," or does it just *sound* like it to an immigrant's ear? Could it be "one-hour" transcript—the duration of a language test? Or one-hour transit—a bus schedule? I was left to ponder.

As critics have noted, no comfortable decidability or stability defines Kim's subjectivities. At times, personal recollection mingles with cold, objective assertion. For instance, in one segment of *Penury* the clinical intrusion of a distant observer interrupts the memories of an unknown persona who is in the process of recalling a world debauched by pollution, sickness, and (most probably) forced prostitution, a leveling of human culture to that of "dogs":

obverse view k

nitrogen oxides, heavy metal (mercury) deposits

not people—dogs, lowly animals—we were taught

the dead framed in black cardboard

obverse view t

sacrifices to those who have died in epidemics

the demand for young slender women

she thought she heard the photos (73)

The "obverse views" sound like calculated schematics on a construction diagram—all for a world undone.

In the boldest display of absence, Kim offers twenty lines of single and double slashes along with five periods, a pattern that suggests a trace of a poem without words, a trail of emphatic blank phrases measured with ambiguous symbols (104). I found myself intrigued by this pointed emptiness, always trying to discern a pattern; I was a restless partner in this interplay. Was this the skeleton of a well-known poem? Or the bare-bones scheme from a segment of *Penury* itself? As the poverty of language presents itself in much of Kim's poetry, it provides a spectacle in which absences are as provocative as text.

A study in mystery and restraint, *Penury* is embellished with Kim's trademark enigmas. For example the following bold-faced markings divide one poem from another:

. . .
. . .

Are these dots a unique organizational marker or a code? An American reader may wonder if this block of periods has some meaning in Korean texts. Kim also defamiliarizes traditional punctuation with unusual spacing; for instance, she blunts the pronounced, declarative stops that periods provide by adding spaces around the periods that suggest unspoken or missing text. Yet her de-periodization permits emphatic deliberation. Take for example the following section:

> we are late . flower boxes mistaken antidote . shrubbery money .
>
> vacant boarded . steps of the courthouse . grateful that one pan is clean
>
> and cooking can begin . seen nothing but the insides of things .
>
> forlorn me in my house | forlorn you in yours (44)

This section mingles disappointment with what should be upliftment—"flower boxes mistaken antidote"—and the isolation of "vacant boarded" empty interiors. These interiors are apparently "nothing but the insides" and are equally "forlorn" for all involved. Kim also employs non-traditional signs to evoke the unknown—syntactic actions unfamiliar to the reader—*or* perhaps she posits these markers as open invitations for *attributing* meaning or connection. Take for example this section:

> spar wanton drear dear forbid || rest cleft hold avarice swift
>
> regard ally press fray reason || rights tie wallow heaving cause
>
> hold facing simple adore one || (86)

As her reader, I do not know how to voice these marks or how long to pause, if I should pause at all. How is the event of this text mediated by these parallel lines? Do they indicate a balanced caesura? An emphatic barrier? Do they suggest an analogy meant to compare one side to the other? Or do they perhaps suggest parity where one side equals the other? What sort of energy does this passage embody—what sort of life? Verbs are used as nouns here and vice versa. What is the play of thinking in such a world where even the spare foundations of meaning-making are ambiguous? Certainly it is deliberate but not fixed, associative but not from a unified or monovocal standpoint, concrete yet unmoored.

The section entitled "[Reader of the Announcement of the Spirit]" especially demonstrates the equivocal play in Kim's work. This section suggests step-by-step directions for a Korean funereal or death ritual. The body is mindfully prepared:

> Place in the nose a piece of blue paper
>
> The hair is combed and parted in the middle
>
> Any fallen hair is collected and put in a pouch
>
> With a spoon carved from a willow tree
>
> Place three spoonfuls of rice in the mouth
>
> Seven times bound with rope (63)

The rites seem exotic and precise; the audience is drawn in and asked to project onto these rites their significance. And who is the "reader" invoked in what appears to be an aside, a parenthetical detail, or a moment of authorial substitution in the place where a defining title might go in more traditional verse? After this ritual, three blank pages follow; these pages are an example of what is distinct in Kim's poetic environment: silence. An evocation of not-knowing. Kim offers this quietude with a question: "What happens during a collaboration between the impossibility of utterance and a search for the means by which to utter?" That special space is "never a decided, resolved, fixed point" but is instead "constantly in motion, constantly reshaping itself" ("Generosity of Method"). Kim locates that edge as her preferred site of play: "I suppose any poem is that, and really is always on the cusp of coming into legibility—formally, psychically, politically. For me those works that keep reinvigorating that space of silence and erasure, the space of the seemingly untranslatable, are the ones in which you really feel some sort of endurance and power" ("Generosity of Method").

The *energeia* of Kim's verse—the pulse of life, the drift of being that her poetry brings forth—is an ecstatic struggle. Voices in her verse stand out and stand open amid pauses and great silences. Kim's texts serve as witnesses to worlds and histories but also initiate an intimate unfolding of strangeness: of being outside and apart, waiting for the whisper of possibilities. Not only do Kim's poems wait for language to speak but so do these poems' readers, who can easily get lost tarrying "on the cusp of . . . legibility" (Kim "Generosity and Method"). As a result, Kim's verse demands elasticity from readers. Some poems permit readers to maintain a safe distance; they require minimal play, little exertion. Not Kim's; with her verse, we must choose to tarry in, patiently embrace, or even openly grapple with her implosive bursts. As Gadamer might suggest, the engaged reader is a participant in *Penury*. In the game of self-forgetting—in ways dynamic, unique, and enigmatic—the reader *becomes* the poem—one version of it—with each temporal experience of the text. In the case of Kim's poetry, the reader travels with the words and the quiet, pursuing dialogues with strangers.

In my response to Kim's poetry, I sense that she reconstitutes the alchemy of reading, in particular the dialogue with "the other." While certainly texts "are [not] equivalent to persons," for Gadamer ". . . the process by which the truth . . . is revealed is instructively similar to the unconcealing that goes on in the ethical hermeneutics of being open to . . . the truth of another person" (Haney 38). Innovative texts such as Kim's can open social spaces wherein thinkers are revealed but not subjugated. The author's experience of creating the text invites readers to create their *own* experiences. In other words, these texts make palpable a "nearness" of thought. It is as if Krzysztof Ziarek was describing this dialogue with Myung Mi Kim's verse when he wrote:

> [It] induces language to "pay attention" to the inscriptions of otherness, of the unsaid, in what it brings to words. In the end, at stake is not a hermeneutics of knowing or understanding but one of listening . . . of letting come into one's own—efforts summed up by the enigmatic sense of nearing. It is a hermeneutics that . . . attempts to deliver a message, to let it say itself, without covering or explaining away what remains baffling and other in it. (Ziarek 10)

Experiencing contemporary American innovative poetry requires a revised sense of what reading can be. It asks us to move beyond apparent outcomes and locate an appetite for experience. Gadamer explains:

> Experience stands in an ineluctable opposition to knowledge and to the kind of instruction that follows from general theoretical or technical knowledge. The truth of experience always implies an orientation toward new experience. . . . The consummation of his experience, the perfection that we call "being experienced," does not consist in the fact that someone already knows everything and knows better than anyone else. Rather, the experienced person proves to be, on the contrary, someone who is radically undogmatic. (*Truth and Method* 1990 ed. 355)

To be experienced is to be hungry for *more*: experience, Gadamer explains, "has its proper fulfillment not in definitive knowledge but in the openness to experience that is made possible by experience itself" (*Truth and Method* 1990 ed. 355). Gadamer here may have defined the ideal reader of innovative poetry. Later in his career, Gadamer emphasized that, "It is the untiring power of *experience*, that in the process of being instructed, [a human being] is ceaselessly forming a new preunderstanding," and this achievement, he asserts, could be called "a transformation" ("On the Scope and Function of Hermeneutical Reflection" 38). In the context of Gadamer's assertions, reading innovative verse should not only valorize the pragmatic—questioning the ontic character of poetic structures—but invite the "radically undogmatic": the openness and buoyancy of experienced readers who remake the event of understanding, and, in so doing, remake themselves and how they stand out in the world. In Gadamerian terms, an innovative aesthetics of reception belongs not to the avant-garde fringe but to *the center*; it brings "nearness" and makes us more available to moments of self-forgetting, though this forgetting is not a loss of self but rather a movement that pushes us beyond ourselves. In its happily unpredictable, free-fall nature, innovative verse makes possible an experiential *ethos*. It fosters a nearness to the experience of thought that surprises, perplexes, and can awaken in us an appetite for more experiences and "games." In other words it offers us events capable of revealing both who we are and who we *can be.*

Note

The author wishes to thank the Faculty Grants Committee of Millersville University of Pennsylvania for providing released time that made this chapter possible.

The Utopian Textures and Civic Commons of Lisa Robertson's Soft Architecture

Christopher Schmidt

What is *Rubus armeniacus*? How does Lisa Robertson's essay on this botanical invader to the Pacific Northwest—commonly known as Himalayan blackberry—constitute a manifesto about globalism, urban architecture, and, most of all, Robertson's own dandy poetics? Such is the power of this Canadian-born, peripatetic writer to unify an astounding array of aesthetic and political concerns in a consideration of something as seemingly innocuous as a fruit-bearing vine. Robertson notes that the non-native plant—not really Asian but European in origin, transplanted to California in an Orientalist vogue before snaking its way up into Canada—possesses a tendency to "garnish and swag and garland any built surface it encounters" (*Occasional* 109). Of the plant's "morphological lust," she says that this "alien is the dystopian epitome of the romance of botanical pattern as applied architectural decoration" (110). In other words, the plant is the Jamesian real thing: a living model of the ersatz bellflowers and festive husks that might adorn the top of a Corinthian column. The important difference between these two types of ornament is not that one lives while one is artificial. Rather, the vine shows Robertson how ornament can transform even a ruin into a new structure; the geometric patterning of the plant—which endeared it to its Orientalist transplanter—*is* the structure. The scaffolding lust of the *Rubus armeniacus* inspires Robertson, with a little help from Ruskin, to propose a liberating reversal of the structure-ornament binary that has traditionally subordinated style to content.

Criticism, as dandy stylist Oscar Wilde declared in *The Picture of Dorian Gray*, is at best a form of self-description. Robertson's attention to ornament in her essay on the *Rubus armeniacus* is indeed a sidelong description of her own dandiacal poetics. Although Robertson is known as a poet, the essay comes from a relatively early collection of lyric prose entitled *Occasional*

10.1. Rem Koolhaas's CCTV Headquarters. Photo (CC) by Kevin Poh.

Work and Seven Walks from the Office for Soft Architecture, first published in 2003. Embedded in the playful heteronym used throughout the book, Office for Soft Architecture (inspired by architect Rem Koolhaas's Office for Metropolitan Architecture), is Robertson's belief that the hard structural form of a building, city, or poem is less important than the "soft" environment created by its surface effects.

Surfaces, too, possess import. Koolhaas's own recent buildings demonstrate how a reversal of the surface/structure binary has not just theoretical but real applications. For example, note how Koolhaas's CCTV Headquarters in Beijing (see Fig. 10.1) alters the traditional modernistic grid for reasons integral to the building's structure: the concentration of external ribbing provides additional support where the structure of the building is weakest; thus, the surface ornamentation becomes integral to the structure's form (Ouroussoff). The relationship between structure and skin is similarly developed in Robertson's work when, for example, she describes the *Rubus armeniacus* as: "an exemplary political decoration, a nutritious ornament that clandestinely modifies infrastructural morphology" (112). Likewise, in Robertson's poetry, the groomed difficulty of her style is not a screen that prevents the reader from accessing the interior—the poem or essay's subject. The clandestine subject most often is some version of soft architecture, for in *Occasional Work*, Robertson considers the most ornamental of possible subjects: color, clothing, furniture, and fountains.

The value that Robertson places on ornament brings into binocular focus her difficulty and her dandyism, which accommodates both an aesthetic transport (in the way of Pater) and an aesthetic-political resistance to capital (in the way of Baudelaire). Robertson's dandiacal prose, to say nothing of her verse, is anti-absorptive in the manner identified by Charles Bernstein in his seminal "Artifice of Absorption" essay in *A Poetics*. However, Robertson largely eschews the poetic effects—disjunction, collage, and radical parataxis—first exercised by Bernstein's generation of L=A=N=G=U=A=G=E writers. While Robertson has identified Lyn Hejinian as an important influence, an equal and perhaps more revealing affiliation is her provisional identification with another group, the New Narrative writers largely centered in San Francisco and its environs, which include Dodie Bellamy, Kevin Killian, Robert Glück, and Matthew Stadler (who first published Robertson's *Occasional Work*). This affinity is evinced in Robertson's playfulness regarding authorial presence, the cerebral incisiveness of her sentences, and her frequent recourse to walking literature; Bruce Boone's "My Walk with Bob" comes to mind as one model for the walks that conclude *Occasional Work*. (Rousseau's peripatetic writing is another clear and avowed template.)

Robertson's aestheticism is not merely a stylistic effect but rather a thoroughgoing merger of surface and structure. In *Occasional Work*, Robertson quotes Ruskin and William Morris in essays entitled "Pure Surface," "How to Colour," and "Arts and Crafts in Burnaby: A Congenial Soil." Robertson's aestheticism extends as well to the book's "Seven Walks," which are not Wordsworthian rural amblings but rather urban fantasias of hyperbolized taste-making befitting the *flâneur*: "We shall not enter this establishment: we do not care for the lucrative sugaring of glutinous cakes" (205). Elegance is refusal, as Baudelaire might have said. And yet, Robertson's writing is notable not only for what it excludes (narrative closure, piety) but also for what it includes: the sometimes antiquated diction of the sources she rewrites. Especially in her early poetic projects—*XEclogue, Debbie: an Epic, The Weather*—Robertson indulges in a hothouse lyricism and period diction that is undercut by flashes of erotic sadism and academic rhetoric (and in the process draws out the affective sadism latent in the rhetoric of academic theory). Robertson's *XEclogue* (1993) is a rewriting of various pastoral traditions; *Debbie: an Epic* (1997) re-imagines Virgil. *The Weather* (2001) mines English meteorological descriptions researched in a rare books archive while Robertson was a visiting poet in Cambridge. *R.'s Boat* (2010) models itself on Rousseau, using Robertson's own notebooks as the archive. While these appropriations are indeed conceptual in formation, Robertson's style resists the machinic anti-expressivity of the Conceptual writing movement; her hothouse lyricism makes every book humidly intimate (with the exception, ironically, of *R's Boat*, which in spite of its use of notebook material creates a more arid ambience.)

Throughout the remainder of this chapter, I will attend to the ways the mannered surfaces of Robertson's *Occasional Work* conflate the civic surfaces of her putative site—turn-of-the-millennium Vancouver—and the soft architecture of her own writing project, which she positions as a response to globalist politics. During the time in which Robertson wrote *Occasional Work*, Vancouver underwent a rejuvenation and renovation fueled by an influx of global circuits of capital—specifically, she writes during a period of booming construction between the 1983 Expo and the 2010 Olympics. While the rise of condominiums and urban renovation in Vancouver fascinates Robertson, and gives rise to her *flânerie*, she ultimately disdains the "utopia of the new" in favor of a "dystopia of the obsolete" (McCaffery 23). Yet Robertson's soft architecture is no simple opposition of the local to the global. A telling feature of *Occasional Work* is how Robertson tacks between contemporary Vancouver and aesthetic taxonomies that transcend geography and the contemporary moment (often taking her to fin-de-siècle England or Paris, habitat of the original *flâneur*). Robertson alternates between these so as to confuse the categories of old and new, near and far, and show that the site of writing, to say nothing of the site of reading, is never fixed like a landmark but is mobile and porous.

Michael Davidson, while defining "soft architecture" slightly differently than either I or Robertson herself would, trenchantly situates Robertson's work within the larger frame of what he calls "cosmopoetics": that is, a literature that exceeds any grouping in a locality or school but which instead emerges from a recognition of hemispheric economic interdependence post-NAFTA. The goal of such poetries is to describe and critique the economic injustices such a system exacts on its subjects. Davidson writes, "[t]he architecture of the new global city, as Lisa Robertson points out, is 'soft,' its glamorous surface permeated by investment capital from East Asia and elsewhere" (738). (A correlation between capital invasion and the propagation of the "non-native" Himalayan blackberry may be inferred.) Although Robertson is sensitive to the changes wrought on Vancouver, her approach is not literally documentary. Instead, Robertson's response (even in the ostensibly discursive prose of *Occasional Work*) is more poetic and formally innovative. Instead of approaching the effects of globalism as a resistant outsider, Robertson instead invents an authorial persona—an architectural office—that inscribes the logic of global capital into its cultural production. Like a star architect, the Office for Soft Architecture freely roams over geography and history in response to site-specific commissions (many of the pieces were born out of magazine assignments). Just as Koolhaas's work takes him from London to Rotterdam to Beijing, so does Robertson's research triangulate Amsterdam, China, Walden Pond, Burnaby, and of course Paris in its attempts to describe the historical and contemporary flows that constitute Vancouver in its late capitalist liquidity.

Another way that Robertson resists a reductive contrast of the local to the global is by showing how even the humblest-seeming "pastoral" site is in fact a palimpsest of global traffic. Like language, space too fossilizes historical change. In perhaps the most rhetorically straightforward essay in *Occasional Work*, "Site Report: New Brighton Park," Robertson reveals a history of official and subverted uses that are elided in the parceling of this landscape. This essay strikes a similar stance as Robertson's *Rubus armeniacus* essay, in which the seemingly natural is read as a construction. Here, however, Robertson's reading is less fancifully imaginative than it is scrupulously factual. The site, New Brighton Park, was once designated as the official township of Vancouver (a public commons), then made into a spa hotel (a private recreational retreat for the privileged), before serving as an internment center for Japanese Canadians during World War II (governmental disciplinary territory). After a period of decay, it has more recently been transformed into a park for the city's gentrifying classes. As Robertson notes in a Philly Talks conversation with the poet Steve McCaffery, "This overlay—old world fantasy, leisure and industrial, racial and natural constructions—defines for me the pastoral. This is the pataphysical Utopia here in Vancouver. I want to represent its politics, as they appear fragmented in the landscape" (McCaffery 24).

Pastoral is not for Robertson a positive value but rather a fantasy space constructed in response to nationalist insecurities around the vestiges of empire. The *Rubus armeniacus* offers one such example of how "nature" hides a history of ideological baggage in its seemingly innocent reproduction: "The plant's swift rhetorical trajectory from aestheticized exotic, to naturalized species, to invasive alien, all the while concealing a spurious origin myth, displays a typically hackneyed horticultural anthropomorphism" (109). Robertson is able to expose this history of the plant's rhetorical uses while finding poetic—and arguably anthropomorphic—inspiration in its ornamental/structural form. This metaphorical legerdemain shows that even Robertson's discursive prose possesses the metaphorical compression and syntactically charged energy of lyric.

Nature is often construed as the "site" of the poetic, yet Robertson imagines alternatives to this *locus classicus* not just in the soft architecture of *Occasional Work* but in many of her poetic projects. Even when she is addressing nature tropes directly, it is with a revisionist impulse. In the preface to Robertson's ambitious second book of poetry, *XEclogue*, the poet targets some of the nationalist and gendered dynamics animating pastoral fantasy. Yet even here, Robertson is able to find surface-level pleasure in the act of critique. In the passage below, Robertson first creates a bond between reader and writer ("Let's pretend") that in some sense imitates the collusion and bossiness of empire. The sentences that follow lead the reader through a confident and changeable pageant of rhetorical stances, metaphors, and personifications:

> Let's pretend you "had" a land. Then you "lost" it. Now fondly describe it. That is pastoral. Consider your homeland, like all utopias, obsolete. Your pining rhetoric points to obsolescence. The garden gate shuts firmly. Yet Liberty must remain throned in her posh gazebo. What can the poor Lady do?! (unpaginated)

The defensive gendering in this passage underlines the ways that "nature" has traditionally been constructed to the advantage of privileged male classes of noble persons, explorers, and adventurers, who loot and bound the "feminine" land. In *XEclogue*, as in her essays on the *Rubus armeniacus* and the New Brighton Park, Robertson critiques the notion of a nature independent from human preconception, showing instead how our descriptions of nature are often anxious and fantastical projections onto landscape. Such projections constitute a history, and dwelling within this history imaginatively creates soft architecture, a dwelling that is temporal as well as spatial. Robertson concludes her essay on New Brighton Park by noting, "Soft Architects believe that this site demonstrates the best possible use of an urban origin: Change its name repeatedly. Burn it down. From the rubble confect a prosthetic pleasure ground; with fluent obliviousness, picnic there" (41). If Situationist drift relies on a strategic ignorance of a space's intended use, Robertson's ironies imply that such tactics have been overtaken by the picnicking gentrifier. The soft architect, however, possesses an acute awareness and resuscitation of a site's previous uses and decay: the fundament of a pleasure ground may contain sinister buried ideologies. One way of resisting globalist whitewashing is to recall the fragmented histories that may color the featureless renovation of urban architectural surface. Robertson's soft architecture—not so much a bounded place as a poetic-intellectual approach to the sediments and ruins of urban facades—updates *flânerie* to the 21st-century global metropolis. The *flâneuse* archly observes patterns of consumption while remaining herself an arbiter of surface; the soft architect is similarly interested in the surface but attends to the waste and excess that might resist the "utopia of the new."

Nature is often counter-posed as the antidote to, or more often, the victim of capitalism's logic of waste-making. In one version, this nature appears as mythic pastoral; in a more recent fantasy, it is cast as purified "wilderness" that functions as a commons (e.g., the United States' national parks). Robertson's critique of the pastoral in *XEclogue* and "Site Report: New Brighton Park" problematizes this fantasy. Contra a natural commons, Robertson's soft architecture construes urbanity—and particularly urban ruins—as a commons *requiring* gender, class, and racial diversity for its production. As Michael Hardt and Antonio Negri argue in their book *Commonwealth*, urban space itself is a kind of "factory for the production of the commons" (250). Here "factory" is of course used metaphorically, to echo the traditional Marxist site of community building, the factory floor ("the metropolis is to the multitude what the factory was to the industrial working class" [Hardt and Negri 250]). It is in the warp and weft of various creative, social, and yes, economic activities between different classes that this urban commons is woven. This fabric constitutes Robertson's soft architecture—not the city's gridded structure but its "ornamental" texture, subject to growth as well as decay and ruin.

This soft architecture is often generated in specific locations, as Robertson explores in her essay on Vancouver's New Brighton Park. Another writer, Samuel Delany, has persuasively argued in his *Times Square Red, Times Square Blue* (2001) that the elimination of seedy Times Square movie theaters removed from the fabric of New York City an important site of inter-class and inter-racial sexual contact; local character was sacrificed to global capitalist branding and hyper-speculative development. While such notions of an urban commons do depend on specific sites, underlying them is a less literal notion that the value of a city lies not in its built architecture but in its character and capacity for generating and fostering communities through dynamic interactions between subjects and places. O'Hara's "city eclogues" (as

Robertson calls them in *XEclogue*) are one model for this, and the "New York School" was indeed no literal site or even a unified aesthetic approach but a dynamic network of personalities, attitudes, and collaborations. The danger is that a successful soft architecture like New York City's risks becoming a global stand-in for the urban: a "logarithm / Of other cities" (as John Ashbery terms it) or a grid by which other urbanities are colonized, synthesized, and in turn exported (75). One impetus for *Occasional Work* is Robertson's worry that Vancouver will fall prey to a similar formulaic urbanity through a cynical combination of relentless development and selective preservation of the attractively "authentic." What of Vancouver's soft architecture is specific to Vancouver? What is generic, simulacral, imported from elsewhere, or designed to appeal to the tourist? And how does Robertson's own embodied experience, and the mental maps she has formed of other cities she has lived in, inform her reading of Vancouver?

If a subject is a palimpsest of all the places it has traveled, it is the body housing this subject that registers what travels to it: food, commodities, goods, "lifestyle." Robertson notes in an interview, "The interesting thing about bodies too is that they move around, both physically and cognitively! So the sensing, thinking, remembering, desiring body becomes a way to specifically situate . . . larger scales, where scale pertains also to discursive fields" ("Lisa Robertson" 99). In *Occasional Work*, as in Delany's *Times Square Red, Times Square Blue*, an insistence on embodiment—in sexual practices, life practices, sentences, and subjectivity—stands in stark opposition to the globalist reduction of persons into consumers and laborers, parts in a vast global eating and wasting machine. As Robertson notes in the same interview, "globalising politics erase—violently or much more insidiously—the particularity of bodies, and thus histories, replacing these with the theology of the market" (100). In *Occasional Work*, Robertson theorizes this interaction by considering the body's own soft architecture: its clothing. In an essay on a secondhand clothing store in East Vancouver, "The Value Village Lyric," Robertson is concerned as in her peregrinations around Vancouver—with the interplay between the situated and the dispersed, between the actual garment and the global semiotic system in which this garment travels and signifies. Through the garments it dons, the body circulates and signifies within the larger discursive field ("the garment italicizes the body and turns it into speech," Robertson writes [*Occasional Work* 182]). Through the garments that clothe it, a body articulates within the global economies of status and value. The analogy between this semiotic fashion system and what Robertson means by the city's soft architecture is apparent in a litany of "houses" (akin to Parisian couture houses) that appear in her essay: "House of V . . . House of Vreeland, House of Viva, Luxe, Calme, et Volupté, House of Wordsworth, House of Versace, the Blessed V, House of Valentino" (182). In choosing to purchase a Versace dress, the consumer is not just buying a flattering skin but situating herself within the semiotics of global branding, which are built on top of other historical systems of status (House of Wordsworth, House of . . . Luxe, Calme, et Volupté). The wearer of "obsolete" Versace, however, resists enthrallment to the commodity as fetish and its machinery of desire: "We finger the bad judgments in mass-market branding; we fraternize with frayed and gaudy trousers as if we remembered them; we mimic the seaminess of markets. We choose among lurid failures" (183). Waste is the logic of capitalism but also the chink in its armor. In the failures of the system, in its cast-offs and ruins, Robertson finds a way to perform capitalist renovation—"we mimic the seaminess of markets"—without capitulating to its entreaties to buy only the new and trash the secondhand.

Robertson's incisive style prevents this "dystopia of the obsolete" from collapsing into a romanticism that the thematization of the ruin and the fragment sometimes risks. As an alternative, I offer one last trope from *Occasional Work* as the *ne plus ultra* of Robertson's soft architecture: a skin that is structure, an agent of renovation that is also a subject of decay, something that is both perilously situated and fluidly abstract: scaffolding. Robertson titles her essay "Doubt and a History of Scaffolding" as a partial joke, since there is no extant history—only a missing study and a dossier of photographs to guide us. To write a history of scaffolding, ever-present yet endlessly mutable and fleeting, would be like writing a history of language. In fact, Robertson sees scaffolding *as* language, as a system of T's and X's that structures by skinning: "Scaffolding is analogy. It explains what a wall is without being a wall. Perhaps it describes by desiring the wall, which is the normal method of description" (*Occasional Work* 139). For Robertson, scaffolding is the labile agent of money—construction and reconstruction—but also of decay, because its demolition is inherent in its construction, and it leaves only traces of its existence. Here Robertson's soft architecture is inspired again by Koolhaas, who, in refusing the gridded totality of modernism, substitutes instead a changed modernism of fracture and disassembly. Koolhaas writes, "More important than the design of cities will be the design of their decay. Only through a revolutionary process of erasure and the establishment of 'liberty zones,' conceptual Nevadas where all the laws of architecture are suspended, will some of the inherent tortures of urban life—the friction between program and containment—be suspended" (Koolhaas 201). Scaffolding is a literal soft architecture—ornamental but structural, descriptive, and fluid—that creates a kind of negative utopia, a salutary "return of entropy and dissolution to the ephemeral" as Robertson describes it:

> All the ceremonies of transition take place on such a makeshift planking: judgments, executions, banquets and symposia, entertainments and recitals, markets and bazaars, funerals, births and weddings and illicit fuckings are rehearsed and performed to their witnesses on this transient stage, which is sometimes decorated with drapes or swags or flags or garlands, sometimes padded for the comfort of the performing body, sometimes left bare as if to state the plain facts of life. The scaffold is a pause, an inflection of passage. It accommodates us in a shivering. (*Occasional Work* 139)

Like many of the poetries described in this volume, Robertson's scaffolding is a textural surface that some may regard as aesthetically unpleasing. Yet if engaged rather than abjured, the scaffolding emerges as the mobile site of life's great passages, wisely prefiguring its own dissolution and decay in its construction. Soft architecture's work is evanescent and occasional, and when the occasion passes, so too does it. While Robertson's writing is more garlanded than bare, the visible patterns of its soft architecture open it generously to the reader's imagination.

Let me conclude with a few final thoughts about the self-reflective nature of Robertson's soft architecture. While the thorned, hyper-mannered surfaces of Robertson's writing connect her soft architecture to the critical *flânerie* of Baudelaire and Benjamin, its anti-absorptive manner stages at the same time a very contemporary resistance to global hegemony. As Robertson notes, "style is dangerous" because it radically individuates ("Lisa Robertson" 100). In "Artifice of Absorption," Bernstein reminds us that absorption is a social-political metaphor with particular resonance for Canadians, who do not wish to be "absorbed into the U.S./ cultural orbit" (20). Robertson's dandiacal soft architecture even resists absorption into Bernstein's own school of L=A=N=G=U=A=G=E writing as well as into more recent Conceptual writings. Robertson's publishing history reflects this caginess about assimilation. *Occasional Work* was first publication by the Oregon-based Clear Cut Press; this demonstrated a regional affiliation (the Northwest) that also transcended national borders. Robertson's book, like the scaffolding she describes, then disappeared from the civic sphere until it was reissued in similar form by the nationally-supported Coach House Books of Toronto. Robertson's difficult text was absorbed into the Canadian canon of avant-garde writing only after its transplantation from foreign soil. Is it an accident that this history in some ways echoes the travels of the *Rubus armeniacus* from Europe to Western America to Canada? In Robertson's hybrid style—a mixture of European aestheticism and experimentalist difficulty—we indeed see the mutual interdependence of the global and the local in the production of soft architecture.

Problems of Context and the Will to Parsimony

Reading "Difficult" Recent U.S. Poetry

Thomas Fink

In his 1982 essay "Migratory Meaning," Ron Silliman—with the help of linguists Charles Fillmore and Paul Kay's conceptual apparatus—identifies and questions fundamental ways in which readers make sense of texts. "Envisionment," a reader's sense of a unified understanding of a text, depends upon the development of a "*frame* or *schema*"(112). The "frame" is a context in which structures order worldly and textual experience through associations and the application of "the Parsimony Principle"; it involves the emergence of particular kinds of "confidence" as well as "levels of importation of detail and nuance" (113). These "levels" include interpretation "explicitly justified by the material of the text," "inferences which the text is seen as clearly inviting," readings resulting "from schematizations *brought* to the text to situate its events in common experience," and manifestations of "idiosyncratic experience and imaginings of individual readers" (113).

Crucial to the components of envisionment, as presented by Fillmore and Kay, is the "Parsimony Principle," which allows "the latency of the text and the ideological dimensions of presupposition into an actual envisionment combining frames always to a maximum of unification with a minimum of effort" (Silliman, *The New Sentence* 115). Smaller contexts involving local details of a text during the process of reading are eventually placed within a larger one. Fillmore holds that "whenever it is possible to integrate two separate schema into a single larger frame structure *by imagining them as sharing a single common participant* the reader will do so" (qtd. in Silliman 115, 120). Silliman not only argues that the experience of reading texts like Joe Ceravolo's poem "Migratory Moon" disrupts and eventually derails the quest for a single total envisionment, but he seeks to show that "the experience of contact and unity is not" a natural attainment of interpretive truth "beyond the experience of words at all but is itself just an effect" (112). Further, while "each [poetic] device is determined by its relationship to the whole" text, no actual "whole" exists, as reading is temporal: "The reader is always *at some point* with regard to the reading" (122).[1]

In "Signature Event Context" (1971), Jacques Derrida elucidates what disrupts envisionment and the Parsimony Principle. Stating that "a written sign carries with it a force of breaking with its context, that is, the set of presences which organize the moment of its inscription," he foregrounds the possibility of lifting "a written syntagma from the interlocking chain in which it is caught or given without making it lose every possibility of functioning" and "eventually . . . inscribing or *grafting* it onto other chains" (317). "No context," Derrida asserts, "can enclose it." Any interpretation of a literary text involves such "grafting." "The unity of the signifying form," states Derrida, can be "repeated in the absence . . . of a determined signified or current intention of signification, as of every present intention of communication" (318). "Citationality,"—the fact that "every sign . . . as a small or large unity, can be *cited*, put between quotation marks"—ensures that the sign "can break with every given context, and engender infinitely new contexts in an absolutely nonsaturable fashion" (320). Even though a context needs to be assigned for any "mark" to be legible, "there are only contexts without any center of absolute anchoring."

The force of citationality is evident when one wishes to determine whether a sentence should be read literally or ironically. Writing that both "irony" and "literalness" are "ways of reading," with "neither . . . prior to the other," Stanley Fish holds that these "interpretive ways" are "set in motion by cues and considerations that are themselves in place as a consequence of an interpretive act" (195).[2] According to Annette Kolodny, "*Insofar as we are taught how to read, what we engage are not texts but paradigms*," and so "we appropriate meaning from a text according to what we need (or desire), or . . . according to the critical assumptions or predispositions (conscious or not) that we bring to it" (505). Like Silliman's fourth kind of confidence in envisionment, involving individual "experiences and imaginings," Kolodny's point accurately debunks the idea of interpretive "objectivity."

Even conscious need and desire do not necessarily preside over individual interpretation; reading can be influenced by forces beyond a reader's control. In section 27 of "The Chinese Notebook," a long Wittgensteinian metapoem (originally published in 1986 and probably written ten years earlier), Silliman ponders how a reader is influenced by external forces: "Your existence is not a condition of this work. Yet let me, for a moment, posit it. As you read, other things occur to you. You hear the drip of a faucet, or there's music on, or your companion gives a sigh that represents a poor night's sleep.

As you read, old conversations reel slowly through your mind, you sense your buttocks and spine in contact with the chair. All of these certainly must be a part of the meaning of this work" (*The Age* of *Huts* 152). Silliman suggests that the interruption of and interference with a reader's focus (on authorial intention, for example) is more or less unavoidable. In fact, a reader cannot be aware of all elements of interference/influence and how they affect reading. Perhaps these factors limit the reader's freedom, or perhaps one chooses to consider these contingencies as generative conditions for a richer interpretation—one that is somewhat different with each successive reading.

In the past quarter century or so, proponents of New Historicism, cultural studies, and postcolonialism have studied interpenetrating contexts of various literary and many other cultural/historical texts to discern what they reveal about discursive formations and power relations, but they tend to eschew close reading. Marjorie Perloff insists on the pedagogical necessity of "close reading" that "accounts for all the elements in a given" innovative poem, to be followed by a succession of "larger frames," including "genre and stylistic conventions," as well as "cultural and historical markers vis-à-vis other comparable poems of the period" (*Differentials* 247). For Perloff, "the adoption of a theoretical model always puts the literary work in a secondary position . . . where the poem tends to be no more than an example of *X* or a cultural symptom of *Y*" (262). In a text subtitled "The Status of the Subject of the Humanities in an Age of Cultural Studies," Charles Bernstein humorously exclaims: "Behind every successful artist is a new historian who says it's all just a symptom. Behind every successful new historian is an artist who says you forgot to mention my work—and, boy, is it symptomatic!" (*My Way* 48). To read the most "difficult" poetry as "cultural symptom" is to use the Parsimony Principle in ways that ignore what is *not* symptomatic.

In general, interpretation takes place between the pressure for parsimonious re-presentation—since institutions set spatial and temporal limits on acts of reading—and counter-pressure generated by the Proliferation Principle (citationality). Without some proliferation of interpretive possibilities, how could the condensing or gathering force of a Parsimony Principle have any relevance? How could the discovery of unity offer much pleasure or potential edification without the experience of multeity? In reading contemporary innovative U.S. poetry closely, the mere re-marking of/on undecidability or contextual vertigo as derealization ignores how different texts produce differing effects. The development of forms of close reading that do not privilege the end-point but examine intricacies of contextualization, decontextualization, and recontextualization in a poem's temporal unfolding, along with those moments where the location of a context seems impossible, is much more promising. When Jonathan Culler, explicating Derrida's analysis of context, articulates a dynamic in which the binary opposition of inside/outside is subject to continual reversal and displacement,[3] I would assert that he is presenting not an impasse, but part of a map for the elucidation of process: "Any given context is open to further description," as "there is no limit in principle to what might be included in a given context," and "any attempt to codify context can always be grafted onto the context it sought to describe" (123-4).

In the readings of the three recent poetic texts that follow, I will adopt a provisional beginning context as a way of entering the encounter with the work; I will then follow contextual juxtapositions, ambiguities, opacities, and transformations without either losing contact with the beginning context or establishing it or any other context as an interpretive "center" or "anchor." (Obviously, other beginning contexts could be used.)

Tom Beckett, first known as editor of *The Difficulties*, an important venue for the dissemination and interpretation of Language writing in the 1980s, is the author of an anaphoric catalog poem "This Poem" (2008). This work features a constraint that helps me find a beginning context: his third-person "narrator" indicates "this poem's" intentions and actions, as well as properties and attributes, as though no author has intended the "actions" represented. Thus, Beckett is testing—whether seriously or humorously—a concept that, about forty years earlier, had gained currency in French poststructuralist circles and, to some extent, in Language Poetry during its emergence in the 1970s. In "The Death of the Author" (1968), Roland Barthes identifies a beginning point in France of the critical will to remove the privilege accorded to authorial intention:

> Mallarmé was doubtless the first to see and to foresee in its full extent the necessity to substitute language itself for the person who until then had been supposed to be its owner. For him, for us, too, it is language which speaks, not the author; to write is . . . to reach that point where only language acts, "performs," and not "me." Mallarmé's entire poetics consists in suppressing the author in the interests of writing (which is . . . to restore the place of the reader). (*Image, Music, Text* 143)

Barthes's pronouncement of "the death of the author" seems to suggest that we can and should disregard authorial intention altogether. Michel Foucault's "What Is an Author?", published a year after Barthes's essay, challenges the belief in "the author" as "an indefinable source of significations which fill a work" and "a certain functional principle by which, in our culture, one limits, excludes, and chooses," impeding "the free circulation, the free manipulation, the free composition, decomposition, and recomposition of fiction" (119). Studying the "author function" (108), Foucault articulates the "matter of depriving the subject (or its substitute) of its role as originator, and of analyzing the subject as a variable and complex function of discourse" (118). Discursive formations precede, influence, and often determine (hence, *originate*) decisions that an author makes in composing a text. Therefore, reliance on authorial intention as a primary or exclusive source for contextualization of a text would be extremely limiting and inadequate. But it is important to note that Foucault does not wish to "suppress the author" altogether; "recomposition" of the text may still include a consideration of the one who is not an "originator" but plays a part in the circulation of discourse.

If Barthes is right that "it is language which speaks, not the author," then why does "language" need an authorial ventriloquist "to reach that point" where it can "perform" alone? Is textuality really a solo act, or do the author, language, and the reader all speak? In "This Poem," Beckett's third-person narrator's repeated use of personification provides a context for the imagining of this solo act, whereas the (extra-textual?) fact of his *intention* to utilize these devices seems to undermine it. Here are the poem's first ten strophes:

This poem
Proffers
Its ass.

This poem
Penetrates me.

This poem
Is blue.

This poem
Is colored
Outside
Its lines.

This poem
Is parenthetical.

This poem
Is embedded
Within______.

This Poem
Operates among
Focal points.

This poem
Eschews
The copula.

This poem
Is fucked.

This poem
Sucks. (7-8)

A reading of the opening strophe that takes the noun "poem" literally indicates that language on a page, as opposed to at a public reading, exists without the presence of its author. However, within the context of language's "action," the existence of an audience is included. The ambiguity of the noun "ass"—its potential inclusion within at least three contexts—prevents or at best defers confidence in an envisionment of the opening strophes. There are multiple possibilities of reference derived from "common" linguistic "experience" at the time of the poem's writing. Exposure of the poem's "ass" could be an offer of sexual/textual fulfillment (making it an object of desire for the reader, a means of sublimating desire for another human being, or an experience apart from any requirement to engage with authorial intentions). It could be an indication of written language's vulnerability to the endless contexts of readers' differing interpretations, an indifference to audience comprehension, or a disdain for audience incomprehension. The alternative contextualization of "poem" as a figure that identifies the poet as ventriloquist allows the sexual/textual come-on, the admission of vulnerability to readers, or the humiliation of the audience to stem from the poet through the mediation of the text.

In the second strophe, one can detect a shift from the poem as agent of either its own activity or passivity to a purveyor of activity influencing someone outside itself. However the use of the pronoun "me" engenders a doubling of contexts based on different conventions for identifying a first-person reference in a literary text. The "me" can refer to the author *or* the "character" who, in all but two strophes, is the third-person narrator, and, in each case, the text—most sensibly, a metonymy for psychological content interpreted from the words—is said to exert an emotional influence on him/her or perhaps even to "nail down" a sense of the "essence" of that person. Here, a framing of poet as ventriloquist suggests a process of de- and re-contextualization: the writer uses words to intend particular representations, and then becomes the reader of his own text and thus comes to be influenced emotionally by psychological content or acute self-awareness that may or may not have been available to him in the process of writing; alternatively, the writer stages how a third-person narrator is influenced (or even "read") by the object of his/her narration.

The implication of emotion within the context of textual agency in the second strophe triggers an association with emotion linked to color ("blue") in the third, as though a poem can have feelings rather than evoke feelings in others (of course, a poem can literally be written or typed or typeset in blue ink, and "blue" can have other connotations). The next four strophes, the first of which continues the association with color, involve context *as* context or, if you will, meta-context, and three of the four substitute a frame of passivity for that of activity in the poem's opening two sentences. The text's language does not speak, but when "colored" (interpreted) "outside/ Its" formal arrangement ("lines"), unidentified interpreters—the reader? the writer?—"speak" it. "This poem/ Is embedded/ Within _____" points to the Derridean notion of the endless proliferation of contexts, while its parenthetical aspect can refer to its being within a frame or its framing of something considered to be inside it. "Focal points" as loci of operation imply that the text has a multiplicity of contexts that cannot be framed through reference to a center or a simple notion of unity. The eighth strophe, whose statement about "eschew[ing] the copula" is proven (literally) inaccurate because of the fact that the verb "is" had already occurred twice by itself and twice as the auxiliary for a passive construction, suggests a rejection of metaphorical equivalences or centralizing correspondences that would shore up a central perspective or a fixed identity and, hence, an overall governing context.

Mention of "the copula" is followed by a reminder of copulation and another use of "is" in a passive verb. Returning to the kind of frank sexual imagery in the poem's first two sentences, the ninth and tenth strophes feature a collision of contexts of activity/passivity and externally based evaluation of the text's aesthetic quality. In the ninth, "this poem" is either violated or "satisfied" by interpretation or it is denigrated beyond hope of evaluative redemption, and in the tenth, it either gives sensual pleasure through linguistic action, feeds off its environment, or is deemed a poor aesthetic product. Not only are the judges, their qualifications, and criteria for castigation *not* identified, but ambiguity does not allow the context of judgment to wield authority over other possibilities.

Roughly three pages later, another form of meta-context emerges, only to be reframed:

This poem
Stares into
A mirror.

This poem
Plays
With itself.

This poem
Is the body
In question.

This poem
Works
The room.

This poem
Is an
Empty
Container.

This poem's
Raptures rupture
A repertoire.

This poem's
Reversals are
Rehearsals for
A dance. (11-12)

Many references to mirrors and mirroring could be cited as "common experience" contributing to an "envisionment" or context for the first strophe above. Thinking, for example, of Jacques Lacan's much-bruited 1936 and 1949 papers on "the Mirror Stage," the second of which speaks of "the transformation that takes place in the" infant "subject when he assumes an image" (76), one can imagine the personification of Beckett's sentence as a reversal of the process whereby an influential interpretation ("mirror") of a poem freezes the public reception of that text into a (verbal) image; if the poem itself is said to happen upon the mirror-image that "arrests" it, then the agency of the author is bypassed. A second way of aligning this passage with "the Mirror Stage" is to suggest that the poem incorporates particular language from the culture (outside) and brings it *inside* its "room" to constitute its identity.

Another possible reference in Beckett's mirror-sentence could be to John Ashbery's long poem, "Self-Portrait in a Convex Mirror." Stephen Paul Miller writes that Ashbery's poem "repeatedly returns to the basic issue that the painting" by the Mannerist Parmigianino "poses—one's existence in the context of a convex mirror that modifies one's existence" (*Seventies Now* 144). According to Miller, "we look into a mirror because we are unsure of what we are and therefore do not know what to expect." Again, if we can set aside the fact that a poet selects words, a poem like Beckett's does not proceed from a pre-established center of identity but puts into play language about its own process of construction and representation to explore what it might be and do; making itself "the body in question," a "body" questioning itself, it is receptive to modifications in the framing of its identity.

The idea that "this poem" is playing "with itself" can be interpreted as repeating the drowning of vain Narcissus in his "mirror." However, if the context of self-referentiality or what Miller calls "self-surveillance" is invoked, it can be said that language's play with its own signifying and sound-based resources embodies a testing of capacities that include openness to and representation of what is outside. And so, like comedians trying out contexts of possible rapport with an audience, a text "works/ The room." If a text "Plays/ With itself," the text does not constitute itself as a single entity but establishes a division of inside/outside. "The positing of a self as a site for this play, if only as a site which eventually may be undermined," Miller writes of Ashbery's "Self-Portrait," "is necessary to facilitate this play of difference" (159-60). The doubling effect of the poem/mirror, poem/itself, and poem/room is at odds with the notion of the text as "an/ Empty/ Container," since language in the latter strophe is no longer represented as doing something but as a receptacle to be filled—at a later point—by external agents. This emptying of the frame either grants all power to the interpreters, allowing their "envisionments" to be as "idiosyncratic" as they want, or it indicates that all contextualization performed on a text to make it readable is an illusion that obscures an absence of meaning, a fundamental severing of signifiers from signifieds. In other words, the sentence does not tell us whether the "container" is temporarily or permanently "empty."

Rather than dwelling on emptiness or stasis, the last two strophes in the passage above entertain contexts involving movement. Whereas the penultimate sentence, featuring alliteration and a slant-homonym, accounts for disjunction as a consequence of intense pleasure—including the delight of sound effects—the last one, also including a slant-homonym, figures continual "reversals" of perspective in the poem as a preparation for some later aesthetic play of differences. But who are the dancers? If author and readers are involved, and this is not merely a deferred dance of the differing elements in the poem's language, the text neither specifies nor denies the possibility.

The concluding four strophes of "This Poem" build toward what *may* be an undoing of the premise, articulated by Barthes, of the drive to refuse the author much of a say:

> This poem
> Multiplies.
>
> This poem
> Subdivides.
>
> This poem
> Posits
> A rhetorical
> Stance.
>
> This poem
> Pretends not
> To know me. (13)

The "multiplication" attributed to "this poem" returns to the proliferation of contexts, while "subdivision" indicates heterogeneous aspects within a formal totality or the posited "rhetorical/ Stance" described in the last strophe. The irony of the poem's final personification—if we take the "me" as Beckett and not just the third-person narrator—is that language can neither "know" the one who has chosen it for a poem nor can it fake ignorance. The poet constructs a narrative situation in which the text seems to operate by itself, with no mention of an author, and finally, he exposes that situation as duplicitous. (As Charles Bernstein puts it in the essay I cited earlier, "[t]he theory death of the author seems to apply to other people's authors" [*My Way* 45].) Beckett’s strategy serves to test Barthes’s concept and to locate the extent to which it possesses and lacks explanatory power. Given the implication at the end that the poet has something to do with the shaping of what the poem “posits,” even if interpretation “multiplies” well beyond the writer’s intentions, a reader would be justified in adding the poet’s influence while recontextualizing a sizeable number of “This Poem”’s sentences. For example, could the poem posit “A rhetorical/ Stance” if the poet did not consciously or unconsciously assemble the words to make such a context legible? The author comes back from playing dead but does not return to the sovereign position that Barthes and Foucault critique. While the pronoun “me” is used twice in Beckett’s poem, “you” appears only once—“This poem/ Wants to/ Get to/ Know you” (9), and yet one may frequently draw implications of a reader’s power.

Sheila E. Murphy is a poet whose work is less discursive and involves more phrase-by-phrase or sentence-by-sentence disjunction than Tom Beckett’s work. In a review of Murphy’s work, Jen Tynes states:

> the language of [Murphy’s] voice scatters into different categories: the language of the everyday; the language of lyric intimacy; the language that seems descended from a larger and/or higher voice or choir; the language that ascends from newspapers, eavesdropped conversations and streets; the language that resembles the detritus an owl leaves behind, the little bits of bone and fur coat that are indigestible but full of presence and information, shells both impenetrable and empty. Murphy allows us both the pleasure of their cleaving together and the pleasure of their cleaving apart.

The multiplicity of Tynes’s catalogue of voice categories is equally relevant to the flux of subject matter in Murphy’s writing, but one might take the statement on the back cover of Murphy’s 2010 book-length poem, *Toccatas in the Key of D,* as an invitation to concentrate exclusively on its music: “Each of these 72 numbered poems is a toccata, literally *touch piece*. Syllables become strings on an instrument that sings conceptual music alive within a vivid and timeless present tense.” Jessica Lewis Luck’s contribution to this volume, “The Musical Phenomenology of Lisa Jarnot,” demonstrates how criticism could elucidate this “conceptual music” in Murphy’s work, but I choose to perform a reading that is more attuned to the possibilities of what Tynes calls “presence and information.”

Surely, no two sections of these *Toccatas* contain the same trajectory of topoi, and an attempt to analyze the whole closely would probably prove too great a strain on critics’ and their readers’ desire for a semblance of parsimony. Therefore, I will examine a single section, Poem 21, the first three words of which offer the promise of a stable context:

> This is home, with fish oil, sanctity, replacement
> Therapy. Abrupt encyclical disjunction.
> Thirty years to life.
> An episode connotes the space in privilege.
> Pawns trill evidence of upper registers
> Gone wrong. With nothing changed. (21)

"Home" is a context that often refers to the demarcation (and protection) of the inside (self) from the potentially dangerous outside, but the three objects of the preposition following the opening declaration indicate that "home" has a "subdivision": physical/spiritual (or psychological). In the case of "fish oil," this useful item to have in one's refrigerator or vitamin cabinet may come from outside the home, but its function is to protect the body against disease. As for "sanctity"—as abstract as fish oil is concrete—the dweller's spiritual feelings can be perceived either as an ultimate interiority (being "at home" with the divine) or something transmitted by an external religious institution that animates the hearth. "Replacement/ Therapy" most obviously refers to the physical section of the divide: a "hip," "knee," other "joint," or "hormone" may have been replaced, and rehabilitative exercises occur at home. However, couldn't this refer to efforts to recover from a psychological upheaval? Couldn't it involve the substitution of a new significant other, pet, or hobby for a departed parent, pet, or life-partner? Then again, "home" could refer not only to a literal dwelling place and psychological security but also to language (or even the pronominal adjective "this") that serves as a "home" for what the poet does—namely, point to things and ideas or point to the process itself. Language (naming) may be a capsule promoting mental health, an attempt to characterize unrepresentable spirituality, and a "replacement" for the absent signified.

If one is reading closely, a proliferation of possible contexts—physical, spiritual, and psychological—threatens even a moderate application of the Parsimony Principle as a neat ordering of inside/outside just as this section of an already unwieldy poem has gotten under way. In the fragment that follows, "encyclical disjunction," in which a noun is strangely used as an adjective, further complicates the matter of competing contexts in the opening sentence through adding features to the spiritual context of "home." An "encyclical" is a circular letter, generally entering the home from the external institution of the papacy and intended, like an encyclopedia, its etymological relative, to be an integrative force, but Murphy's phrase suggests its creation of a "disjunction"—perhaps between the doctrine or dogma propounded and one's personal sense of "sanctity" or how to be "at home" with oneself. Considering the proximity of this fragment to the one following it, which fits the common context of prison-sentencing—a dwelling-place or "inside" that offers the opposite of the security, stability, and sense of well being that a home is supposed to provide—the believer could feel sentenced by papal command to adopt thoughts and behaviors that seem irksome or else feel compelled to reject actions that would otherwise be desirable. But must the adjective "encyclical" refer to the context of a religious institution? A decree of separation or a "sentence" of banishment could come from an affectively authoritative lover, thus occasioning "replacement/ Therapy" in the home to compensate for a sentence of sorrow. Murphy's speaker generalizes about what "an episode connotes"—the "privileging" of a particular "space," the setting of a contained story or drama—but this meta-statement does not help determine a context that would identify the presentation of a particular kind of "home" or a dismantling of home.

In the fifth line, tropes of music, the "motif" directly linked to the long poem's title, contribute to the saturation of contexts. "[P]awns," or lowly chess pieces and/or human victims of more powerful people, institutions, and social dynamics, provide "evidence" of problems in the area of musical production (or domestic management) that may be most challenging. Given this cryptic information, the idea of continuity in the isolated clause that follows seems puzzling: how can "disjunction" not change the characteristics of "home"? If one does not read "nothing changed" as a cliché for the status quo but (as the word is commonly glossed in *King Lear*) perceives "nothing" as an entity that *is* changed, then the "nothing" or void that used to have the potential to trouble home's security is now another emptiness indicating what has "gone wrong." Murphy follows the "nothing" with two more negations as a tonal bridge between the first and second halves of the text: "No partial print. No first/ Coat of paint. Barometer/ Of written pressure and precise" (21). Musical "registers" a few lines earlier have given way to other forms of measurement: "print," what is "written" and in terms of criminology, identifiable, and even the numerical "writing" of a "barometer." Lacking even a layer of "paint," the home's and hence the individual's walls are especially vulnerable to assault. The overlapping of musical, visual, and scriptive contexts do not coalesce into a master image or context, but they heighten a sense of anxiety. Is psychological or physical "pressure" recorded by the harshly "precise" instrument? Is the "this-ness" of home in general or just the impact of a single episode "being" measured? Poem 21's last six lines create further complication:

> The tangled ossified new bloat of ice
> On different days. Some practical lamps
> Whose glare goes watched over
> The night's linoleum, made responsible
> For what is loathe to shelving Pavarotti
> High into the rippling trees. (21)

Although a piece of "ice" often floats on water like a boat, Murphy's implied rhyming substitution makes it "bloat" like an iceberg. To call ice "ossified"—not so similar to "bloat(ed)"—is to venture a fresh comparison of fossilization and the freezing of water, but the preceding adjective "tangled," like "bloat," has disrupted the association in advance. If ice is thin and bent, how can it not break or liquefy at once? The sentence may refer to an excess of emotional frigidity—one that is either "on . . . days" that are "different" in character from one another or simply on separate days—that stems from a rigidity of thinking or a "tangle" of psychological issues that cannot be combed into a parsimonious explanation. But we do not know who or what is creating or enduring the chill. If we choose to contextualize the text as a fragmented narrative, the actors are not necessarily human beings, but rather they are the abstract and concrete nouns that Murphy has placed in the subject and object positions throughout the poem to stand in obliquely for people who experience inner or interpersonal turmoil.

The complex tangle of clauses and phrases that ends Poem 21 could be a fragment or a complete sentence, and if language itself is "home," then indeterminacy of syntax makes home difficult to conceive within a single context. Even if I read "watched" as the main (past tense) verb and thus argue for completeness, more questions follow: What is "made responsible": "lamps," "glare," or "linoleum"? Does the lamps' "glare" depart ("goes") and if it "goes," does it proceed while being "watched over"? Why is the gerund form "shelving" used instead of "shelve"? Is Pavarotti being "shelved" (put on a shelf inside or "thrown" outside "shelving") or is he not shelved at all, since someone "is loathe" to do it? Does "shelving" lack an object? Is the last line bizarrely linked to Pavarotti or to earlier antecedents? Such questions can only be resolved through arbitrary decisions. Perhaps emblematic of the possibilities of (psychological) perception and foundation respectively, "lamps" and "linoleum" are objects *inside* a domestic context and "rippling trees" are *outside* the house but still, perhaps, inside the property that can be interpreted as the boundary of "home," while Pavarotti's singing, released from the "container" of a CD, does not seem to be confined to or kept out of the inside. Since grammar and syntax engineer so much decontextualization here, I can point to no contextual evidence about whether Pavarotti "ripples" as a trope of liberation from "encyclical disjunction" or whatever has "gone" glaringly "wrong" in a domestic situation, a symptom of the problems. There is no frame to organize this heterogeneity.

The fashioning and identification of "home" as interiority depends on the importation of resources from the outside and on the ability of those elements to lose their exteriority and "cooperate" in the development of a demarcation between inside and outside. Murphy's poem illustrates how this idealizing process is doomed practically from the start; decontextualizing/recontextualizing movements of "homing" and "un-homing" continually shift inside elements to outside ones and outside to inside. The temporal struggle to trace a succession of contexts for the poem foregrounds provisional, unpredictable discoveries.

Mei-mei Berssenbrugge's poetry is stylistically different from the work of both Sheila E. Murphy and Tom Beckett, but she shares with these two slightly younger poets an abiding concern with exploring the conditions of representation. In a powerful reading of her 1983 book *Empathy*, Charles Altieri argues that Berssenbrugge practices a "'phenomenological materialism'" (63) that aims to help readers experience language's facilitation of their ability "to connect to a world beyond the ego" (55), where empathy and intimacy can be released. According to Altieri, Berssenbrugge's poetry of "conjecture" entails "an ongoing process of constant mobile adjustments content with a series of imaginative leaps" (59). Here, "temporality modifies, extends, and complicates our experiences of intimacy," as "spatial and temporal access to other persons is best achieved if we can imagine ourselves as cubist painters bringing multiple overlapping perspectives together as a kind of parallax view projecting beyond what can only be dimly realized in specific images" (61).

In the 2006 poem "Concordance," I believe that Berssenbrugge takes as her beginning context something adjacent but not identical to the contexts of intimacy and empathy; she considers the mapping of relationships between communicating entities. Typical of Berssenbrugge's work of the last quarter century or so, "Concordance" is divided into three sections of what might either be called monostichs (though the long sentence can spill over to a second or even third line), single-sentence strophes that consist of between one and three lines, or prose paragraphs that contain one sentence each. I think of this work as lineated poetry, but it could just as easily be considered prose-poetry. The first section begins:

> Writing encounters one who does not write and I don't try for him, but face-to-face draw you onto a line or flight like a break that may be extended, the way milkweed filling space above the field is "like" reading.
>
> Then, it's possible to undo misunderstanding from inside by tracing the flight or thread of empty space running through things, even a relation that's concordant.
>
> Seeds disperse in summer air. (133)

Like John Ashbery, Berssenbrugge utilizes most of the pronouns in the rainbow; here, there are three in a single long sentence. If the notion of "writing" as "encounter" with an "other" is not an effort to "win" a reader, then the writer's effort at communication entails the "drawing" of a "you" (a direct addressee, not the previous third-person "him") into the trajectory of the text, which itself is meant to map a process of relation. Even if there is an inherent discontinuity ("break") between what the writer transmits and the reader receives and tries to decode, words can "extend" the respite ("break") from the problem of that separation of experiences. In the delicate simile of "milkweed filling" a visual "field," the poet compares the writing of a substance on a "page," a dispersal of a plenitude occurring in time, to reading as an act of interpretation, not mere reception. The optimistic idea that the casting of a "line" or "tracing" of what runs "through things" can "undo misunderstanding" seems to be founded on the common "thread of empty space"—the nothing around which all transient material circles and which makes everyone mortal "concordant." The context of communication is further complicated by problems of mediation among writer, text, and reader:

> Sunrays cease to represent parallel passages in a book, i.e., not coming from what I see and feel.
>
> Relation in the middle, relay, flower description *to* flower becoming of my eye between light and heart.
>
> Now, information has released imaginative function from authors.

> I send an interrupted line over the top of space, past the middle cinematically, when you can no longer stand what you put up with before.
>
> At night, part of her numbed to pain and part woke to what occurred.
>
> Working backward in sleep, the last thing you numbed to is what wakes you. (133)

Much that is "not coming from what" the writer can "see and feel" may interfere with transmission and reception of her communication, which depends on a "relation in the middle" or "relay" that is not assured in advance. For both the writer and a reader who is turning the words into images, any single "flower description" obviously depends on how "eye" encounters "flower," including the framing effects of "light," at that time, as well as how shifting emotions affect the viewer. Conventions of linguistic representation are also part of the "relation," and authors' "imaginative function" does not stem from a unique, mystical stroke of genius but from varieties of "information" that the human, natural, and (of course) verbal environment presents. The writer cannot control either her own or the reader's subtle experiential transformations—for example, rejecting what was once acceptable and being "numbed to pain" and suddenly reaching awareness or "waking." Enduring the interruption of her "lines," affective and perceptual disjunctions, the speaker persists at efforts to communicate; she keeps sending lines. The first section concludes with a sense of the fragility of the "concordance" of "feeling" and "knowing" for the two principals (whom I call poet and reader):

> What if that image were Eros as words?
>
> I write to you and you feel me.
>
> What would it be like if you contemplated my words and I felt you?
>
> Animals, an owl, frog, open their eyes, and a mirror forms on the ground.
>
> When insight comes in a dream, and events the next day illuminate it, this begins your *streaming* consciousness, synchronicity, asymptotic lines of the flights of concordances.

> An owl opens its eyes in deep woods.
>
> For the first time, I write and you don't know me.
>
> Milkweed I touch floats. (134)

Berssenbrugge's speaker wants the "miracle" of mutual understanding that writing and reading in the absence of the other "should" provide, as well as mystical communion with animals and dreams that guide later experience. Knowing that the "milkweed" of a sense of contact can "float" away any time, the poet suggests through the juxtaposition of sentences that the context of communication should be considered within or beside various other frames: the desire for unity with a human other, an animal other, and with all sentient and insentient beings, the desire to anticipate an overall narrative of one's life as a progression, and fear of the failure of such desires to be actualized. The second section of "Concordance" elaborates on these contexts and also further explores how frames of perception (as exemplified by tropes of light) impinge upon communication. The felicitous perception of "sunrise frequencies emanat[ing] from your body like music" in the fourth sentence seems to push against the anxiety emanating from the previous three, including "One can experience another's energy as stress" (134). Sentences in this part of the poem vacillate between the possibilities for communicative approach, a detachment designed either to protect the self or prepare for contact, and a fear of communication's negative consequences:

> Attention gives light: shine on a baby's calf; as he hears what I say, I become that.
>
> Look at my body as light reflecting the thought and feeling, it's not safe to be here.
>
> Remove anxiousness over persons you yearn for, stepping back to observe, like an animal in the fourth dimension. (135)

If the "calf" is comparable to a reader and the speaker to a writer, we can surmise that the poet here represents the reader's conflation of the writer with the text; some writers might regard this reception as evidence of "perfect" communication, whereas others may consider it an illusion that is "not safe."

The contextual flux in the first seven sentences of the third section brings into relation the being/productive power of language, the influence of desire on belief, and a sense of trans-species concordance and discord:

> My words unroll a plane of consistence they do not pre-exist—particles, fluxes, the color of spring.
>
> Desire individuates through affects and powers I place on a page or plane of light vibrations, like a flowering field.
>
> His autonomic response is to constrict breath against the feminine, magnetism of gems, consciousness emanating from stars symbiotic with individuation.
>
> When I hear ants are telepathic, I hear tiny words trying to communicate.
>
> Then, they file across my clock, it's time to go.
>
> Life manifests everywhere in the cosmos, but as we eliminate species here, we lose access to other realms.
>
> So, discovering a new species is a great event. (135-6)

Words are not the only entities doing important "unrolling." Although language (textuality as an available reservoir) precedes the act of perception and composition, the specific combination of signifiers that the writer uses does not exist before the "plane of consistence," a set of organizing principles that makes the worldly signifieds perceivable and hence able to be represented. Before the words "unroll," an experience for the reader and the re-collecting writer, "particles" and "fluxes" separately supply sensory impressions for the two perceivers. But the writer is also influenced in her compositional "placements" by the "individuating" force of her own "desire," which affects her reception of sensory data. If she wants to confirm a belief not only in "life" but in communication that "manifests everywhere in the cosmos," the burgeoning array of those who are "writing to" and "reading" each other, including "new species," she is encouraged when hearing strange ideas like the one about ants' "telepathy." The charming image of the "tiny words" is a product of imagination fueled in part by desire. Similarly, the reader's desire and fear can push his or her interpretation of the text in particular directions. The male reader may unconsciously fear "the feminine" in a text or a woman he encounters and thus "constrict breath against" it rather than open himself to the generative potential of this otherness. Contrary desires for "numinous" "connection" and self-protection against external danger, equally important for writers and readers, animate the closing sentences of "Concordance":

> Numinousness in the psyche emerges as from morphic fields, our wish for the animal tuning to its light or waveform, like the light of sex.
>
> When you doubt this, you place a piece of "someone" on a pedestal to examine, a gap.
>
> Breathe the shard back into yourself.
>
> In your memory, scarlet feathers of a beloved macaw begin a glow arising from the exact color of connection.
>
> Warmth, which was parallel, moves across the shard, smoothes and makes it porous, matter breath, light materializing ants and words. (136)

As Berssenbrugge ties "numinousness in the [human] psyche" to the desire for an experience of attunement or illumination (related to "the animal") and ties aesthetic distancing to fear of such intense intimacy, she gently commands her audience to transcend "doubt" and separation from otherness through incorporation of the feared "shard" or "gap." Writer ("I") addresses reader ("you," which can include "me," or a conversation with the self) to enable a presumed "memory" of the possibility of "connection" based on animal presence and vivid color to reassure the audience that such contact is the best path to take. The miracle of ant speech somehow "materializes" as rhetorical proof of the triumph of widespread "connection" and communication over doubt. Those who read the end of a poem as evidence of closure's authority might locate a chain of influence: the power of mystical, "universal" experience has taken hold of the writer, who has then found language to lead the reader to surrender to this epiphanic state. However, I believe that the complexities of relations among a writer's intentions and perceptual contexts, the natural environment, language, and reader's desires and perceptual contexts in "Concordance" as a whole are not "solved" or resolved. This point is not a privileged one but an ending—at which particular desires are being articulated—that could be otherwise.

In "Concordance," the Proliferation Principle frequently threatens to overwhelm the will to parsimony as much as it does in Murphy's *Toccatas* even if the former, like Beckett's "This Poem," includes longer stretches of the discursive. The reading I have just completed has honored the practical need for interpretive thrift in a critical text like this, not only by not reading every part of the poem equally closely, but by following some contextual possibilities and ignoring others, even as I try to indicate proliferating processes that defy rigid applications of parsimony. Implying a similar balancing act, Altieri asserts that we can read Berssenbrugge's "kind of poetry" if we "make frequent leaps of faith enabling us to stay in touch with a mobility of mind always on the verge of dissipating into pure contingency," and then manage to "find [our] way around within a field of loosely related but evocative tiltings of the sense-making process" and become engaged "in processes of attuning which align us with others without providing pictures of either the object known or the knower's confidence"; the "reward," he suggests, is "a feeling for how emotional connection can be maintained through fluidly shifting perspectives" (67-8). Thus, for Altieri, the poet *can communicate* through her linguistic "line or flight," but in ways that differ tremendously from ordinary, "transparent" communication. And perhaps she can *reinvent* what it might mean to communicate by not explaining away or reifying what is unclear, indeterminate, and not exactly communicable.

To produce a partial map of the proliferation of "pure contingency," Derrida's boundlessness of context, in one's encounter with "difficult" poetry would demonstrate the impossibility of reading accurately or truthfully. I have tried to indicate that forms of interpretation that situate themselves between an acknowledgment of such boundlessness and an imposition of a single overarching context (in strict adherence to the "ideals" of the Parsimony Principle) can permit the poems to serve as sites of discovery about "the sense-making process" and not as fodder for foregone conclusions.

Notes

1. In "Migratory Meaning," Silliman calls for a thorough theorization and cataloging of poetic devices (120) so that an alternative "envisionment" can be achieved. This is not my task here, but it would be interesting to see someone rise to Silliman's challenge.

2. Fish contends in *Is There a Text in This Class?* that an "interpretive community" governs the perspectives of individual readers; inherited strategies constitute "a way of thinking" that "shares" its members "and implicates [them] in a world of already-in-place objects, purposes, goals, procedures, values, and so on" (303-4).

3. See Jacques Derrida, *Positions*, 41-43.

Some Notes on bpNichol, (Captain) Poetry, and Comics

Paolo Javier

1. In 2006, the Canadian cartoonist Seth (né Gregory Gallant) offers the following provocation to Marc Ngui in the spring issue of *Carousel*: "I have felt, for some time, a connection between comics and poetry. It's an obvious connection to anyone who has ever sat down and tried to write a comic strip" (17). Apparently, "the idea first occurred to [Seth] . . . in the late '80s when [he] was studying Charles Schulz's *Peanuts* strips" and found his "four-panel setup . . . just like reading a haiku; it had a specific rhythm to how he set up the panels and the dialogue. Three beats: doot doot doot—followed by an infinitesimal pause, and then the final beat: doot." There is a "sameness of rhythm" between haikus and the strips, while "the haikus mostly [end] with a nature reference separated off in the final line."

Here, we see a contemporary cartoonist indirectly challenge the rebranding of the comic book as a "graphic novel," first coined by Will Eisner in 1978, then later adapted by a publishing industry with declining book sales seeking to attract new readers.

2. At the 2009 Museum of Comic and Cartoon Art Festival in New York City, I attended Seth's panel with fellow *Drawn & Quarterly* author Adrian Tomine. Well-groomed and shiny in a tailored suit, the bespectacled cartoonist repeated similar sentiments to Tomine from his *Carousel* interview years before:

> As time passed I began to see this connection as more and more evident in how I went about writing my own work. Certainly, it is not a process that is very tightly worked out—but when I am writing a comics page (or sequence of pages) I am very aware of the sound and "feel" of how the dialogue or narration is broken down for the panels. If you have to tell a certain amount of story in a page then you have to make decisions on how many panels you need to tell it. (19)

Seth's decisions, which "affect how the viewer reads the strip," involve the arrangement of "these panels—small, big or a combination of the two"—the way of "[sitting] them on the page." The reader experiences "an inherent rhythm created by how" the cartoonist sets "up the panels. Thin panel, thin panel, long panel." He adds: "I am very aware of how I am structuring the sentences: how many words; one sentence in this panel; two in this one; a silent panel; a single word. These choices are ultra-important in the creation of comics storytelling, and this unheard rhythm is the main concern for me when I am working out a strip" (*Carousel* 19). Seth compares his deliberations to "how poets who write in 'free verse' decide how to break the thoughts apart and structure them, often in a way that defies a system."

This drew the ire of the audience, clearly made up of readers who privilege comics for their storytelling value. In the Gary Panter spotlight that followed Tomine and Seth's talk, moderator Frank Santoro went so far as to mock the Canadian cartoonist by exaggerating the pronunciation of the word "poetry" in a faux British accent, replete with an effeminate wave of the hand, much to the delight and applause of the mostly heterosexual fanboys packing the room.

For a poet like myself, who has been experimenting with comics the past decade in collaboration with visual artists, hearing a celebrated cartoonist speak to this simpatico between our two disciplines was much-needed encouragement and relief.

3. Seth does not appreciate how "'words & pictures' that make up the comics language are often described as prose and illustration combined"; he sees "poetry and graphic design" as a more apt characterization: "Poetry for the rhythm and condensing; graphic design because cartooning is more about moving shapes around—designing—than it is about drawing" (*Carousel* 22).

Of course, experimental poets and poet-artists have known about and explored this relationship since the advent of the modern cartoon, often to virtuosic effect. In *obb aka The Original Brown Boy*, my experimental comic that is ongoing since 2005, I engage a long poem about a catfish and an octopus moving through New York at the end of the millennium via drawing, illustration, collage, and painting—cues that I shamelessly take from the hybrid comics, collages, and collaborations of the Dadaists, Surrealists, Jess Collins, Joe Brainard, Frank O'Hara, Kenneth Koch, and Ted Berrigan.

Poets' interest in comics continues into the present; it blossomed in a respected anthology, Gary Sullivan's *Chain 8: Comics*; and it is evident in small-press chapbooks such as Sommer Browning's *I Wonder If Balzac Had a Good Pianist* and Jai Arun Ravine's *The Spider Boi Files* as well as in full-length collections such as Donato Mancini's *Ligatures*, Sonja Ahlers's *The Selves*, Monica Youn's *Ignatz*, and my own *The Feeling Is Actual.*

4. Following Seth's ideas here, one might also consider the work of underground or independent comics creators whose orchestrations are attuned more to the rhythms of the poem. Seichi Hayashi (*Red-Colored Elegy*), Terry Moore (*Strangers in Paradise*), Dino Buzzati (*Poem Strip*), Craig Thompson (*Goodbye, Chunk Rice*), Jillian Tamaki (*Skim*), Matt Madden (*99 Ways to Tell A Story: Exercises in Style*), John Porcellino (*Thoreau at Walden*), and the serial drawings of Raymond Pettibone come to mind. But Korean American Richard Hahn's Xeric grant winner *Lumakick* wears poetry's influence proudest. Discussing the first volume, Gary Sullivan notes that Hahn displays his awareness "of a general prejudice against sentiment"; his "protagonist . . . opens a book by T. S. Eliot and reads the lines, 'Amateur poets imitate; great poets steal,'" then "literally steals a book by Wallace Stevens" from the library, and, safely at home, "is nonplussed to discover Stevens's statement: 'Sentimentality is a failure of feeling.' After a single-panel reaction shot from the protagonist, the comic abruptly ends" ("The Poetics of Comics").

Hahn embraces language slippage like a seasoned New York School poet; when he visited my course on comics in the fall of 2010, he revealed to us that the title of his comic book derives from a mishearing of the word "lunatic" by Popeye in the E. C. Segar syndicated strip. So it wasn't surprising to learn that while an undergraduate at Columbia University, he took a poetry class with Kenneth Koch, who also introduced him to Brainard's *I Remember*, a miracle of a book that avoids sentimentality in spite of its title.

5. But poetry isn't on the radar of underground or indie creators exclusively, as mainstream giants like Neil Gaiman (*Sandman*), Mike Mignola (*Hellboy*), Todd MacFarlane (*Spawn*), Alan Moore (*Swamp Thing*, *Promethea*), and Grant Morrison (*Doom Patrol*, *Arkham Asylum*, *The Invisibles*) demonstrate in their occult-themed books that are overtly lyrical in the telling. They revel in poetic allusion and de-center their narrators; they experiment with negative space and interrupt straightforward action-to-action panel sequences with non sequitur transitions, thereby inviting greater closure from the reader. (Moore, it should be noted, once ran his own publishing imprint called Mad Love, after André Breton's key surrealist text, *L'Amour Fou*.) The visual design of their comics teems with pagan and religious symbols that look and read like illuminated versions of William Butler Yeats and Alistair Crowley's magick diaries.

6. Grant Morrison became a superstar as a result of his work writing for the D.C./Vertigo books *Doom Patrol*, *Arkham Asylum*, and *The Invisibles*. These comics were deeply influenced by his abiding interest in the poetry and praxis of the Romantics, Arthur Rimbaud, Dada, Surrealism, Futurism, and the Beats. Reinventing the B-superhero squad and calling them "Doom Patrol" (a team led by a genius in a wheelchair that emerged the same year

as Stan Lee and Jack Kirby's better-known X-Men), Morrison conceptualized the group as "the only superheroes disturbed enough to deal with the kind of menaces to sanity and reality that not even Superman could hope to confront" (Morrison, *Supergods* 221). Adapting techniques by his favorite avant-garde poets to his process, he embraced:

> [S]urrealist writing methods: automatic writing, found ideas, and even my word-processors' spell-check functions to create random word strings with syntax. I'd type in strings of nonsense words, which the computer would dutifully connect to the nearest equivalent, giving my dream horrors dialogue exchanges like this: "'DEFEATING BREADFRUIT IN ADUMBRATE.' 'CRASHLAND FOR AWARD PRIMATE'. 'YUCCA OR PRIORITY?' 'LEMUR NEVER HIBERNATE.'" (222)

Morrison's run even features a villainous syndicate called the Brotherhood of Dada and a wild storyline about a painting that eats up the entire city of Paris. You would expect such "surrealist folderol" to doom the prospects of accruing mainstream readership, when, in fact, *Doom Patrol* enjoyed a four-year run of killer sales and a rabid fanbase, which continues to this day.

7. At the time of *Doom Patrol*, Morrison had already developed a following with his 1989 collaboration with British artist Dave McKean on the original Batman tale *Arkham Asylum: A Serious House on Serious Earth*, which sold an improbable 500,000 copies, making it the most successful graphic novel of all time. Most remarkable about this book is its overtly surrealist and occult designs, inspired, of course, by "surrealism, Eastern European creepiness, Cocteau, Artaud, Svankmajer, the Brothers Quay, etc." Morrison "wanted to approach Batman from the point of view of the dreamlike, emotional and irrational hemisphere, as a response to the very literal, 'realistic' 'left brain' treatment of superheroes which was in vogue at the time" (Morrison, *Arkham Asylum*, notes to script).

The book's subtitle is taken from a Philip Larkin poem, but the ghosts of European outsider poets, artists, and writers such as Rimbaud, de Sade, Breton, Jung, Ernst, Cahune, Kahlo, Crowley, and Francis Bacon haunt its conception and design. Morrison invites the readers to engage in the page layout of *Arkham Asylum* with a strategy similar to the poem, so that they are welcome to read it "up and down rather than left to right; McKean's tall, narrow panels evoke church windows, test tubes, the cracks between shuttles, and many other things, and they create a bad fairy-tale sense of confinement and of toppling, falling dominoes set in motion a long time ago" (Morrison, *Supergods* 227).

McKean's illustrations collapse drawing, collage, photography, and painting, and thus fill the pages with symbols that point to ancient and modern occult, pagan, and religious sources. Constantly alluding to literary, artistic, and philosophical characters and authors, *Arkham Asylum* aspires to read like the grandchild of *The Waste Land* and the *Pisan Cantos*. (Not coincidentally, the character of Amadeus Arkham, founder of the infamous asylum for Batman's villains, resembles Ezra Pound).

Morrison would use the royalties from the book years later to fund a trip around the world, where he set out to experience Rimbaud's derangement of the senses through psychotropic drugs that yielded visions and mind-altered states he would later write into his next major work, *The Invisibles*—a seven-volume occult conspiracy thriller featuring an anarchist superhero squad that includes a chaos magician, a transvestite shaman, and a Liverpool street punk destined to become the next bodhisattva.

8. Writing about the King of Comics, Jack Kirby, who co-created the Marvel Universe with Stan Lee, Morrison describes his Fourth World series of crossovers as the magnum opus of a poet-seer: "I can even see beyond the Beats to Ginsberg's solar sunflower muse, William Blake, whose titanic primal figures Orc and Urthona are given new dress as Kirby's Mister Miracle and Mantis. The dark fires of Urizen burn again in the firepits of Darkseid's death planet, Apokolips. In Blake and Kirby both, we see the play of immense revolutionary forces that will not be chained or fettered, the Romantic revolution of the 1800s and the hip sixties" (*Supergods* 125).

But Jack Kirby and Grant Morrison are chiefly narrative comic creators who use poetic methods in the service of story. The creator who interests me is the reverse—the poet who engages the language of comics in the poem. And this leads me to consider the great Canadian poet bpNichol (1944-1988), who produced, in his short life, a remarkable body of poetry and comics that foreground and experiment with the intrinsic similarities between the two language art forms, arguably far more than any other poet and comics writer/artist.

9. bpNichol is *a poet*, first and foremost, and his work presciently holds up a mirror to my own interrogations: "if we are to break free of the TYPE oriented trap then we must break thru into the non-linear languages—here we use language in the broad sense of VESSEL container & carrier of messages both emotional & intellectual—SEMIOTIC POETRY is intriguing but depends on LINEAR keys—the COMIC STRIP offers a FUSION of linear & NON-linear elements" (Nichol, *bpnc* 198).

I only discovered Nichol's extensive body of comics in 2008, when I bought a copy of Carl Peters's *bpNichol Comics*, while browsing the shelves of a Chapters branch in Toronto. So my interest here is an initial consideration of his comics work in light of Seth's ideas, as Nichol may be the one poet in the past century to explore the connections between our art and comics with singular devotion and persistence. I also would like to get to the heart of such an engagement, i.e. why comics?

10. Nichol certainly anticipates Seth's views by several decades. For the poet, writing and drawing comics seem never to serve merely as a distraction or an occasional experiment to interrupt the writing of poetry; too often, it performs as the poem itself. Nichol even writes about the importance of comics in the same sentence that he describes his major long poem, *The Martyrology*, for which he is better known:

> Comics establish their own mythic base. D.C.'s incredibly complex mythology covers over ten centuries, includes multi-dimensional worlds (including the vital concept of Earth 1 & Earth 2) as well as endless galaxies. Leaning heavily over into dreams & science fiction it is a literature of possibilities (Aldiss defines as "speculative fiction") entirely open-ended. (Nichol, *bpNichol Comics* 76)

It's tempting to trace his interest in comics as an extension of his experiments in concrete and sound poetry, wherein a material interest in the printed and spoken word would seem to preface comics' engagement with language in the panels and across the page on a visual-before-semantic basis. But Nichol himself indicates that *The Martyrology* "grew out of a scifi comic strip milieu" (*bpNichol Comics* 81); significantly, he did not cite an avant-garde poet or poetry movement as an influence on its conception in his essay. Given the devotional nature of his long poem, it makes perfect sense that Nichol would draw (pun intended) from the well of a language art that, unlike any other, made his own heart quicken in his youth: "The love of my young life was Nora Nal, Dream Girl, who had limited ability to see into the future thru prophetic dreams. A Bene Geseritt in her own right she is everything Herbert describes in DUNE or Blish in JACK OF EAGLES. So it was (epic opener a la Thor) I established my own mythologic base" (*bpNichol Comics*, 77).

In "My Love Affair with Winsor McKay," the other one of the pair of critical statements on comics that Nichol wrote (dashed off in longhand, no less), the poet clearly privileges comics:

> Before surrealism, before (more importantly) Dada, there was Winsor McKay. DREAMS OF A RAREBIT FIEND, LITTLE NEMO IN SLUMBERLAND, LITTLE SAMMY SNEEZE, showed us thru the impossible corridors of his mind, so that me, coming to it years later, picking up

> my collection of early McKay masterpieces, thot 'here he is, the logical pre-logical discoverer of the language of the dream in art.' (*bp Nichol Comics* 73)

11. *obb aka The Original Brown Boy* emerged from a rekindling of my own love affair with comic books in 2003, the year I resumed collecting monthly pamphlets and trades. Comics were the only books that sustained my attention throughout childhood, but my mom put a ban on collecting soon as I turned thirteen because of her generation's prejudice against its literary value. In 2005, I published my second book of poems but felt creatively spent. Unable to find inspiration from poetry community factions, I threw myself into a serious study of comics, devoting the latter end of 2005 to absorbing Mike Mignola and Osamu Tezuka's oeuvre, in addition to (re)discovering the work of the artists mentioned above in notes 4 and 5 of this chapter. Comics helped restore my sense of wonder and discovery in writing, and shortly after this, my idea for *obb* came to life.

12. Why poetry and comics? It would seem paradoxical to pair the two, given the small press economy of the former versus the massive print industry of the latter. Setting aside such disparities for now, let's consider bpNichol's merging of these language arts as a progression of his interest to "write the way I draw and draw the way I write" (Peters, quoting Nichol documentary, *bp Nichol Comics* 71). Often in his comics, words exist two-dimensionally like figures before a landscape. Simultaneously, in works such as *Scraptures 12*, *Tegnikal Notes*, *Bullsheets*, *Lonely Fred*, *MASQUE and Unmasking of Captain Poetry*, Nichol will illustrate the contours of his figures with the shapeliness of a letter rendered by a calligrapher.

In his introduction to Nichol's essay "Comics as MYTH," Peters cites the poet's assertion about "'the relation between [an] overt use of space on the page and the structure of the poem,'" as something much more crucial than the fact of "'a merely decorative use of letters,'" which "'would scarcely justify a new style of poetry'" (*bp Nichol Comics* 71). Peters considers "this very relation" the element "that is creative." This is reminiscent of Charles Hatfield's lucid assertion that the reader's experience of comics as "radically fragmented and unstable" comprises "their great strength: comic art is composed of several kinds of tension, in which various ways of reading—various interpretive options and potentialities—must be played against each other" (132).

Much of Nichol's comics are non-narrative, where the story truly is in the tension the poet creates between the illustrated nature of the text and the written nature of the image. Hatfield observes how "comics, like other hybrid texts, collapse the word/image dichotomy"; "visible language," he holds, can "be quite elaborate in appearance, forcing recognition of pictorial and material qualities that can be freighted with meaning" (133). But Nichol's comics seem to proceed with the following idea that he recorded in a journal note from 1964, and with which he opens his seventh book of *The Martyrology*:

> To go beyond THE WORD.
> exercise control over it? No
> NO NO—BEYOND THE
> WORD. not to merely control
> it but to overcome it, go be-
> yond the point where it is
> even necessary to think in
> terms of it (Nichol, *Gifts*, ii)

In volume one of his long poem, Nichol writes:

> a future music moves now to be written
> w g r & t
> its form is not apparent
> it will be seen (Nichol, *The Martyrology 1&2*, 2)

With comics, Nichol's poem can "go be-/ yond the point where it is/ even necessary to think in/ terms of." His oeuvre can lay claim to a couple of breakthroughs: Canada's first original underground comic publication in *Scraptures 12*, and avant-garde poetry's first superhero in *The Captain Poetry Poems Complete*.

13. In April 2011, the influential Toronto small press Book Thug reprinted *Captain Poetry Poems Complete* in a new edition that features an afterword by bill bissett, a poet and close friend of Nichol's whose blewointment press issued the original edition in 1971. As the first superhero of poetry comics, *The Captain Poetry Poems Complete* reads with surprising immediacy and relevance. Outwardly, the book is highly reflective of the medium of comics: not only does it feature the same dimensions of the current *Arkham Asylum* or *Doom Patrol* trades, but it also includes illustrations of our superhero on the front and back cover by an artist other than Nichol. Inside, the poems offer a hilarious, touching, and pointed deconstruction of the alpha male superhero. (Bear in mind that this book appears eighteen years before such important metanarrative comics as Alan Moore's *Watchmen*, Grant Morrison's *Animal Man*, and Garth Ennis's *The Boys*. Also, Nichol's primary text is *poetry*.)

Shifting between the voice of the author, the omniscient narrator, ex-lovers, haters, and eyewitnesses, we are introduced to a Captain Poetry who is a romantic: "when did you learn/ Captain Poetry/ that you had placed her too high/ for even you/ to fly" (*Captain Poetry*, unpaginated); to a "rye-bald" chauvinist pig: "now slaps her fanny/ when he can"; to a superhero who writes "trite" poetry that baldly mimics Robert Creeley: "O/ vellum stars/ he cries/ (i./ e./ she's the one for/ he"; and to an aspiring Lothario who has to take out ads in the paper to attract dates: "Attractive young man wearing/ cape and hood wishes to meet/ lady with similar interests./ Object-mutual enjoyment."

According to Nichol, the idea behind the book "was an attack on the macho male bullshit tradition in Canadian poetry where if you were male & wrote poems you had to make damn sure you could piss longer, shout harder, & drink more than any less obviously effete (i.e. they weren't writing poems) on this national block" (*Captain Poetry*). There's no mistaking Nichol's parody with the front cover illustration of CP, pounding his chest at the full moon, his washboard abs defined, clad in nothing but a mask and speedos. His mask is a comb-less rooster head with a visor covering his eyes similar to Cyclops of the X-Men. Hilariously, a wattle the shape of a pair of testicles dangles from under his mask's chin.

But CP is a character whom Nichol won't quickly disavow, because "in certain ways i liked the idiot. & at certain points his idiocies became my own. . . . but since I'm male & probably occasionally macho in spite of myself it's somewhat understandable that the parody slipped briefly into the subjective mode. one thing i do believe tho is that you let the mistakes stand" (*Captain Poetry*, some words. . . .").

14. I actually find CP endearing in the second section of the book, "The Unmasking of Captain Poetry: a series of stills for dj." With his mask off, our superhero is none other than Nichol's signature icon, Milt the Morph, who guest-appears in the poet's countless other comics and cartoon strips. For the most part, in this second section, the page serves as the panel for the illustration or "still" that's printed single-sided, so that we experience the blank page on the other side when we turn it like a pause or a beat.

This second section opens with an unmasked, smiling CP hiding inside the higher dimensions of the uppercase letter *A*, a variation of which we see four pages later. Inside these letter *A*'s are mountains, clear skies, birds, and trees—a natural world. Other stills include CP riding the letters but with parts of the illustration whited-out or erased as if to suggest that anti-matter or the negative space has entered the poem; no problem: CP continues to smile through it. The third and last page of the section features panels, or "frames", as Nichol liked to call them. There is just one frame on the third but seven on the last page, neither of which can contain CP; he not only stands outside but in front of the two middle and bottom panels, with his feet planted on the fifth, laid out on the floor of the page like a doormat. The top row of panels and the left frame on the second row showcase scenes that include a celestial two-dimensional letter *B*, a white picket fence with hints of mountains behind it, and a sunny sky filled with birds. Inexplicably, the remaining three frames are empty. Perhaps this might have to do with CP cleaning house? After all, his thought balloon reads: "like leaving my roots behind me!!!"

15. Perhaps poetry and comics offer such an appealing hybrid language art for poets and artists to explore because of its potentially rich "means by which to reach out and touch the other" (Nichol, *bpNichol Comics* 49). Especially to a poet/artist like Nichol, a lay therapist by trade, as Nichol says, "[t]he other is emerging as the necessary prerequisite for dialogues with the self that clarify the soul & heart and deepen the ability to love. [He] place[s him]self there, with them, whoever they are, wherever they are, who seek to reach themselves and the other thru the poem by as many exits and entrances as possible" (qtd. in Peters 49).

Crossing the Corpus Callosum

The Musical Phenomenology of Lisa Jarnot

Jessica Lewis Luck

Lisa Jarnot's *Night Scenes*, published in 2008, begins with a casserole of poems cooked up with some Gertrude Stein, slices from Alexander Pope and Oulipo, and a pinch of Dr. Seuss. It's definitely a dish best served out loud, as shown in "Zero Onset":

> an eagle added attaboy ongoing outboard oak
> of after agile april airs in inner age awoke
> apparent oaten apple arcs, amazing amish ax
> and undulating ache of air in archival attacks
> o agitation angrily, o okra ocracoke
> and after orange onset ilk upon update approach
> all-knowing error out of earth, o undulate aardvark
> applicable of oft aft oars, androgynal embark
> antagonistic afterburn, appalling anvil adze
> adversity, ambivalence, ashore ashore advance
> astrology all edible, of aging update om
> and opening and opening, unpacked allowed aroma
> authentic arching anarchist, allowance all awry
> an afternoon, albanian, unurgent and espied. (18)

Like many poems in the book, "Zero Onset" contains traditional lyric meter, form, and rhyme. Not only is this a sonnet in rhymed couplets, it's also a perfect Fourteener with seven iambic feet per line. But, to be sure, there's something different going on here than in, say, Philip Sydney's 16th century Fourteeners. Most significant is the absence of the lyric "I"; this poem is generated through constraints rather than from the personal experience of the poet. "Zero onset" is a linguistic term. The "onset" is the first of three sounds comprising a syllable. For example, in the word "ball," /b/ is the onset and /all/ is the rhyme. A zero onset occurs when syllables begin with vowel sounds, as is the case with almost all the words in Jarnot's poem. (An exception is the word "all," which contains only the rhyme and no onset sound.) The poem highlights the absence of the lyric "I" in the constraint itself—only four words out of ninety-six begin with "I." Jarnot's poem thus seems to enact a surrender of the lyric "I" to the rhyme and meter at play behind the sonnet form.

This is a helpful description of Jarnot's experimental poetics in *Night Scenes*, but in this essay I'd like to consider the work and the effects of *reading* such a text. It's especially important to focus on this because the poetry, as it eschews the lyric "I", also seems to effect a surrender of the reader's "I" and promote a kind of ecstatic loss of self in the rhythm and music of the poems. Indeed, that the poetry's music is so "catchy" that it becomes difficult to even pay attention to the meaning of the words. What happens when the brain encounters such catchy nonsense? Using theories of literary and musical emotion from contemporary cognitive science, I will argue that Jarnot's use of infectious musical language promotes a kind of cognitive border-crossing in the reader, from the more logical left cortex to the more emotional and musical right cortex. But I also consider how Jarnot's poems question that ecstasy even as they invoke it, re-crossing the corpus callosum from right to left, in order to harness that readerly feeling of jouissance to résistance. But before we get to the poetic pathology report on the effects of her infectious poems, I'd like to consider the resurrection of "catchiness" as a significant category in post-Language poetry.

I. The Catchiness of the Avant-Garde

According to the *Oxford English Dictionary*, though the term "catchy" originally referred more to visual effects that grabbed the attention, it now most commonly describes infectious bits of language and music, such as in "catchy titles" or "catchy tunes." The word also has a sinister subtext: something catchy may be deceptive and liable to trip one up or be difficult to manage or execute (OED). Catchiness, of course, lies at the historical foundation of the genre of poetry. To preserve the customs, manners, and stories of an oral culture, the medium had to be catchy, easily memorized, recalled, and repeated by performers and listeners (Bernstein, "The Art of Immemorability" 505). In fact, "[t]he Greeks used the same word, *mousike*, to describe dance, music, poetry, and elementary education" (Preminger and Brogan 804). With the advent of alphabetic writing, however, this catchy quality became less significant. As Charles Bernstein writes, it freed poetry from its "epic function" of memory storage, so that poetry increasingly became defined by an individual voice, a "lyric function" ("The Art of Immemorability" 505), though we might say that the catchiness of the epic lived on in the lyric, like a vestigial organ.

The history of poetic catchiness over the millennia is perhaps yet to be written, but the twentieth century is certainly a significant turning point in its evolution. During this century many modernist poets eschewed the catchy jingle-jangle of the past in favor of more complex rhythms. As Ezra Pound famously put it, the poet should "compose in the sequence of the musical phrase, not in sequence of a metronome." Yet with several contemporary experimental poets, we hear the tick-tock and jingle-jangle return; poetry gets its groove back. As Harryette Mullen says of her own catchiness in *Muse & Drudge*, "rhyme is too powerful a tool to be abandoned to advertising, greeting cards, or even platinum rap recordings" (Caplan 164).

"Catchiness" is related to "cuteness," an aesthetic that Sianne Ngai defines in her wonderful essay on "The Cuteness of the Avant-Garde." She finds that avant-garde visual art and poetry often feature small, concrete, even adorable, everyday things: Williams's red wheelbarrow and tasty plums, Ashbery's cocoa tins, Creeley's rocks, Bernadette Mayer's puffed wheat cereal, and, perhaps at the apex of the cuteness pyramid, Gertrude Stein's "tender buttons" (815). The avant-garde, of course, conventionally imagines itself as sharp, pointy, and cutting edge, while cute things are soft, round, childlike, and feminine (814). Ngai points out that, consequently, modernist critics have actively avoided discussing Stein's cute aesthetic in *Tender Buttons* (814). Ngai's article works to recover the avant-garde's very cuteness as a critical, even transformative minor aesthetic. She notes how cute objects often provoke a violent response in their viewers, a desire to squish or even to *eat up* the adorable little thing. Paradoxically, at the same time, cute things have a destructive power over their viewers. On the popular website cuteoverload.com, for example, commenters use language that suggests paralysis and even head explosions to describe the effects of viewing whatever cute "morsel" is served up that day. Ngai uses the work of the visual artist Takashi Murakami and Stein's poems to show how avant-garde work makes it difficult to ingest its cute objects by "becoming something *slightly less easy to consume*," or something that, when consumed, results in "heavy choking" (to use Stein's phrase) (834). Stein's roast beef is tender, but it also grows blisters and teeth; her soft "ribbon" bites (831).

Jarnot's poems, too, are filled with huggable furry critters. Her menagerie includes squirrels, lemurs, fennec foxes, basset hounds, cats, pigs, horses, deer, sheep, cows, sparrows, and other "cheeping beaked things," and even an aardvark. Like the aforementioned avant-garde practitioners, she also links violence to this aesthetic of cuteness in many of her poems. For example, her poem "Christmas Prelude" begins in a kitschy holiday land but suddenly grows teeth:

O little fleas
of speckled light
all dancing
like a satellite

O belly green trees
shaded vale
O shiny bobcat
winter trail

Amoebic rampage
squamous cock
a Chinese hairpiece
burly sock

A grilled banana
smashes gates
and mingeless badgers
venerate. . . . (12)

But while Ngai focuses a great deal on the *visual* aspects of cuteness—mouthlessness, squishiness, and the hyperintensification of the thingishness of things—I want to turn to the cuteness—the catchiness—of things that *sing*. This shift in focus is significant, I think, because it begins to illustrate some of the potential *distinctions* between a modernist and postmodernist avant-garde aesthetic. Ngai treats the cuteness of the avant-garde rather monolithically across the twentieth century, from Stein to Francis Ponge to Bob Perelman and Francie Shaw. Marjorie Perloff, of course, has argued that "[a]s we move into the twenty-first century the modern/postmodern divide has emerged as more apparent than real" (*21st Century Modernism* 164). But I find myself on the side of critics such as Jennifer Ashton who want to argue for some very real historical and theoretical differences. And I think "catchiness" offers potential *aesthetic* and *affective* differences to consider as well.

Lisa Jarnot's poem "Stein Meat Work" suggests an instructive modern/postmodern catchiness comparison. Let's begin with Stein's modernist portrait of "ROASTBEEF" from *Tender Buttons*:

> In the inside there is sleeping, in the outside there is reddening, in the morning there is meaning, in the evening there is feeling. In the evening there is feeling. In feeling anything is resting, in feeling anything is mounting, in feeling there is resignation, in feeling there is recognition, in feeling there is recurrence and entirely mistaken there is pinching. All the standards have steamers and all the curtains have bed linen and all the yellow has discrimination and all the circle has circling. This makes sand (21).

Stein's recursive style has certainly proven to be "catchy" for some readers, particularly her detractors. One publisher, Arthur C. Fifield of London, rejected her manuscript for *Three Lives* with a letter that begins: "Dear Madam, I am only one, only one, only one. Only one being, one at the same time. Not two, not three, only one. Only one life to live, only sixty minutes in one hour. Only one pair of eyes. Only one brain . . . ." As compelling as Stein's soundscapes are, however, they aren't catchy like a Rihanna song or a Dr. Seuss poem that goes straight into our long-term memory. If there is a catchiness to Stein, it's a logical, mediated, left-brain catchiness. As Jonah Lehrer claims in *Proust Was a Neuroscientist*, Stein's lines seem to reveal the Chomskian scaffolding of grammar embedded in the brain's architecture (145).

In "A Retrospect," Pound advises the poet to "[c]onsider the way of the scientists rather than the way of an advertising agent for a new soap." While Stein follows Pound's logico-scientific approach to poetic language, Jarnot seems to embrace her inner ad man. Listen to what happens when very nearly the same content that appears in Stein is recast by Jarnot in a catchy form, in this case the Shakespearean sonnet:

> And in the inside there is sleeping sleep
> and in the outside there is reddening red
> and in the morning there is meeting meat
> and in the evening there is feeling fed
>
> in feeling anything is resting rest
> in feeling anything is mounting mount
> in feeling there is resignation best
> in feeling there is recognition round
>
> in feeling there recurrence has recurred
> entirely mistaken pinching there

all standards have their steamers in a fur
and all the curtains, linen beds are here

yes all the yellow can discriminate
and every circle circles on the plate. (6)

If Stein's lines show us the structure of grammatical language in the left brain, then I would suggest that Jarnot's catchy forms reveal the scaffolding of emotional, musical language in the right. The metaphor of "scaffolding" is apt because of its suggestion of three-dimensionality. Jarnot's musical poems remind us—despite, or perhaps even because of, their closed forms—that a stanza is an open "room" in which the reader's embodied mind is invited to dance. In Stephen Fredman's recent book on the art of assemblage he points out that after World War II, collage in the visual arts started to move from a two-dimensional to a three-dimensional approach. I wonder if we might think of Jarnot's postmodern poems transforming traditional forms in a similar way. Emptied of intentional, semantic content, distilled down to the pure catchiness of language, these musical forms become attentional, a kind of 3-D kinetic sound sculpture—not a work of art we stand in front of or walk around, but one that we step into, drawn in by its catchiness, and step out infected and transformed.

II. Right Brain Poetics

Now I'd like to turn to the etiology of this poetic infection and transformation. In Lisa Jarnot's poems, I argue, it occurs by engaging a deep musical phenomenology in the reader. The epigraph to *Night Scenes* captures her sonic ambitions: "O, to release the first music somewhere again, / for a moment / to touch the design of the first melody!" These lines from Robert Duncan's poem also titled "Night Scenes" emphasize the musical nature of her poetics, inspired by artists such as Bob Dylan and Johnny Cash. (Her second book is titled *Ring of Fire.*)[1] She explains in an interview, "Bob Dylan has probably had the biggest influence on the intonations of my work (in getting the sources to be sources of energy in addition to subject matter)" (*Verse* 201). She connects his resonance to the Buddhist mantra, in which "each syllable penetrates a different realm of existence." Similarly, in performances, Dylan "finds the word, then begins to bend the vowel until it hits the pitch, until it rings" (201). The epigraph from Duncan suggests that a poem's music could also make a connection to the reader's body; it suggests that somewhere in the brain there is some fundamental design or rhythm or melody that a poem can "touch" and "release," like the ringing of a mantra during meditation.

But how might we test such a hypothesis? We can turn to the work of cognitive linguist Reuven Tsur, which explores how the brain processes language sounds. According to Tsur's work, the right hemisphere processes sounds that are not speech—such as birdsong, traffic noise, music, etc.—in which the noises we hear are very similar to the acoustic signal that conveys them. When we perceive *speech* sounds the left hemisphere takes over and recodes the noise into abstract phonetic categories. Tsur describes these two forms of sound perception as non-speech mode and speech mode; however, he argues for a third "poetic" mode of sound perception in which some of the rich sensory detail of non-speech sound is perceived (as in the noisy /s/ sounds in Poe's line "the silken sad uncertain rustling of each purple curtain"). In this poetic mode, right and left hemispheres work together (18).[2] Tsur's work goes on to focus on very specific poetic devices such as alliteration and assonance, but I'm more interested in focusing on his holistic view of poetic sound. I want to consider how sound and rhythm come together to create a musical experience for the reader, "touching the design of the first melody," as Jarnot aspires.[3]

Recent studies of music in cognitive science seem to support Tsur's work on poetical sound processing. The neurologist and best-selling author Oliver Sacks recently compiled some of these studies in his book *Musicophilia*. In this book he considers how and why music has such power over us—over our emotions, our memory, and even our bodily movement. According to Sacks, music occupies more areas of our brain than language does. We are a species wired for the enjoyment of rhyme, rhythm, and tone, and much of this enjoyment is out of our conscious control. Music can become an "earworm" playing again and again in the mind; it can conjure up lost memories, make us feel elated or depressed, or it can make us start to dance. One of the most compelling insights from Sacks's book is the close relationship between our motor and auditory systems. We pick up on the beat of music very quickly and begin to anticipate and establish an internal template for its pattern. And despite some of the dance moves that I've seen on nights out at academic conferences, rarely does anyone have full rhythm deafness—rhythm is represented widely throughout the brain (Sacks 99). Interestingly, listening to music activates the motor cortex even if the listener is not moving or keeping time to the beat (241). Thus music, and I would argue musical poetry as well, can produce an ecstatic response in the listener, a release of self in the sound of the rhythm.

On the Bookslut blog, Dale Smith described Lisa Jarnot's *Black Dog Songs* (2003) as "poems you could almost dance to." I think Jarnot took this as a challenge because you can definitely dance to some of the poems in *Night Scenes*. Listen to the sonnet "Thricemost Field Mouse Song," which seems to be a postmodern remix of Robert Burns's "To a Mouse":

Thricemost field most fidelitous mice of sun
mice most field toast rebellion riven gunned
of rice mice most field glow of the one
christ mass field task resting mice and run
run most field roast, mossy mice of one
arm's length mouse flank, felicitous and sunned
tan glow field row mouse is underdone
cooked roe built of field greens overrun
run mouse field house tent inside the sun
love paste arm's haste mouse toes moon and hum
shaped wave, spare pace, mouse face dusted on
under taken leaves all raken, golden fur begun
open out the field of mouse, the field of mouse begun. (11)

Lewis Turco's book of poetic forms suggests that a dispondee (four stressed syllables in a row) doesn't really exist, but Jarnot seems to have written nearly fourteen of them here.[4] These four strong beats at the beginning of each line are similar to the opening four taps of a drummer setting the beat at the beginning of a song, thereby giving the rest of the band as well as the audience a feel for the song's beat pattern. The four strong beats are followed by the caesura, after which we hear a "riff" on the initial beat in the form of three more mixed feet of iambs, trochees, and anapests. This back-and-forth 4-3-4-3 rhythm reveals the common meter or ballad meter within the Fourteener line. The pleasure induced by these lines seems to arise in part from that familiar and "catchy" form. Robert Duncan, another major influence of Jarnot, believed that classical forms echo fundamental energies of the universe. Perhaps Jardot's use of the sonnet form and the common meter "touches the design" of some foundational rhythm of the human body.[5]

Cognitive scientists have studied the ways that background music in films can trigger particular emotional responses in viewers, such as panic in a horror film. Joseph LeDoux in his book *The Emotional Brain* calls this "the low road" to emotional response (Hogan 174). Certain sounds, like a growl or a hiss, or images like the shape of a snake, bypass slower systems of the brain and are processed immediately by the amygdala. The "high road," on the other hand, is cognitively mediated; for example we hear a story that makes us angry or a joke that makes us laugh. Most critics of literary emotion take this "high road" when exploring the emotional effects of a text and consider, for example, why we feel anger toward King Lear and pity for Cordelia, or why we weep when little Eva dies in *Uncle Tom's Cabin*. (Such powerful emotional reactions are especially mysterious to cognitive scientists because these are, of course, fictional characters.) The critic Patrick Colm Hogan even goes so far as to claim that "literature (apparently) must forego the 'low road' of direct emotive stimulation" (176). But what about poems? While the sound dimension of poetry certainly doesn't evoke emotion in exactly the same way as the screeching violins in the movie *Psycho* (though, come to think of it, I'd love to hear a poet try this), I think that the sonic or aural elements in Jarnot's work prove that some poetry, at least, can still travel that low road. Caught up in the catchy rhythms and rhymes of her poems, the reader experiences a kind of joyful ecstasy of dance.

Considering the focus on sound in Jarnot's poetry, is it a form of glossolalia? Oliver Sacks explains that while the bulk of our language function is housed in the left brain, the right brain also has linguistic potential (221). Aphasics who have lost all ability to produce propositional speech can still sing the lyrics to songs, list memorized sequences of words, curse, and, significantly, recite whole poems (217). Hughlings Jackson described this right-brain language as "emotional," "ejaculate," or "automatic" speech (Sacks 217). One is tempted to put Jarnot's sound poems in this category of right-brain emotional language. Steve McCaffery writes in his avant-garde sound poetry manifesto that "[s]ound poetry is *the* poetry of direct emotional confrontation: there is no pausing for intellectualization . . . the repetition of sound . . . liberates the elemental regions and most primitive impulses of the human self" (Scobie 216). But there is also a potential danger in such an emotional release of "primitive impulses" with no "intellectualization." Advertisers know all too well the power of a catchy tune to embed product names and even phone numbers in our brains. If poetry is to accomplish anything more than just giving readers warm feelings or a brain dance, it must be something more than a parallel language. As McCaffery writes, it must "situate within the critical interiorities of the sociolect and its possible transgressions" (Cazé 46); that is, it must harness the power of an advertiser's song for good rather than evil.

The opening poem of *Night Scenes*, "Sinning Skel Misclape," seems to accomplish this feat. It does this by situating a critique of voyeuristic local news culture within a catchy ballad form.

O sinning skel misclape thy lock
from frenzied felbred feefs
and longitudes of long tongued fuels
unpebble-dashed deceased.

Unpebble-dashed, unpebble dashed,
Unpebble-dashed unrose,
up from the theme that random flaps
in news flash rancid hose. (3)

According to the Urban Dictionary (urbandictionary.com), "skel" is a slang term that is short for "skeleton" and was first used by the NYPD to describe crack users because they were often so emaciated. Now the term refers to criminals more generally. The "sinning skel" addressed in the poem seems to have been killed ("deceased," "dashed" against something that is not a pebble), but the "frenzied" "long tongued fuels" of the media seem to be unwilling to let him rest in peace. Like some kind of zombie he is "unrose" via the "random flaps" of the "rancid hose" of the "news flash," which sprays shocking stories at us 24/7. The third stanza seems to give us the cheery newscaster live at the scene: "A morning dress of morning field / redrenched upon the sun." Even the blazing sun itself seems to be watered down or, punningly, "retrenched," that is, cut down or reduced by "the wobble of the / air" shot through with news waves. (Notice how the line break literally wobbles the ballad here.) The poem ends with the money-shot of the victim's body:

The red-black innards laid up bare
for all to see and spy,
tradition for the form of those
belingered, cheerful, nigh. (3)

Coining the term "belingered" for the voyeurs gathering around the crime scene—both in person and virtually via the "air" waves—Jarnot suggests that their seemingly innocuous "cheerful" lingering is also a kind of second siege on the victim, who is thereby "beleaguered" and beset by a new and different destructive force.

The reader who gets caught up in the cheery sounds of this ballad finds herself chastened for such "ecstasy" by the end of the poem. Dancing to the easy common meter of the song with no regard for its dark content mirrors the act of the bad news junky, who is always rubbernecking for the next fix of raw, shocking imagery. Jarnot seems to connect these two very different media consumers in the line "tradition for the form of those." The traditional form of the folk ballad is known for manifesting a phenomenon known as "leaping and lingering," "meaning that it skips from high point to high point, ignoring details of the narrative" (Turco 96), and thereby behaves much like today's sound bite news cycle. The poem's Jabberwockian wordplay and rollicking rhythms induce an almost childlike delight in the reader, but instead of selling us a product with its catchiness the poem re-crosses the corpus callosum to critique media culture (the ballad included) and its unquestioned "primitive" delights.

This crossing happens in some of Jarnot's poems even at the level of the individual word. Saussure famously argued that linguistic signs are split into a sound image and a concept, the signifier and the signified. Derrida calls the mechanism between these parts a "hinge," and Jarnot's poems seem to play upon that hinge between sound and sense. A good example of this play appears in "Vulpes Zerda Sonnet," which takes its title from the scientific name for the fennec fox. It begins:

> O fine fennec fenéstrated and full
> fennec, I've never seen one in the cold
> fennec, a moor, with long ears, sharpened toes,
> near fennel I would place you in font bold (7)

Note how the poem toggles back and forth between "fennec" as signified and "fennec" as signifier. The actual signified fennec fox has "long ears, sharpened toes," but it is the signifier fennec that appears in the dictionary "near fennel . . . in font bold." The poem continues to open and close the hinge of the sign with the fennec who "romps and bounds" but is also "so close to fenks: the blubber of the whale" in the dictionary. Even the book's cover plays this game. Look carefully behind the dark stars of the "night scene" and you can see the outline of a fennec fox. This image illustrates how we process language and look through the slippery, arbitrary signifier that blurs the furry, physical signified. It is important, however, that the fennec fox's enormous ears make him hyper-sensitive to sound. Jarnot's signifying mascot for the book thus seems to highlight the power of sound itself in the shell game of our language system. The sound of poetic language allows Jarnot to keep "one foot in the realm of the real and one in the realm of artifice" (Foust 170).

The poet and critic Graham W. Foust offers a savvy reading of a similar move in Jarnot's poem "Dracula" from *Black Dog Songs*. The poem begins with an epigraph from the 1931 film version of *Dracula*: "To be dead, to be really dead. That must be glorious" (12). Jarnot attributes the quote not to the writers of the film (the "real" authors of the quote) or to the character Count Dracula (the artificial character), but to Bela Lugosi, the actor who played the role. Lugosi is the "real" speaker of the quote, but he also speaks it in an "artificial" capacity; the words are not "his." Interestingly, Foust also points out that Lugosi, who could not speak English when he first came to the U.S. from Hungary, is said to have "learned his part phonetically" for the original stage production of *Dracula* in 1921 (171). Despite the fact that Lugosi had a ten-year learning period before the film, Foust still finds the language of Lugosi's performance memorably foreign and musical in sound. Foust uses this information to highlight the performative nature of the authorial self behind Jarnot's work: "making up what is the sum of me," to quote the poem (170).

I would argue that Jarnot's catchy poems also put the *reader* in a kind of Bela Lugosi position. The cheerful music of her poetic language gets the brain dancing and pushes language processing out of the intellectual left frontal cortex and into the more distributed network of music processing, or even into the right brain's emotional language centers, touching the design of the first melodies housed there. It's as if her poems break down the language into its musical parts for us so that we see and hear it afresh and defamiliarized, as a foreign speaker would. Her lyrics help us "learn our part phonetically," but they don't leave us in that state of ecstatic emotional response. Indeed, even as they invoke ecstasy, they point to the potential dangers of such a state. Ultimately, like Bob Dylan's songs they become catchy sources of energy that engage and empower the reader for protest.

Notes

1. Jarnot says of her book *Some Other Kind of Mission*, "I think of poetry as related to song. Repetition helps a reader read a poem rhythmically. I also think that there is a psychological construct at work. One goes through repetitions of thought neurotically, and a lot of this book tries to document that. I wanted to chart out what was happening in my head, to make a map of the mind at work. Those repetitive phrases brought me closer to writing exactly what was going on in my brain at particular moments" (*What Is Poetry* 83).

2. See J. Kane's "Poetry as Right Hemispheric Language" for an interesting compilation of cognitive linguistics and psychology research dealing with the connection between poetry and the right hemisphere.

3. As Marjorie Perloff and Craig Dworkin point out in their essay collection *The Sound of Poetry / The Poetry of Sound*, though sound is often consid-

ered one of poetry's key distinguishing features, no element is currently so neglected in contemporary poetry scholarship (1).

4. I also hear a metrical echo of John Donne's "Thou hast made me and shall thy work decay?"

5. Stephen Cushman calls this notion the "physiological fallacy," but many poets still seem to buy it (Golston).

Extrapolatia

Sheila E. Murphy

The culture argues for homogamy
while smashing mirrors
against foreign things.

An unordered issue of *Dwell* arrives.
I shred the corner rectangle
that leads to where I live.

From next door, my brother sends
a font called "My Old Remington,"
invoking smudged veracity.

Our ancestry, amounting to
"another species," yields intuition
ill-fitted to the shallows.

An inadvertent disciple keeps phoning
to show off friendliness
she hopes to have acquired.

How many mascules does it take
to oust the impulse
to feel feminine?

Literal fracking
means I can inflate the very fire
I want to quench.

I tell myself
one can, with skill,
remove prevailing code.

I go out to fetch the mail
and hear my neighbor's mezzo chanting
I can't hear you.

Works Cited

Alter, Robert. *The Art of Biblical Poetry*. New York: Basic Books, 1985. Print.

Altieri, Charles. "Intimacy and Experiment in Mei-mei Berssenbrugge's Poetry." *We Who Love to Be Astonished: Experimental Women's Writing and Performance Poetics*. Ed. Laura Hinton and Cynthia Hogue. Tuscaloosa: U of Alabama P, 2002. 54-68. Print.

———. *The Particulars of Rapture: An Aesthetics of the Affects*. Ithaca, NY: Cornell UP, 2003. Print.

———. *Postmodernisms Now: Essays on Contemporaneity in the Arts*. University Park: Pennsylvania State UP, 1998. Print.

Andrews, Bruce. "FROM 'Poetry as Explanation, Poetry as Praxis.'" *Postmodern American Poetry*. Ed. Paul Hoover. New York: Norton, 1994. 668-672. Print.

———. *Paradise & Method: Poetics & Praxis*. Evanston: Northwestern UP, 1996. Print.

——— and Charles Bernstein, eds. *The L=A=N=G=U=A=G=E Book*. Carbondale: Southern Illinois UP, 1984. Print.

Arthos, John. *Speaking Hermeneutically: Understanding in the Conduct of a Life*. Columbia, SC: U of South Carolina P, 2011. Print.

Ashbery, John. *Selected Poems*. New York: Penguin, 1986. Print.

——— and Peter Stitt. "John Ashbery." [Interview.] *Poets at Work: The* Paris Review *Interviews*. Ed. George Plimpton. New York: Penguin, 1989. 387–412. Print.

Attardo, Salvatore. *Humorous Texts: A Semantic and Pragmatic Analysis*. Berlin: Mouton de Gruyter, 2001. Print.

Augarde, Tony. *Oxford Guide to Word Games*. Oxford, UK: Oxford UP, 2003. Print.

Augustine, Saint, Bishop of Hippo. *Confessions*. Tr. and Intr. R. S. Pine-Coffin. Harmondsworth, Middlesex, UK: Penguin, 1961.

Bares, Karel. "On the Anagram and Its Functions." *Zeitschrift Fur Anglistik und Amerikanstik* 23.2 (1975): 141-52. Print.

Barthes, Roland. *Image, Music, Text*. Trans. Stephen Heath. New York: Hill and Wang, 1977. Print.

———. *Le Plaisir du Texte* (*The Pleasure of the Text*). Paris: Seuil, 1973. Trans. Richard Howard. New York: Hill and Wang, 1975. Print.

———. *The Responsibility of Forms*. Trans. Richard Howard. New York: Hill and Wang, 1985. Print.

———. *The Rustle of Language*. Trans. Richard Howard. Berkeley: U of California P, 1989. Print.

———. *S/Z*. Trans. Richard Miller. New York: Hill and Wang, 1974. Print.

Baudrillard, Jean. *Simulacra and Simulation*. Trans. Sheila Faria Glaser. Ann Arbor: U of Michigan P, 1994. Print.

Beckett, Tom. *This Poem/ What Speaks?/ A Day*. Rockhampton, Australia: Otoliths, 2008. Print.

——— and John Bloomberg-Rissman. "An Interview with John Bloomberg-Rissman." *Otoliths* 12 (Feb. 2009). Web. 10 April 2013. http://the-otolith.blogspot.com/2009/01/tom-beckett-interview-with-john.html

Bedient, Calvin. "Solo Mysterioso Blues: An Interview with Harryette Mullen." *Callaloo: A Journal of African-American and African Arts and Letters* 19.3 (1996): 651-69. Print.

Benjamin, Walter. *The Arcades Project*. Trans. Howard Eiland and Kevin McLaughlin. Cambridge: Harvard UP, 1999. Print.

———. *The Correspondence of Walter Benjamin, 1910-1940*. Ed. Gershom Scholem and Theodor W. Adorno. Trans. Manfred R. Jacobson and Evelyn M. Jacobson. Chicago: U of Chicago P, 1994. Print.

———. *Selected Writings: Volume 1, 1913-1926*. Trans. Rodney Livingstone, et al. Eds. Marcus Bullock and Michael W. Jennings. Cambridge: Harvard UP, 1996. Print.

———. *Selected Writings: Volume II, Part 1, 1927-1930*. Trans. Rodney Livingstone, et al. Eds. Howard Eiland, Michael W. Jennings, and Gary Smith. Cambridge: Harvard UP, 1999. Print.

———. *Selected Writings: Volume II, Part 2, 1931-1934*. Trans. Rodney Livingstone, et al. Eds. Howard Eiland, Michael W. Jennings, and Gary Smith. Cambridge: Harvard UP, 1999. Print.

———. *Selected Writings: Volume III, 1935-1938*. Trans. Edmond Jephcott, et al. Eds. Howard Eiland and Michael W. Jennings. Cambridge: Harvard UP, 2002. Print.

———. *Selected Writings: Volume IV, 1938-1940*. Trans. Edmond Jephcott, et al. Eds. Howard Eiland and Michael W. Jennings. Cambridge: Harvard UP, 2003. Print.

____ and Gershom Gerhard Scholem. Trans. Gary Smith. *The Correspondence of Walter Benjamin and Gershom Scholem, 1932-1940*. Cambridge: Harvard UP, 1992. Print.

Berlin, Adele. *The Dynamics of Biblical Parallelism*. Bloomington, IN: Indiana UP, 1985. Print.

Bernstein, Charles. *All the Whiskey in Heaven*. New York: Farrar, Straus and Giroux, 2010. Print.

———. "The Art of Immemorability." *A Book of the Book: Some Works and Projections about the Book and Writing*. Ed. Jerome Rothenberg. New York: Granary Books, 1999. 504-17. Print.

———. *Artifice of Absorption*. Philadelphia: Singing Horse Press/Paper Air, 1987. Print.

———. *Attack of the Difficult Poems*. Chicago: U of Chicago P, 2011. Print.

——. *Content's Dream: Essays, 1975-1984*. Evanston, IL: Northwestern UP, 2001. Print.

——. *Dark City*. Los Angeles, CA: Sun and Moon P, 1994. Print.

——. "The Economics of the Small Press: Poetry Publishing." *Talking the Boundless Book: Art, Language, & the Book Arts*. Ed. Charles Alexander. Minneapolis: Minnesota Center for Book Arts, 1995. 33-44. Print.

——. *My Way: Speeches and Poems*. Chicago: U of Chicago P, 1999. Print.

——. *A Poetics*. Cambridge: Harvard UP, 1992. Print.

——. *Rough Trades*. Los Angeles: Sun & Moon, 1991. Print.

——. *Shadowtime*. Los Angeles: Green Integer Books, 2005. Print.

——. "Writing and Method." *In the American Tree*. Ed. Ron Silliman. Orono, ME: National Poetry Foundation, 1986. 583- 598. Print.

——, ed. *The Politics of Poetic Form*. New York: Roof Books, 1990. Print.

Berssenbrugge, Mei-mei. *I Love Artists: New and Selected Poems*. Berkeley: U of California P, 2006. Print.

Bewes, Timothy. *Reification, or the Anxiety of Late Capitalism*. London: Verso, 2002. Print.

Blaser, Robin. *The Fire: Collected Essays of Robin Blaser*. Ed. Miriam Nichols. Berkeley, CA: U of California P, 2006. Print.

Bloom, Harold. *A Map of Misreading*. London: Oxford UP, 1975, 2003. Print.

Bloomberg-Rissman, John. *2nd NOTICE OF MODIFICATIONS TO TEXT OF PROPOSED REGULATIONS, REGULATION AND POLICY MANAGEMENT BRANCH, CALIFORNIA DEPARTMENT OF CORRECTIONS AND REHABILITATION*. Nottingham, U.K., and Claremont, CA: Laughing Ouch Cube Publications/Leafe Press, 2010. Print.

Booth, Stephen. "Preface." *Shakespeare's Sonnets*. Ed. Stephen Booth. New Haven: Yale UP, 1977. ix-xix. Print.

Breton, André. *Nadja*. Trans. Richard Howard. New York: Grove Press, 1960. Print.

Britt, Brian. *Walter Benjamin and the Bible*. New York: Continuum, 1996. Print.

Brodersen, Momme. *Walter Benjamin: A Biography*. Trans. Malcolm R. Green and Ingrida Ligers. New York: Verso, 1996. Print.

Caplan, David. "Reduced to Rhyme: On Contemporary Doggerel." *The Antioch Review* 67.1 (2009): 164-80. *Academic Search Premiere*. Print.

Cazé, Antoine. "An Interview with Karen Mac Cormack & Steve McCaffery." "Echoes from American Poetry Today." *Sources Revue d'études Anglophones* No. 8 (Printemps), Université d'Orléans, 28-47. Print.

Clanchy, M. Thomas. *From Memory to Written Record: England 1066-1307*. Cambridge: Harvard UP, 1979. Print.

Culler, Jonathan. *On Deconstruction: Theory and Criticism after Structuralism*. Ithaca: Cornell UP, 1982. Print.

Delany, Samuel. *Times Square Red, Times Square Blue*. New York: New York UP, 2001. Print.

Derrida, Jacques. *Margins of Philosophy*. Trans. Alan Bass. Chicago: U of Chicago P, 1982. Print.

———. *Positions*. Trans. Alan Bass. Chicago: U of Chicago P, 1981. Print.

Dever, William G. *Who Were the Early Israelites and Where Did They Come From?* Grand Rapids, MI: Eerdmans, 2003. Print.

Duncan, Robert. *The Opening of the Field*. New York: Grove Press, 1960. Print.

Evans, Steve. "After a Fashion: Reading Roland Barthes Today." *Third Factory: Notes to Poetry*. 2009. Web. 2 January 2012. http://thirdfactory.net/barthes.html

Fifield, Arthur C. "Letter to Gertrude Stein. 19 April 1912." MS. *Letters of Note*. Web. 11 July 2011. http://www.lettersofnote.com/2011/02/hardly-one-copy-would-sell-here-hardly.html

Fish, Stanley. *Doing What Comes Naturally: Change, Rhetoric, and the Practice of Theory in Literary and Legal Studies*. Durham: Duke UP, 1990. Print.

———. *Is There A Text in This Class?* Cambridge: Harvard UP, 1980. Print.

"Flarf Poetry." *Wikipedia*. 19 Oct. 2011. Web. http://en.wikipedia.org/wiki/Flarf_poetry

Foucault, Michel. "What Is an Author." *The Foucault Reader*. Trans. Josue V. Harari. Ed. Paul Rabinow. New York: Pantheon, 1984. Print.

Foust, Graham W. "'Not [Not] the Poet, Not [Not] Me': Frederick Seidel and Lisa Jarnot after 9/11." *Ideas of Order in Contemporary American Poetry*. Ed. Oliver Scheiding. Würzburg, Germany: Königshausen & Neumann, 2007. 159-72. Print.

Frost, Elisabeth, A. "An Interview with Harryette Mullen." *Contemporary Literature* 41.1 (2000): 397-421. Print.

———. "Signifyin(g) on Stein: The Revisionist Poetics of Harryette Mullen and Leslie Scalapino." *Postmodern Culture* 5.3 (May 1995). Web. 29 Dec. 2011. http://pmc.iath.virginia.edu/text-only/issue.595/frost.595

Gadamer, Hans-Georg. "Aesthetics and Hermeneutics." *The Gadamer Reader: A Bouquet of the Later Writings*. Ed. and Trans. Richard E. Palmer. Evanston, IL: Northwestern UP, 2007. 123-131. Print.

———. "The Artwork in Word and Image." *The Gadamer Reader: A Bouquet of the Later Writings*. Ed. and Trans. Richard E. Palmer. Evanston, IL: Northwestern UP, 2007. 192-224. Print.

———. "Composition and Interpretation." *The Relevance of the Beautiful*. Trans. Nicholas Walker. Cambridge: Cambridge UP, 1989. 66-73. Print.

———. "On the contribution of poetry to the search for truth." *The Relevance of the Beautiful*. Trans. Nicholas Walker. Cambridge: Cambridge UP, 1989. 105-115. Print.

———. "Language and Understanding." *The Gadamer Reader: A Bouquet of the Later Writings*. Ed. and Trans. Richard E. Palmer. Evanston, IL: Northwestern UP, 2007. 89-107. Print.

———. "Man and Language." *Philosophical Hermeneutics*. Ed. and Trans. David E. Linge. Berkeley: U of California P, 1976. 59-68. Print.

———. "On the Problem of Self-Understanding." *Philosophical Hermeneutics*. Ed. and Trans. David E. Linge. Berkeley: U of California P, 1976. 44-58. Print.

———. "The Relevance of the Beautiful." *The Relevance of the Beautiful.* Trans. Nicholas Walker. Cambridge: Cambridge UP, 1989. 3-53. Print.

———. "On the Scope and Function of Hermeneutical Reflection." *Philosophical Hermeneutics.* Ed. and Trans. David E. Linge. Berkeley: U of California P, 1976. 18-43. Print.

———. "Text and Interpretation." *Dialogue and Deconstruction.* Eds. Diane P. Michelfelder and Richard E. Palmer. Albany: SUNY P, 1989. 21-51. Print.

———. *Truth and Method.* 2nd rev. ed. Rev. Trans. Joel Weinsheimer and Donald G. Marshall. New York: Crossroad, 1990. Print.

———. *Truth and Method.* 2nd rev. ed. Rev. Trans. Joel Weinsheimer and Donald G. Marshall. London: Continuum, 2004. Print.

———. "On the Truth of the Word." *The Gadamer Reader: A Bouquet of the Later Writings.* Ed. and Trans. Richard E. Palmer. Evanston, IL: Northwestern UP, 2007. Print.

Gates, Henry Louis Jr. *The Signifying Monkey: A Theory of African American Literary Criticism.* New York: Oxford UP, 1988. Print.

Gell-Mann, Murray. "Complexity and Complex Adaptive Systems." *The Evolution of Human Languages.* Eds. John A. Hawkins and Murray Gell-Mann. New York: Addison-Wesley, 1992. Print.

Gilbert, Alan. *Another Future: Poetry and Art in a Postmodern Twilight.* Middletown, CT: Wesleyan UP, 2006. Print.

Golston, Michael. *Rhythm and Race in Modernist Poetry and Science.* New York: Columbia UP, 2009. Print.

Green, Daniel. "Tangibility of the Word." *berfrois: Intellectual Jousting in the Republic of Letters.* Aug. 2011. Web. 31 December 2011. http://www.berfrois.com/2011/08/get-silli/

Haney, David P. "Aesthetics and Ethics in Gadamer, Levinas, and Romanticism: Problems of Phronesis and Techne." *PMLA* 114.1 (January 1999): 32-45. Print.

Hardt, Michael and Antonio Negri. *Commonwealth.* Cambridge: Harvard UP, 2009. Print.

Harryman, Carla. *Under the Bridge.* Berkeley: This P, 1980. Print.

Harvey, David. "Commonwealth: An Exchange." *Artforum* November 2009: 210-214; 259-262. Print.

Hatfield, Charles. "An Art of Tensions." *A Comics Studies Reader.* Eds. Jeet Heer and Kent Worcester. Jackson, MS: UP of Mississippi, 2009. 132-148. Print.

Hayles, N. Katherine. *How We Became Posthuman: Virtual Bodies in Cibernetics, Literature, and Informatics.* Chicago: U of Chicago P, 1999. Print.

Heidegger, Martin. *Being and Time.* Trans. John Macquarrie and Edward Robinson. New York: Harper and Row, 1962. Print.

———. *What Is Called Thinking?* Trans. J. Glenn Gray. New York: Harper and Row, 1968. Print.

Hejinian, Lyn. *The Language of Inquiry.* Berkeley: U of California P, 2000. Print.

———. "The Rejection of Closure." In *Writing/Talks.* Ed. Bob Perelman. Carbondale: Southern Illinois UP, 1985. 270-91. Print.

Heller, Michael. *Conviction's Net of Branches: Essays on the Objectivist Poets and Poetry*. 1985. New York: Spuyten Duyvil, 2002. Print.

———. *Uncertain Poetries: Selected Essays on Poets, Poetry, and Poetics*. Cambridge, UK: Salt Publishing, 2005. Print.

Hinton, Laura and Cynthia Hogue, eds. *We Who Love to Be Astonished: Experimental Women's Writing and Performance Poetics*. Tuscaloosa: U of Alabama P, 2002. Print.

Hoffman, Eva. *Lost in Translation: A Life in a New Language*. New York: Penguin, 1990. Print.

Hogan, Patrick Colm. *Cognitive Science, Literature, and the Arts: A Guide for Humanists*. New York: Routledge, 2003. Print.

Hogue, Cynthia. "Beyond the Frame of Whiteness: Harryette Mullen's Revisionary Border Work." *We Who Love to Be Astonished*. Eds. Laura Hinton and Cynthia Hogue. Tuscaloosa: U of Alabama P, 2002. 81-89. Print.

Hoover, Paul, ed. *Postmodern American Poetry*. NY: Norton, 1994. Print.

Howitt, Dennis and Kwame Owusu Bempah. "Race and Ethnicity in Popular Humor." *Beyond a Joke: the Limits of Humour*. Eds. Sharon Lockyer and Michael Pickering. New York: Palgrave Macmillan, 2005. 45-62. Print.

Huehls, Mitchum. "Spun Puns (and Anagrams): Exchange Economies, Subjectivity, and History in Harryette Mullen's *Muse & Drudge*." *Contemporary Literature* 44.1 (2003): 19-46. Print.

Hunstberger, David W. *Procedural Form in Postmodern American Poetry: Berrigan, Antin, Silliman, and Hejinian*. New York: Palgrave MacMillan, 2010. Print.

Iser, Wolfgang. *The Implied Reader: Patterns of Communication from Bunyan to Beckett in Prose Fiction*. Baltimore: Johns Hopkins UP, 1974. Print.

"Isidore of Seville" (Anonymous review of *The Etymologies of Isidore of Seville*, trans., intr. and notes. Stephen A. Barney, W. J. Lewis, J. A. Beach, and Oliver Berghof [Cambridge: Cambridge UP, 2006]). *Wordtrade*. Web. 21 January 2012. http://www.wordtrade.com/philosophy/medieval/isidoreseville.htm

Jameson, Frederic. "Postmodernism, or the Culture of Late Capitalism." *New Left Review* 146 (July/August 1984): 53-92. Print.

Jarnot, Lisa. *Black Dog Songs*. Chicago: Flood Editions, 2003. Print.

———. Interview with Daniel Kane. *What Is Poetry: Conversations with the American Avant-Garde*. Ed. Daniel Kane. New York: Teachers & Writers Collaborative, 2003. 78- 85. Print.

———. Interview with Rod Smith. *The VERSE Book of Interviews: 27 Poets on Language, Craft, and Culture*. Eds. Brian Henry and Andrew Zawacki. Amherst, MA: Verse, 2005. 199-203. Print.

———. *Night Scenes*. Chicago: Flood Editions, 2008. Print.

———. *Ring of Fire*. Cambridge, UK: Salt Publishing, 2003. Print.

Kane, Daniel, ed. *What Is Poetry: Conversations with the American Avant-Garde*. New York: Teachers and Writers Books, 2003. Print.

Kane, Julie. "Poetry as Right-Hemisphere Language." *Journal of Consciousness Studies* 11.5-6 (2004): 21-59. Print.

Keats, John. *The Complete Poetical Works and Letters of John Keats, Cambridge Edition.* New York: Houghton, Mifflin and Co., 1899. Print.

"Kenneth Goldsmith." *Academy of American Poets.* 2011. Web. http://www.poets.org/poet.php/prmPID/1965

Kim, Myung Mi. *Penury.* Richmond, CA: Omnidawn, 2009. Print.

Kimmelman, Burt. *The Poetics of Authorship in the Later Middle Ages: The Emergence of the Modern Literary Persona.* New York: Peter Lang, 1996. Print.

———. "Text and Selfhood in Medieval and Postmodern Worlds." *Readerly/Writerly Texts* 10.1, 10.2 (Spring/Summer-Fall/Winter 2002 and Spring/Summer 2003): 51-60. Print.

Kolodny, Annette. "Dancing through the Minefield: Some Observations on the Theory, Practice, and Politics of a Feminist Literary Criticism." *Critical Theory Since 1965.* Ed. Hazard Adams and Leroy Searle. Talahassee: Florida State UP, 1986. 499-512. Print.

Koolhaas, Rem and Bruce Mau. *S, M, L, XL.* New York: Monacelli, 1995. Print.

Lacan, Jacques. *Ecrits.* Trans. Bruce Fink. New York: Norton, 2006. Print.

Lazer, Hank. *Days.* New Orleans: Lavender Ink, 2002. Print.

———. *INTER(IR)RUPTIONS.* Mentor, Ohio: Generator Press, 1992. Print.

———. "N20PG1." Unpublished poem from ongoing series *Notebooks (of Being & Time)*, 2012. Print.

"Lectio Divina." *Idaho Monks, Monastery of the Ascension.* 2011. Web. 15 Dec. 2011. http://www.idahomonks.org/sect810.htm

Lehrer, Jonah. *Proust Was a Neuroscientist.* Boston: Houghton Mifflin, 2007. Print.

Lee, Sueyeun Juliette. "shaped like relation suggested like progress: Celebrating Myung Mi Kim's *Dura.*" *Building is a Process/Light is an Element: essays and excursions for Myung Mi Kim.* Eds. Michael Cross and Andrew Rippeon. State U of New York/Buffalo: *Electronic Poetry Center.* 2008. Web. 18 Dec. 2011. http://epc.buffalo.edu/authors/kim/building/

Levinas, Emmanuel. *Entre Nous: Thinking of the Other.* Trans. Michael B. Smith and Barbara Harshaw. New York: Columbia UP, 1998. Print.

Lin, Tan. Interview with Katherine Elaine Sanders. *Bombsite.* March, 2010. Web. http://bombsite.com/issues/999/articles/3467

———. *Seven Controlled Vocabularies.* Middletown, CT: Wesleyan UP, 2010. Print.

——— and Charles Bernstein. "Tan Lin in Conversation with Charles Bernstein." *Close Listening.* MP3 (29:09) *PennSound: Center for Programs in Contemporary Writing.* 23 May 2005. Web. 23 Aug. 2011. http://writing.upenn.edu/pennsound/x/Lin.php

Lowi, Michael. *Fire Alarm: Reading Walter Benjamin's "On the Concept of History."* New York: Verso, 2005. Print.

Luck, Jessica Lewis. "Entries on a Post-Language Poetics in Harryette Mullen's *Dictionary.*" *Contemporary Literature* 49.1 (Fall 2008): 357-383. Print.

Lukacs, Georg. *History and Class Consciousness: Studies in Marxist Dialectics*. Trans. Rodney Livingstone. Cambridge: MIT Press, 1971. Print.

Mack, Anne, and J. J. Rome. "*The Alphabet*, Spelt from Silliman's Leaves (A Conversation on the 'American Longpoem')." *The South Atlantic Quarterly* 89:4 (Fall 1990): 734-759. Print.

Malpas, Jeff. *Heidegger's Topology: Being, Place, World*. Cambridge: MIT P, 2008. Print.

Matthews, Harry and Alastair Brotchie. *Oulipo Compendium*. London: Atlas Press, 1998. Print.

McCaffery, Steve. *Prior to Meaning: The Protosemantic and Poetics*. Evanston: Northwestern UP, 2001. Print.

——— and Lisa Robertson. "Emails." *PhillyTalks* 17. 3 October 2000. Web. 12 Jan. 2012. http://slought.org/files/downloads/domains/phillytalks/pdf/pt17.pdf

McGann, Jerome. *A Critique of Modern Textual Criticism*. Charlottesville, VA: U of Virginia P, 1999. Print.

Meisel, Perry. "Dylan and the Critics." *Raritan* 26.3 (Winter 2007): 103-4. Print.

Miller, Stephen Paul. *The Seventies Now: Culture as Surveillance*. Durham: Duke UP, 1999. Print.

———. *There's Only One God and You're Not It*. East Rockaway, NY: Marsh Hawk P, 2011. Print.

——— and Daniel Morris, eds. *Radical Poetics and Secular Jewish Culture*. Tuscaloosa: U of Alabama P, 2010. Print.

Morrison, Grant. *Supergods: What Masked Vigilantes, Miraculous Mutants, and a Sun God From Smallville Can Teach Us About Being Human*. New York: Spiegel & Grau, 2011. Print.

——— and Dave McKean. *Batman: Arkham Asylum*. 15th Anniversary Ed. New York: DC Comics, 2004. Print.

Morrison, Yedda. "Generosity as Method: An Interview with Myung Mi Kim." *Electronic Poetry Center*. State U of New York/Buffalo: December 1997. Web. 16 Dec. 2011. http://epc.buffalo.edu/authors/kim/generosity.html

Motte, Warren F. Jr., ed. and trans. *Oulipo: A Primer of Potential Literature*. Lincoln, NE: U of Nebraska P, 1986. Print.

Mullen, Harryette. "Imagining the Unimagined Reader: Writing to the Unborn and Including the Excluded." *Boundary 2: 99 Poets /1999: An International Symposium*. 26.1(1999): 198-203. Print.

———. *Muse & Drudge*. Philadelphia: Singing Horse Press, 1995. Print.

———. "Poetry and Identity." *West Coast Line 19*, 1996: 85–89.

———. "'A Silence Between Us Like Language': The Untranslatability of Experience in Sandra Cisneros's *Woman Hollering Creek*." MELUS: *The Journal of the Society for the Study of the Multi-Ethnic Literature of the United States* 21:2 (1996): 3-20. Print.

———. *Sleeping with the Dictionary*. Berkeley: U of California P, 2002. Print.

Murphy, Sheila E. *Toccatas in the Key of D*. West Hartford, CT: Blue Lion, 2010. Print.

Ngai, Sianne. "The Cuteness of the Avant-Garde." *Critical Inquiry* 31 (2005): 811-47. Print.

Nichol, bp. *bp Nichol Comics*. Ed. Carl Peters. Vancouver: Talon Books, 2002. Print.

———. *The Captain Poetry Poems Complete*. Toronto: Book Thug, 2011. Print.

———. *Gifts: The Martyrology Book{s} 7 & 8*. Toronto: Coach House Press, 1990. Print.

———. *Martyrology: Books 1 & 2*. Toronto: Coach House Press, 1994. Print.

The OED Online. Oxford English Dictionary. 2004. Web. 10 Nov. 2007. http://www.oed.com

Ong, Walter J. *Orality and Literacy: The Technologizing of the Word*. Ed. Terence Hawkes. New York: Methuen, 1988. Print.

Oring, Elliott. *Engaging Humor*. Urbana: U of Illinois P, 2003. Print.

Ourousoff, Nicolai. "Koolhaas, Delirious in Beijing." *New York Times*. 11 Jul. 2011. Web. 12 Jan. 2012. http://www.nytimes.com/2011/07/13/arts/design/koolhaass-cctv-building-fits-beijing-as-city-of-the-future.html

The Oxford Dictionary of Modern Slang. Eds. John Ayto and John Simpson. Oxford, UK: Oxford UP, 1993. Print.

The Oxford English Dictionary. 2nd ed. Oxford UP, 1989. Print.

Perloff, Marjorie. *Differentials: Poetry, Poetics, Pedagogy*. Tuscaloosa: U of Alabama P, 2004. Print.

———. "Language Poetry and the Lyric Subject: Ron Silliman's Albany, Susan Howe's Buffalo." *Critical Inquiry* 25.3 (Spring 1999): 406-34. Print.

———. "Modernism Now." *A Companion to Modernist Literature and Culture*. Ed. David Bradshaw and Kevin Dettmar. Oxford, England: Blackwell, 2006. 571-8. *Marjorie Perloff*. Web. 4 July 2012. http://marjorieperloff.com/stein-duchamp-picasso/modernism-now

———. "The Portrait of the Language Poet as Autobiographer: The Case of Ron Silliman." *Quarry West* 34 (1998): 167-81. *Marjorie Perloff*. Web. 2 January 2012. http://marjorieperloff.com/stein-duchamp-picasso/silliman-autobiographer/

———. *Radical Artifice: Writing Poetry in the Age of Media*. Chicago: University of Chicago Press, 1994. Print.

———. *21st-Century Modernism: The "New" Poetics*. Malden, Mass.: Blackwell Publishers, 2002. Print.

——— and Craig Dworkin, eds. *The Sound of Poetry / the Poetry of Sound*. Chicago: U of Chicago P, 2009. Print.

Place, Vanessa. *Tragodía 1: Statement of Facts*. Los Angeles: Blanc P, 2010. Print.

Pound, Ezra. *The Cantos of Ezra Pound*. New York: New Directions, 1970. Print.

———. "A Retrospect." 1918. *Modern American Poetry*. Dept. of English, U of Illinois, Urbana-Champaign. Web. 11 July 2011. http://www.english.illinois.edu/maps/poets/m_r/pound/retrospect.htm

Preminger, Alex and T. V. F. Brogan, eds. *The New Princeton Encyclopedia of Poetry and Poetics*. Princeton: Princeton UP, 1993. Print.

Prevallet, Kristin. "Investigating the Procedure: Poetry and the Source." *Telling It Slant: Avant-Garde Poetics of the 1990s*. Eds. Mark Wallace and Steven Marks. Tuscaloosa: U of Alabama P, 2002. 115-29. Print.

Quartermain, Peter. *Disjunctive Poetics: From Gertrude Stein and Louis Zukofsky to Susan Howe*. Cambridge, UK: Cambridge UP, 1992. Print.

Queneau, Raymond. "Potential Literature." *Oulipo: A Primer of Potential Literature*. Ed. and Trans. Warren F. Motte Jr. Lincoln, NE: U of Nebraska P, 1986. 51-64. Print.

Raffel, Stanley. "Baudrillard on Simulations: An Exegesis and a Critique." *Sociological Research Online* 9.2 (2004). Web. 2 January 2012. http://www.socresonline.org.uk/9/2/raffel.html

Rasula, Jed. "Ron Silliman." *Contemporary Authors*. Detroit: St. James P, 1996. 1009. Print.

Ratcliffe, Stephen. *human/nature*. Ubu editions: Publishing the Unpublishable 026, 2007. Web. 14 Dec. 2011. http://www.ubu.com/ubu/unpub/Unpub_026_Ratcliffe_Human.pdf

———. "*human/nature* Campus Flyer." *PennSound*. Web. 15 Dec. 2011. http://media.sas.upenn.edu/pennsound/authors/Ratcliffe/Human-Nature/human_nature_flyer.jpg

———. "Stephen Ratcliffe: Bio & Response." *Double Room: A Journal of Flash Fiction and Prose Poetry* 3 (Fall/Winter 2003). Web. 15 Dec. 2011. http://doubleroomjournal.com/issue_three/Stephen_Ratcliffe.html

Redfern, Walter. *Puns*. Oxford: Blackwell, 1985. Print.

Roach, Joseph. "Performance: The Blunders of Orpheus." *PMLA* 125.4 (October 2010): 1078-1085. Print.

Robertson, Lisa. *Debbie: an Epic*. Vancouver: New Star Books, 1997. Print.

———. "Lisa Robertson." Interview with Lytle Shaw. *Printed Project* 14 (November 2010): 96-107. Print.

———. *Occasional Work and Seven Walks from the Office for Soft Architecture* [2003]. Third ed. Toronto: Coach House Books, 2011. Print.

———. *R's Boat*. Berkeley, Ca.: University of California Press, 2010. Print.

———. *The Weather*. Vancouver: New Star Books, 2001. Print.

———. *XEclogue* [1993]. Rev. ed. Vancouver: New Star Books, 2006. Print.

Rodefer, Stephen. "What I See in the Silliman Project." *Chicago Review* 54.3 (Winter 2009): 53-59. Print.

Rothstein, Edward. "CONNECTIONS: A Daring Theory That Stalin Had Walter Benjamin Murdered," *New York Times*, Arts 30 June 2001. Web. 15 Dec. 2011. http://www.nytimes.com/2001/06/30/arts/connections-a-daring-theory-that-stalin-had-walter-benjamin-murdered.html

Roubaud, Jacques. *Poetry, etcetera: Cleaning House*. Trans. Guy Bennett. Los Angeles: Green Integer, 2006. Print.

Sacks, Oliver. *Musicophilia: Tales of Music and the Brain*. New York: Alfred A. Knopf, 2007. Print.

Scobie, Stephen. "I Dreamed I Saw Hugo Ball: bpNichol, Dada, and Sound Poetry." *Boundary 2: An International Journal of Literature and Culture* 3.1 (1974): 213-26. Print.

Seth, and Marc Ngui. "Interview." *Carousel* 19 (Spring/Summer 2006): 17-24. Print.

Shakespeare, William. *The Riverside Shakespeare*. Ed. G. Blakemore Evans. Boston: Houghton Mifflin, 1997. Print.

Silliman, Ron. *The Alphabet*. Tuscaloosa: U of Alabama P, 2008.

———. "The Chinese Notebook." *The Age of Huts (Compleat)*. Berkeley: U of California P, 2007. 147-177. Print.

———. "Email to Burt Kimmelman." 27 December 2011.

———. *The New Sentence*. New York: Roof, 1995. Print.

———. "Statement for the Guggenheim." "*The Alphabet*, Spelt from Silliman's Leaves (A Conversation on the 'American Longpoem')." By Anne Mack and J. J. Rome. *The South Atlantic Quarterly* 89:4 (Fall 1990): 734-759. Print.

———. "*Who Speaks*: Ventriloquism and the Self in the Poetry Reading [Afterword]." *Close Listening: Poetry and the Performed World*. Ed. Charles Bernstein. New York: Oxford UP, 1998. 360-78. Print.

——— and Carla Harryman, Lyn Hejinian, Steve Benson, Bob Perelman, and Barrett Watten. "Aesthetic Tendency and the Politics of Poetry: A Manifesto." *Social Text* 19-20 (Fall 1988): 261-75. Print.

——— and Gary Sullivan. "Ron Silliman Interview [with Gary Sullivan]." *ReadMe*. 2000. Web. 5 August 2011. http://home.jps.net/~nada/silliman.htm

——— and Thomas A. Vogler. "Ron Silliman Interview." *The Argotist Online*. Web. 5 August 2011. http://www.argotistonline.co.uk/Silliman%20interview.htm

Smith, Dale. "Weighing Words." *Bookslut*. N.p., February 2004. Web. 11 July 2011. http://www.bookslut.com/marsupial_inquirer/2004_02_001525.php

Smith, Mark S. *The Memoirs of God: History, Memory, and the Experience of the Divine in Ancient Israel*. Minneapolis, MN: Fortress P, 2004. Print.

———. *The Origins of Biblical Monotheism*. New York: Oxford UP, 2001. Print.

Spahr, Juliana. *Everybody's Autonomy: Connective Reading and Collective Identity*. Tuscaloosa: U of Alabama P, 2001. Print.

SpanishDICT. 2007. Web. 10 Nov. 2007. www.SpanishDict.com

Stein, Gertrude. "Composition as Explanation." *A Stein Reader*. Ed. Ulla E. Dydo. Evanston: Northwestern UP, 1993. 493-503. Print.

———. *Tender Buttons*. Sioux Falls, SD: NuVision Publications, 2007. Print.

Stewart, Susan. *Poetry and the Fate of the Senses*. Chicago: U of Chicago P, 2002. Print.

Sullivan, Gary. "The Flarf Files." Charles Bernstein. Syllabi. State U of New York/Buffalo: *Electronic Poetry Center*. 22 Aug. 2003. Web. http://epc.buffalo.edu/authors/bernstein/syllabi/readings/flarf.html

———. "The Poetics of Comics: Richard Hahn (Part 1)." *Elsewhere*. 2 Aug. 2007. Web. 15 Dec. 2012. http://garysullivan.blogspot.com/2007/08/poetics-of-comics-richard-hahn-part-1.html

Suzuki, Shunryu. *Zen Mind, Beginner's Mind*. Ed. Trudy Dixon. 6th ed. New York: Weatherhill, 2003. Print.

This, Hervé. *Molecular Gastronomy: Exploring the Science of Flavor*. New York: Columbia UP, 2005. Print.

Tsur, Reuven. *What Makes Sound Patterns Expressive?: The Poetic Mode of Speech Perception*. Durham: Duke UP, 1992. Print.

Tuma, Keith. "Contemporary American Poetry and the Pseudo Avant-Garde." *Chicago Review* 36.3-4 (1989): 43-50. Print.

Turco, Lewis. *The New Book of Forms: A Handbook of Poetics*. Hanover, NH: UP of New England, 1986. Print.

Tynes, Jen. Review of *Proof of Silhouettes* by Sheila E. Murphy. *Verse* 2 Feb. 2005. Web. 23 Dec. 2011. http://versemag.blogspot.com/2005/02/new-review-of-sheila-e-murphy.html

Urban Dictionary. 2004. Web. 1 November 2007. www.urbandictionary.com

Vance, Eugene. "Augustine's Confessions and the Grammar of Selfhood." *Genre* 6.1 (1973): 1-28. Print.

Vendler, Helen. *The Art of Shakespeare's Sonnets*. Cambridge: Harvard UP, 1997. Print.

Wallace, Mark. "Definitions in Process, Definitions as Process/ Uneasy Collaborations: Language and Postlanguage Poetries." *Flash Point*. Web. 16 Jan. 2010. http://www.flashpointmag.com/postlang.htm

Watkin, William. "The Materialization of Prose: *Poiesis* versus *Dianoia* in the Work of Godzich and Kittay, Shklovsky, Silliman and Agamben." *Paragraph* 31.3 (2008): 344-64. Print.

———. "Systematic Rule-Governed Violations of Convention: The Poetics of Procedural Constraint in Ron Silliman's *Bart* and *The Chinese Notebook*." *Contemporary Literature* 48.4 (2007): 499-529. Print.

Wertheim, Christine and Matias Viegener, Eds. *The /n/oulipian Analects*. Los Angeles: Les Figues Press, 2007. Print.

Yu, Timothy. *Race and the Avant-Garde: Experimental and Asian American Poetry Since 1965*. Stanford: Stanford UP, 2009. Print.

Xiaojing, Zhou. "Possibilities Out of an Impossible Position: Myung Mi Kim's *Under Flag*." State U of New York/Buffalo: *Electronic Poetry Center*. June 2002. Web. 19 Dec. 2011. http://epc.buffalo.edu/authors/kim/xiaojing.html

Ziarek, Krzysztof. *Inflected Language: Toward a Hermeneutics of Nearness*. Albany: State U of New York P, 1994. Print.

Contributors

Charles Bernstein is the author of over 40 books, most recently *Recalculating, All the Whiskey in Heaven: Selected Poems*, and *Attack of the Difficult Poems: Essays and Inventions*. Regan Professor of English and Comparative Literature at the University of Pennsylvania, Bernstein is the co-founder and co-editor, with Al Filreis, of PennSound (writing.unpenn.edu/pennsound) and editor and co-founder, with Loss Pequeño Glazier, of the Electronic Poetry Center (epc.buffalo.edu). He has been host and co-producer of *LINEbreak* and *Close Listening*, two radio poetry series. With Bruce Andrews, he edited *L=A=N=G=U=A=G=E*, which was anthologized as *The L=A=N=G=U=A=G=E Book*. Bernstein has served as editor of such volumes as *Louis Zukofsky: Selected Poems* and *Close Listening: Poetry and the Performed Word*.

Carrie Conners is an assistant professor of English at CUNY-LaGuardia. Her chapter "'But he aint never been seen!': The Protean Howard Hughes and Overlapping Capitalist Narratives in Ed Dorn's *Gunslinger*" appeared in *Merchants, Barons, Sellers and Suits: The Changing Images of the Businessman Through Literature*. Her poetry has been featured in *RHINO*, *Tar Wolf Review*, *DMQ Review*, and *California Quarterly*.

Thomas Fink is the author of *"A Different Sense of Power": Problems of Community in Late-Twentieth-Century U.S. Poetry*, a book on David Shapiro's poetry, and eight books of poetry, including *Joyride* and *Autopsy Turvy*, co-authored with Maya Diablo Mason. He co-edited *"Burning Interiors": David Shapiro's Poetry and Poetics*. His work appeared in *Best American Poetry 2007*. Fink's paintings hang in various collections. He is a professor of English at CUNY-LaGuardia.

Kristen Gallagher was a first-generation member of the Kelly Writers House at the University of Pennsylvania and went on to receive a PhD from the SUNY Buffalo Poetics Program in 2005. She is now an associate professor of English at CUNY-LaGuardia Community College. She is the co-editor (with Chris Alexander) for Truck Books and is a co-curator for the Segue Series at the Bowery Poetry Club. Her book *We Are Here* was published in 2011. Other critical work by Gallagher on Tan Lin has appeared in *Criticism* and *Jacket2*.

Judith Halden-Sullivan, a professor of English at Millersville University of Pennsylvania, authored *The Topology of Being: The Poetics of Charles Olson* and critical works on contemporary American poetry, including "Architect / House of Being" in "*Burning Interiors*": *David Shapiro's Poetry and Poetics*. "The Experiential *Ethos* of Advanced Composition" appears in *Principles and Practice: New Discourses for the Vertical Curriculum*. She is currently drafting another book-length study, *Inviting Innovative Writing: A Meditation and Class Plan*, which is a Gadamerian interpretation of experimental movements in contemporary rhetoric, along with both a rationale and strategy for asking college students to compose innovative texts of all kinds. She also serves as a reviewer and book review editor for the *Journal of the Assembly for Expanded Perspectives on Learning*. Halden-Sullivan's own verse has been published in several innovative poetry journals.

Paolo Javier is the author of five chapbooks and three full-length books of poetry, including *The Feeling Is Actual*, *60 lv bo(e)mbs*, and *the time at the end of this writing*. The Poet Laureate of Queens County from 2010–2013, he is the recipient of grants from the New York State Council on the Arts and Queens Council on the Arts. He publishes the online journal *2nd Ave Poetry* and lives with his wife in Queens.

Burt Kimmelman's seven collections of poetry are *The Way We Live*, *As If Free*, *There Are Words*, *Somehow*, *The Pond at Cape May Point*, a collaboration with painter Fred Caruso, *First Life*, and *Musaics*. His poem "Taking Dinner to My Mother" was featured on NPR's *The Writer's Almanac*. He was Senior Editor of the now defunct *Poetry New York: A Journal of Poetry and Translation*. Professor of English at New Jersey Institute of Technology, Kimmelman is the author of *The "Winter Mind": William Bronk and American Letters* and *The Poetics of Authorship in the Later Middle Ages: The Emergence of the Modern Literary Persona*. He edited *The Facts on File Companion to 20th-Century American Poetry* and co-edited *The Facts on File Companion to American Poetry*. He has published scores of essays on medieval, modern, and contemporary poetry. Recent interviews of Kimmelman are available in *Jacket* 40 (text) and at *Poetry Thin Air* (video). More information can be found at Burt-Kimmelman.com.

Hank Lazer, Associate Provost for Academic Affairs and professor of English at the University of Alabama, is the author of *Lyric & Spirit: Selected Essays 1996-2008*, *Opposing Poetries*, and 14 books of poetry, including *The New Spirit*, *Elegies & Vacations*, *INTER(IR)RUPTIONS*, and *Doublespace: Poems 1971-1989*. His poetry was nominated for the 2005 Pulitzer Prize. Lazer edited the collection *What Is a Poet?*

Jessica Lewis Luck is an assistant professor of English at California State University, San Bernardino. She has published essays on Harryette Mullen, Larry Eigner, and Sylvia Plath in such journals as *Contemporary Literature*, *Mosaic*, and *Tulsa Studies in Women's Literature*. Her current book project on the "poetics of cognition" uses cognitive theories of the embodied mind to explore the ways that experimental poems think and the ways we think through them.

Stephen Paul Miller is the author of *The Seventies Now: Culture as Surveillance* and numerous books of poetry, including *There's Only One God and You're Not It*, *Fort Dad*, *Being with a Bullet*, *Skinny Eighth Avenue*, *The Bee Flies in May*, and *Art Is*

Boring for the Same Reason We Stayed in Vietnam. With Daniel Morris, he co-edited *Radical Poetics and Secular Jewish Culture* and, with Terence Diggory, *The Scene of My Selves: New Work on New York School Poets.* His work has appeared in *New American Writing, Best American Poetry, Jacket, Columbia Review, Shofar, Mipoesias, Boundary 2, American Letters & Commentary, EOAGH, St. Mark's Poetry Project Newsletter, Mudfish, The Tribe of John, Burning Interiors,* and elsewhere. Miller is a professor of English at St. John's University in New York and was a Senior Fulbright Scholar at Jagiellonian University in Krakow, Poland.

The second volume of **Sheila E. Murphy**'s long-term collaborative poem sequence with Douglas Barbour, *Continuations 2,* appeared in 2012; *American Ghazals* was also published that year. Originally from South Bend, Indiana, and the author of many previous volumes of poetry, Murphy has lived in Phoenix all of her adult life. There, she has captained her eponymous consulting firm since 1993. Her work in leadership development, both individual and organization-wide, is accompanied by active college teaching, drawing, and writing roles.

Elizabeth Robinson is the author of several volumes of poetry, most recently *Three Novels, Also Known As,* and *The Orphan & its Relations.* Robinson has been a winner of the Fence Modern Poets Prize and was selected for the National Poetry Series, and has received grants from the Fund for Poetry, the Foundation for Contemporary Arts, and the Boomerang Foundation. She also is a co-editor for Ether-Dome Chapbooks and Instance Press.

Christopher Schmidt is the author of a book of poems, *The Next in Line.* Recent poems and essays have appeared in *Tin House, Court Green, Boston Review, Bookforum, Arizona Quarterly,* and *Computers and Composition.* He is currently completing a study on waste in twentieth-century poetry and poetics. An assistant professor of English at CUNY-LaGuardia, Schmidt has also taught at Bard College and the University of Michigan.

Eileen R. Tabios has released nineteen print and four electronic poetry collections, one CD poetry collection, an art-essay collection, a poetry essay/interview anthology, a short-story book and a collection of novels. Recipient of the Philippines' National Book Award for Poetry, she melds ekphrasis with transcolonialism in her work. Her poems have been translated into Spanish, Italian, Tagalog, Japanese, Portuguese, Polish, Greek, computer-generated hybrid languages, paintings, video, drawings, visual poetry, mixed media collages, Kali martial arts, music, modern dance, and sculpture. She also has edited, co-edited, or conceptualized nine anthologies of poetry, fiction, and essays. As part of her poetry-as-performance approach, she blogs as the "Chatelaine" (angelicpoker.blogspot.com), edits a poetry review journal, *Galatea Resurrects (A Poetry Engagement)* (galatearesurrects.blogspot.com), and curates an ongoing inter(net)national "Poets On ___" series whereby poets offer prose and poetry on current events.

Index